NEW PLAYERS, PARTNERS AND PROCESSES: A PUBLIC SECTOR WITHOUT BOUNDARIES

Edited by

Meredith Edwards and John Langford

National Institute for Governance
University of Canberra
Australia

Centre for Public Sector Studies
School of Public Administration
University of Victoria
Canada

TABLE OF CONTENTS

PART 3: DEVOLUTION AND DISCRETION: BUILDING COMMUNITY BASED MANAGEMENT INTO CONTEMPORARY GOVERNANCE

PART 4: HORIZONTAL COORDINATION - HOW FAR HAVE WE GONE AND HOW FAR CAN WE GO?

Foreword

This volume contains the proceedings of a symposium held in Canberra, Australia in April 2001 on *New Players, Partners and Processes: a public sector without boundaries?* Our broad goal was to ask critical questions about the nature of governance in an era when boundaries are blurring across the public, private and not-for profit sectors. We also sought to identify what structures, processes, organisational relationships and human resource capacities will be needed to ensure good governance for a country and its citizens.

We invited leading practitioners and academics from Australia and Canada to draft papers to provide different points of departure for exploring these questions at a day long Symposium. We then assembled an impressive group of practitioners and academics from across the public, private and community sectors, and allowed significant blocks of time for open discussion and debate. As the proceedings of our discussions demonstrate, considerable learning occurred as issues were explored from the perspectives of practitioners and researchers, and of different countries. However, given the diverse career patterns of many participants and the ongoing exchange of insights between practitioners and academics alike in Australia and Canada during the last few years, our discussions did not seem hindered by conventional intellectual boundaries!

We would like to thank the contributors to this volume for the work they put into both their presentations and the editing of their chapters. We would also like to thank the generosity of the various sponsors of this event: PricewaterhouseCoopers Legal, the Association of Canadian Studies at Australia and New Zealand, The Departments of Family and Community Services, Health and Aged Care, Environment Australia, Transport and Regional Services, Finance and Administration as well as Centrelink, and the Australian National Audit Office. We would also like to express our gratitude for the hospitality shown to the symposium participants by the Chancellor of the University of Canberra and the Canadian High Commissioner in Canberra.

Finally, we would like to thank in particular, Professor John Langford of the Centre for Public Sector Studies and the School of Public Administration at the University of Victoria, and Pam Richmond of the National Institute for Governance at the University of Canberra, for the many hours they have put into making this fine publication see the light of day. We are very pleased that a close working relationship developed between the organisers and contributors to the first joint symposium of the National Institute for Governance and the Centre for Public Sector Studies, and we look forward to continuing this collaboration in the years to come.

Meredith Edwards, Director, National Institute for Governance, University of Canberra
and
Evert Lindquist, Director, School of Public Administration, University of Victoria

INTRODUCTION

Boundary Spanning and Public Sector Reform

Professor John Langford, School of Public Administration, University of Victoria, Canada
and
Professor Meredith Edwards, National Institute for Governance, University of Canberra

The most recent cycle of public service reform has been tumbling around within the governments of the western industrial democracies for over two decades. While the pace of reform has been frenetic and often destabilizing, practitioners and students of government in Australia and Canada have had enough experience with new governance institutions and processes that preliminary assessments, at least, of developments to date have begun to appear.[1]

A central theme and four topics

As Davis and Rhodes point out, a transformative phenomenon that was once easily labelled as New Public Management has morphed so often over the last 20 years that its essential features are not easily identified. They set out what they see as six key dimensions of public sector reform: marketization, corporate management, regulation, political control, decentralization and privatisation.[2] A key theme within many of these dimensions is the spanning of traditional boundaries among government departments, between public sector agencies and private and third sector organizations, and between citizens and communities, on the one hand, and government decision making, on the other. Over the last year, this theme has become central to the research and outreach efforts of both the National Institute of Governance at the University of Canberra and the Centre for Public Sector Studies, School of Public Administration at the University of Victoria.

The symposium organizers, therefore, built the symposium around this theme and asked participants to reflect on four significant boundary spanning initiatives in Australia and Canada:

- Engaging private and third sector organizations in the delivery of government services
- Partnerships with private and third sector organizations
- Community-based management of natural resources
- Horizontal coordination among government departments

In the spirit of the boundary-spanning theme, none of these issues forms a separate "silo" unrelated to its three counterparts. For example, the delivery of services is being accomplished through straightforward principal/agent contracts, but it is also being structured, in some cases, as more elaborate forms of collaborative partnership. By the same token, some of the arrangements labelled as partnerships by government are little more than standard contractual arrangements without any of the power sharing characteristics implicit in the notion of partnership. Horizontal coordination may look like a topic unto itself, but many of the values, attitudes and specialized managerial skills central to successful horizontal coordination prove to be precisely the same as those required for partnership management and the integration of community stakeholders into regional resource management regimes.

Comparing Australian and Canadian experience

What made the symposium particularly interesting was the comparative dimension. While the social, economic and technological forces that have driven the reforms of the public sector have been reasonably constant across the industrialized democracies, ideological and institutional contexts have created distinctive patterns of reform in the various western democracies. Superficially, within the Westminster tradition, Canada and Australia share common executive, parliamentary and bureaucratic institutions with largely common inadequacies. But, as these essays reflect, the governance revolution has not proceeded at the same pace or in the same way in both societies.[3] This symposium helped to clarify similarities and differences in boundary-spanning approaches between both countries.

Boundaries between speaker and participant

Another distinctive feature of this volume is the inclusion of the commentary and lightly edited versions of the discussion that followed the delivery of each pair of papers. The quality of the commentaries and verbal exchanges made them key ingredients of the symposium. This reality argued for their retention as part of the manuscript. An equally powerful argument for their inclusion is the way in which it allows the structure of this volume to reflect the theme of the symposium, by reflecting the efforts made to break down the normal barriers between the speaker and the participant. A symposium, when thought of as "a philosophical or other friendly discussion," suggests an environment in which there are exchanges among equals, not pontification followed by respectful questions. As we shall see, the most successful example of boundary spanning may have been the symposium itself.

Reflections on the theme

The central theme of the symposium and these papers is the spanning of boundaries. Two related features of boundary spanning are wider networks of participants in a particular activity and, therefore, increased management and political complexity. As Dobell argues in his paper, what we talk of as boundary spanning may as accurately be thought of as boundary enlarging. Many of the instruments of governance, with which western industrialised nations have been experimenting during this 20 year cycle of public sector reform, reflect the pressure to open up government activities to new actors and to recognize that the state, traditionally structured, lacked the capacity on its own to achieve the ambitious goals it set for itself. Where tasks have not been eliminated completely by governments, their achievement has been made more challenging by the pressures to coordinate internally around more broadly conceived policy problems, to contract out, to partner, and to share decision making and management with affected stakeholders. In a sense, then, our theme begs the bigger question about the ability of parliamentary governments to shed more comprehensively their narrow go-it-alone approach to governance and develop the institutions, processes and skills to work with a wider group of actors to achieve what inevitably must become commonly shared goals.

Unfortunately the experiences of Australian and Canadian governments have not been very positive. Since the founding of both countries, their governments have struggled with the boundary-spanning challenges of managing a federal state. Kath Wellman's paper on community based resource management is *en passant* a damaging critique of the capacity of Australian state and federal governments to coordinate their approaches to environmental management. In the Canadian case, the contemporary healthcare crisis has starkly illustrated the bankruptcy of these efforts and led to widespread demands for a more collaborative approach to cross-jurisdictional decision making.

Similarly, the absence of a boundary between our executive and legislative branches has led to outright executive domination and calls for a rebalancing of the roles of the cabinet and the legislature.[4] Both countries have struggled for years with the problem of developing democratically defensible non-captive relationships with what we now call stakeholder groups.[5] Finally, as both Jenny Stewart and Evert Lindquist make clear in their papers on horizontal coordination, this particular problem did not appear yesterday. The formation of interdepartmental committees have for generations reflected the efforts of ministers and senior officials to bring departments of government together to deal with social and economic problems which were bigger than the mandates of any one of them. Thirty years ago, this coordination effort was stepped up with the creation of policy super-ministries (e.g. environment) or mega-departments and the formation of intricate systems of integrative cabinet committees and supporting central agency bureaucracies. In a reform era in which the primary emphasis is on better steering, however, what was in the 1970s the dream of a few advocates of rational policy making models has today become a key building block of the new governance.

Has boundary spanning been effective?

As noted, the case studies in this volume do not represent a comprehensive assessment of the effectiveness of public service reform efforts to work across traditional boundaries. Having said that, the evidence of the effectiveness of the new arrangements reviewed in the case studies is mixed.

For example, in his study of the contracting out of employment services, Considine condemns the boundary-spanning relationships established between the Australian government and the contractors as pitting contractors against the public sector participants and other contractors in unproductive ways. David Good reports that the program under which the Canadian job-creation partnerships were created was – in the face of a media crisis – first severely restricted and then terminated. Langford argues that despite the rhetoric there have not been enough examples of genuine collaborative partnerships between governments and private or third sector organizations to begin to adequately measure the effectiveness of this mode of boundary spanning.

The grants and incentive route to engaging Australian community based organizations in environmental management gets a mixed review from Wellman. Dobell makes the cautionary point that we can't expect to see the emergence of "win-win" solutions in community-based decision making immediately; such outcomes "can only be possible in the context of commitment to longer term processes promising a generalized reciprocity." He adds: "It remains to be seen whether all these new institutions will simply gravitate toward a new elite, in effect be co-opted in their turn by the existing, large-scale formal institutional apparatus, as they become more abstract and distant in order to be effective in their linkage roles."

Boundary spanning within and across governments also gets mixed reviews. Lindquist reports on the Auditor General's ideologically driven critique of the horizontal initiatives of the Canadian federal government. Stewart suggests that many of the outsourced service delivery "networks" established by departments "exist more in the eye of the department sponsoring them than as a reality for participants or clients." She suggests that the reality of policy networks "is one of cautious incremental change within an overall system which remains inevitably 'Minister-centric.'" As noted below, it is precisely this control/horizontality gulf that Lindquist seeks to bridge through the strategy outlined in his paper.

Boundary spanning and democratic values

At first glance, breaking down boundaries feels intrinsically democratic. Weaker boundaries suggest more open and inclusive government, allowing the direct participation of more players in processes such as policy making, regulation and service delivery. But that is only half the story. Bringing down barriers also sounds alarm bells with respect to the preservation of traditional democratic values.

The most fundamental concern is about who is responsible in a world without boundaries. When individual ministers and departments stop "owning" particular policy issues, when private sector firms are responsible for delivering services, when motley groups of stakeholders exercise real power through participation on community-based management boards, and when governments share power with formal partners, the casual observer can be excused for asking, "Who is in charge here?" The same observer will soon be asking the corollary question: "Did I elect any of these people?"

Questions about the diffusion of power and responsibility almost inevitably lead to concerns about accountability. That is the case for all of the forms of boundary breaking explored in this volume. These reform initiatives challenge traditional notions of accountability, moving away from forms more suited to a command and control environment, and even beyond contemporary fixations with accountability based on results, to complex notions of shared accountability – between those delivering services and those making policy, among government agencies working more collaboratively, among levels of government, and between public agencies and private and community sector organizations. Can we have shared accountabilities and what does that mean? When Dr John Mayne of the Canadian Audit Office spoke in Canberra a few months before this symposium, he emphasised that governments in the twenty-first century would need to tackle greater complexity, encourage more collaboration, and provide means for citizen engagement, all within a framework of acceptable accountabilities. Conceptualizing and building credible frameworks for shared accountability that meet the needs of boundary spanners will test our commitment to traditional Westminster style government.

Anxiety and puzzlement about accountability are visible in almost all the papers in this volume. This value is clearly at play in the efforts to move from vertically oriented "silo" government to a more horizontal, network-oriented model as both Lindquist and Stewart point out in their respective papers. Considine concludes that "it is difficult to see how citizens can hold anyone to account for what is done with their tax dollars when the path from government department, via confidential tender, through an arm's length service delivery agency, to independent contractors motivated by paid outcomes, and to highly vulnerable clients is so complex and obscure." Good observes that:

> [T]he reality is that the objectives in partnerships, as they are in most government programs, are usually multiple, conflicting and vague. Accountabilities among partners are always multiple, inevitably complex and often fuzzy. The roles and responsibilities are often both contradictory and complementary at the same time. And the results information is rarely totally accurate and often incomplete . . . .. The reality is that getting more clarity on one dimension – be it objectives, accountability, or results – will invariably come at cost. That cost might be rigidity, paper burden, slow responsiveness, missed opportunity, or increased resources.

Both McClelland and Dobell support that point in their papers. McClelland, in her analysis of partnerships with community welfare organizations (CWOs), argues that "the role of CWOs in developing innovative ways of meeting needs could be undermined by a requirement to meet rigid output measures that could mean that they are likely to be adventurous in their service delivery." Dobell very bluntly notes in his paper on community-based management structures that "[E]xisting administrative systems and accountability mechanisms are serious barriers to innovation."

The concerns about democratic values don't stop there. Rubbing out boundaries between traditional public service and private and third sectors through partnering or contracting out raises questions about the relevance of other traditional public service values (political neutrality, pursuit of the public interest, fairness, openness, protection of privacy, etc) to boundary spanning public servants. A number of observers have noted the degree to which encouragement of "citizen engagement" in state management structures has the potential to erode the traditional political neutrality and anonymity of the public service by engaging public servants in public displays of what are effectively political negotiation of acceptable tradeoffs with key stakeholders.[6] Good's paper adds an extra dimension to this issue, discussing the political neutrality problems associated with bringing members of Parliament into grants and contributions decision making processes. Such initiatives hold the traditional model of political neutrality up to question on several levels.

Such questions are merely skirmishes prefatory to the wider battle over the merger or hybridisation of public and private sector value sets that public-private partnerships would eventually force us to fight.[7] For example, while boundary busting may feel like it creates more open government, private sector partners are often far more inclined towards secrecy than their public sector counterparts. Theirs is a business model, after all, spawned in the intellectual-property-protecting world of the new economy. Harmonizing the core operating values of the three sectors would be a daunting task.

The ultimate irony is that boundary spanning need not be more inclusive in character although, at first glance, it appears that it should be. Allison McClelland and a number of discussants raised concerns about collaboration sinking into collusion. This essentially revives anti-corporatist arguments; namely that long term partnerships are more often than not with larger organizations and that these arrangements often squeeze out less powerful organizations and make it harder for clients and citizens to become effective participants in decision making and service delivery.

Boundary spanning and capacity

There is one further common thread in the discussion of all four topics that cannot be ignored. It is the issue of the capacity of governments to perform competently in a world without boundaries. The new roles implicit in this world – steering, coordinating, managing contracts, partnering, providing quality service – demand new suites of structures, processes and management skills which have traditionally been in short supply in the public sector.

Most of the skills in question are collaborative in nature. They include the ability to negotiate towards solutions that serve the interests of all parties, to resolve disputes cooperatively rather than by fiat, to share information and – thereby – empower others, to communicate effectively, and to understand and manage the risks inherent in situations in which one cannot exercise ultimate control. These "boundroid" skills, as Diana Leat labels them in the discussion of public-private partnerships, have to be exercised in innovative forums such as strategic alliances, community-based management boards, stakeholder and public meetings, and interdepartmental task forces. The development of these skills and the creation and maintenance of new structures and complex network-style processes represent daunting tasks for public services which already confront staff shortages, a demographic bulge of middle-aged public servants, a shortage of training funds, and a comparative disadvantage in the competition with the private sector for the same skilled people to perform the same market-oriented management and service delivery functions.

This reality is the central theme of Peter Shergold's concluding comments on the Considine and Good papers in which he calls for a new breed of public servants

> who are as committed to the delivery of programs on behalf of the government of the day as they are to providing robust policy advice on the development of those programs. It requires public servants who cannot always be traditionally self-effacing if they are to promote public programs effectively, work in partnership with outsourced providers, stand up to pressure in the very unequal balance of power that is the parliamentary committee, and be willing to respond publicly to press articles that inaccurately portray the departmental management of programs. In other words, it requires public servants with a bias for action, even a passion that can be too readily mistaken for partisanship.

Langford tracks the efforts of the Government of Canada over the last decade to prepare its public service for the daunting challenge of partnership management. He concludes: "[w]hile efforts to improve service quality, break down departmental 'silos' and make public bureaucracies more 'business-like' have implicitly addressed some of the partnership management challenges, no Canadian government has taken on the partnership capacity issue in any organized way." On the other side of the contract or partnership, McClelland sees capacity problems on the part of the community welfare organizations providing services for government. Not surprisingly, the capacity and accountability problems are connected. As McClelland puts it: ". . . twenty years on, there had been very little development in the understanding of community organizations about how to measure the effectiveness of their services . . . . Most community based organizations did not have the resources or the expertise in research and evaluation." The link between success and access to scientific knowledge and leadership skills is reinforced in Wellman's discussion of community-based environmental management.

Dobell insists that capacity building is not just about personal skills, but it is also about recreating organizational settings. He quotes Barry Johnson approvingly: "Perhaps we need a new institutional paradigm that sees management agencies not as providers of solutions, but as facilitators and partners with citizens (i.e. true civil servants) to help find joint solutions." He further argues that the existence of traditional cultural barriers means that new community-based decision making organizations run by skilled people will only succeed if significant energy and resources are put into the "prior activity of building understanding, shared beliefs about facts and visions or norms, and indeed to an extended investment in building understanding and agreement around process and procedure."

Dobell also makes the critical point that successful spanning of boundaries between governments and communities is predicated on the successful spanning of boundaries between ministries and agencies within governments. In short, external boundary spanning capacity is dependent on internal boundary spanning capacity. Lindquist pursues this internal boundary spanning culture question, reporting on the emphasis placed on this aspect of capacity building in Ottawa in recent years. He sets out an integrated strategy for building system support for horizontal initiatives which does not ignore what he argues will be continuing demands for control, accountability and central leadership. Clearly capacity building in this area will depend on significant culture change, involving, among other things, the development of a more positive attitude towards employees who eschew work at the centre of government and its departments in favour of work along the increasingly important margins of government.

Tough Questions for the Future

These brief and incomplete excursions into developments along disputed traditional frontiers by necessity raise more questions than answers. The answers contained in the papers, commentaries and discussions which follow are far from definitive, but they are not particularly encouraging for promoters of new governance arrangements. To date, boundary spanning in the areas examined has been only modestly successful at best.

The mixed results leave us with some tough questions about the future of this "new governance" theme. Is boundary eradication going to become nothing more than a strategy by governments to shift risk and tough challenges to other levels of government and organizations in other sectors? By blurring the boundary of the public sector to include private and third sector organizations as contractors and partners in service delivery agents and collaborators in policy making and regulation, are governments slyly turning watchful stakeholders into state-funded lapdogs? Is the full-blown collaborative partnership model more risk than adverse politicians and our traditional Westminster model governments can really handle? Put another way, are governments and potential private and third sector partners prepared to take the steps required to build trust and longer-term power sharing arrangement? Are central agencies capable of making the shift from central control to guidance so that they can position themselves to offer the advice required by government departments to productively engage in boundary spanning? Will the demands for traditional accountability overwhelm the potential for boundary spanning to drive creativity by turning the relationships into opportunities for innovation and learning? Can governments shed their traditional and distinctive recruitment and retention strategies and compete effectively for the human resources needed to staff a boundary spanning public service?

Even if they don't provide final answers, the following papers, commentaries and verbal exchanges raise these and other tough questions that boundary spanners ignore at their peril. Opening up boundaries and achieving successful outcomes is not going to be the "slam dunk" that some advocates of contemporary public sector reform suggested. In fact, there are already some signs that the boundary-spanning pendulum (as Good put it) has reached its apogee and begun to fall back. Harassed by opposition claims that the new ways of delivering services cost more not less, stunned by media demands for full accountability for activities outside of their control, suspicious of the agendas of power-sharing community groups, and overwhelmed by the capacity gaps in their public services, governments in both countries are beginning to question how far they should voyage beyond traditional boundaries. On the other hand, fiscal realities, the networking and power sharing imperatives of information and communication technologies, and the complexities of contemporary policy agendas ensure that boundary spanning initiatives will not simply be dismissed as a faddish "flavour-of-the-month." The problems explored in this volume will be the subject of continuing debate for some time to come.

Notes

[1] See for instance: B. Guy Peters and Donald J. Savoie, eds., *Governance in the Twenty-first Century: Revitalizing the Public Service*, (Montreal: McGill-Queens, 2000) and *Taking Stock: Assessing Public Sector Reforms*, (Montreal: McGill-Queens University Press, 1998); and M. Keating, J. Wanna and P. Weller, eds., *Institutions on the Edge: Capacity for Governance*, (St. Leonards: Allen and Unwin, 2000).

[2] G. Davis and R.A.W. Rhodes, "From hierarchy to contracts and back again: reforming the Australian public service," in Keating, Wanna and Weller, *Institutions on the Edge*, p.77.

[3] This theme is pursued in more detail in Peter Aucoin, *The New Public Management: Canada in Comparative Perspective* (Montreal: IRPP, 1995).

[4] Donald J. Savoie, *Governing From the Centre: the Concentration of Power in Canadian Politics* (Toronto: University of Toronto Press, 1999); M. Keating and P. Weller, "Cabinet government: an institution under pressure," in Keating, Wanna and Weller, *Institutions on the Edge*, ch.2.

[5] Ian Marsh, "Gaps in policy-making capacities: interest groups, social movements, think tanks and the media," in Keating, Wanna and Weller, *Institutions on the Edge*, ch.7; Herman Bakvis, "Pressure Groups and the New Public Management: From 'Pressure Pluralism' to 'Managing the Contract,'" in M. Charih, and Arthur Daniels, eds., *The New Public Management and Public Administration in Canada*, (Toronto: IPAC, 1997), ch. 13.

[6] Jon Pierre, "Externalities and Relationships: Rethinking the Boundaries of the Public Service," in Peters and Savoie, eds., *Governance in the Twenty-first Century*, pp. 340ff.

[7] John W. Langford, "The Ethical Challenges of Alternative Service Delivery," paper prepared for the OECD Conference on Public Sector Ethics, Paris, November 1997.

PART 1

ENGAGING THE PRIVATE
SECTOR IN SERVICE DELIVERY

Enterprise Governance: The Limits and Shortcomings of Quasi-Markets as a Tool for Social Policy – the Case of Australia's Employment Services Reforms

Dr Mark Considine, Political Science, University of Melbourne

This paper is drawn from a larger study of new governance reforms called ***Enterprising States: The Public Management of Welfare to Work.***[1] As such it will necessarily be a more abbreviated, even skeletal analysis of what are quite major issues and events. And while the paper is based on the Australian case from that study, it does so in the context of a comparative method in which the core governance attributes of systems are reviewed. The particular issues of regulation, accountability and public purpose in quasi-markets are the ones I will focus upon here, because it is these that provide the most interesting lessons for social policy reform more generally.

But first let's agree that from the mid-1990s until now, the Australian institutions involved in what could broadly be defined as *Welfare to Work* have become the most talked about in the OECD. Between 1994 and 1997 two Australian governments set out to attack the country's high rate of long-term unemployment by implementing the most radical root-and-branch reforms. No one has successfully explained why this field was seen as ripe for reform plunder, nor why a Labor government should have preferred a model so clearly indebted to neo-liberal organisation theory. But just as it "took Nixon to go to China," it took a Labor government to dismantle the Commonwealth Employment Service and to hand this highly sensitive service into the hands of contractors.

The hope was that a new organizational architecture (new instruments, new incentives and new agencies) would achieve what the economy and the government had failed to produce – a significant rise in the participation of long term unemployed people. In place of the routine work of the public employment service, the Commonwealth Employment Service (CES) with its suite of regulatory requirements, the unemployed would now face a different, diverse set of expectations. These included some bewilderingly complex alterations in the way services would be delivered, as well as new threats to income support entitlements. So different is the Australian case that it may well be regarded as the most radical OECD experiment in social policy in the post-war period. Certainly those directing it felt that this was their mission.

Background

The core element of the changes adopted first by Labor and then by the Coalition government involved a commitment to privatisation in which a new, more selective welfare model was defined. This was based upon the delivery of core public services by hundreds of small and medium sized contractors.

The first version of this competitive system was defined in the Labor government's White Paper as a part of a new client focus:

> The emphasis will move away from processing large numbers of job seekers through relatively rigid national programs. The key elements of the new strategy are an accurate assessment of the needs of job seekers and an intensive plan to assist disadvantaged people.[2]

The key to the delivery of this approach was stipulated as the harnessing of the non-profit welfare and for-profit recruitment sectors: "Healthy competition will lead to service improvement."[3] The new approach was also frequently contrasted with the weaknesses of the old welfare state with its "universal provision of a highly standardized and centrally controlled group of services," said to result in a "traditional one-size-fits-all approach to service delivery."[4]

The first "Working Nation" reforms occurred between 1994-96 and involved:

- Individual case management for all long term unemployed clients
- Referral of clients to both jobs and subsidized work and training
- Use of both a large public sector service provider (EAA) and many new private providers (CCMs)
- Regulation of this quasi-market by an independent government regulator (ESRA)
- Payment of private providers on a fee-for-success basis
- Competition between providers on quality not price

Empowerment of unemployed clients to choose their preferred agency and negotiate a service contract.

The Labor model imposed a complex and, in the end, unstable regulatory regime upon this new industry. One third of the public assistance effort for long term unemployed people was moved out of the public service and contracted to for-profit and non-profit agencies, and these were subject to regulatory oversight by the Employment Services Regulatory Authority (ESRA), based in Melbourne.

The remainder of the service was left in the hands of a slightly reformed CES, which set up its own version of a case management service under the umbrella of Employment Assistance Australia (EAA). This meant, in practise, that each CES office opened an adjacent counter staffed by CES officers who had been recruited to deliver the new service. They were often drawn from the best and most experienced of the CES corps and they quickly became successful at their new role. EAA was not required to bid for its clients nor to meet the same payment schedule for outcomes as were the new private agencies, a matter that, as we will see, soon caused discontent and pressure for further reform.

But EAA remained firmly tethered to both the CES and to DEETYA and this meant that their separate identify was henceforth somewhat compromised. At the regulatory level EAA was kept out of the purview of ESRA by virtue of deft manoeuvring on the part of DETYA Secretary Derek Volker, aided by Minister Simon Crean. They achieved a high degree of line-management influence over the new system and obviously felt that a full-scale plunge into market competition was either premature or unacceptable. Different reasons were given for the bifurcation of the system back then, and new rationales have been invented by participants along the way ever since. Such is the politics of reinvention.

The central initiative in the reform was the Labor government's Jobs Compact. This guaranteed that job seekers on benefits for 18 months or more would be given access to either employment or training or both. Outcomes were defined as either jobs or placement into a new raft of training programs that Labor was funding with a billion dollar commitment to this new Working Nation program. Many of these highly innovative programs would produce good outcomes for job seekers, while others were of indifferent quality.

I will be returning to these issues later in order to assess the overall impact of these arrangements, but while we are thinking about rationales, justifications and motives it is worth noting one further issue. Like all major reforms this one owed its birth to a confluence of quite different agendas. Having presided over a period of growth in long-term unemployment, the Keating government wanted to make amends before it faced the polls. Their general hostility to public programs and fascination with competitive delivery as an alternative was well known. So too was the Whitlamesque search for glorious victories against the conservatives.

At the launch of the new Employment Services Regulatory Authority (ESRA), Keating described the program as nothing less than "a very revolutionary change," which was "an idea that Simon [Crean] and I dreamed up, and it came from the Austel model in telecommunications." That is,

> . . . we will have a body sitting over this labour market seeking to create a proper market...in such a way that we will not simply see some monolith, and at the same time, involving private sector companies . . . and we will see them (the service providers) proliferate right across the country . . . .

Not only did the prime minister see this new market as a way to improve services, he was also quick to emphasise its political attractions:

> Another good thing about it, . . . one of the things you have always got to do when you think about social reform in Australia is to make it Tory-proof . . . you have got to hermetically seal them so they can't get their nasty little right-wing fingernails under them and tear them away . . . .[5]

But, although powerful, the search for large gestures and politically sustainable outcomes did not exhaust the reform motives. Among the advisers shaping the new policies there was another agenda. When asked about this, one official in the Department of Finance described the need to create "labour market flexibility." I agreed in interview that there were indeed many impediments to long term unemployed people moving freely around the labour market. "Not the unemployed," he interrupted, "public servants." In other words the reforms were driven, at least in part, by a desire to change the working conditions, pay and unionisation patterns among public servants. Central agencies had evidently grown tired of the failed efforts of line managers to reign in service delivery costs and saw this as a dramatic, if not final, solution.

The Rise of Case Management

Although both governments championed the market for employment services as a major experiment in public administration, and both were totally committed to contracting as a means to achieve efficiency, this was not their only common objective. Contracting as a policy tool was to be underpinned by a new and different methodology for deciding treatments. Labor termed this "case management" and the Coalition called theirs "intensive assistance." They meant much the same thing. In place of standardised treatments by staff in the CES, long term unemployed people would now receive an individual or "tailor-made" service in which an adviser or consultant would put together a package of measures to meet the client's needs. Under Labor this might include training programs in new employment sectors such as hospitality or horticulture. It could also include assistance with any personal impediments to employment such as drug dependence or health problems.

Case management, or care management, as it was termed in the first protocols developed in 1991 by the US Department of Health, sought to place an empowered local official at the cross-roads of various practitioner interactions. Their role was to coordinate services for an individual client, making sure there is a "seamless service" and ensuring that the client does not "fall out of the loop" as a result of bureaucratic obstacles and disincentives. Two kinds of ideas were responsible for the popularity of this approach. The first was a well-grounded welfare practice that aimed to treat the "whole client," not merely the symptom being presented. Accordingly, the case manager did more than refer job seekers to vacancies. She sought to understand why the client has been so long out of work and to address these "barriers to work."[6]

The other important idea underpinning the approach came from organisation theory and recent management science. Large organisations were viewed as hostile to customer needs. Typically each division of the organisation was seen to require its own information from clients and its own set of upward permission before a decision could be made. Consequently, each customer or client has to be prepared to pursue his case up and down several separate parts of the organisation (often termed "silos" to indicate their sealed and separate structure). In the Business Process Reengineering account of this problem the approach was to appoint intermediaries to traverse these internal systems on the client's behalf. This agent was known as the "process manager" or "relationships manager." This official took responsibility for linking all relevant services together in a single strategy for meeting the needs of an individual client. To do this effectively in the welfare or health system the theory required that the case manager be granted authority to broker deals with separate agencies that previously dealt with the client as part of a standardised service. As Austin argued, the case management model was viewed as an explicit response to the cost and dysfunction of delivery systems that had been structured "to accommodate providers, funders, and professionals rather than clients."[7]

In the most developed of these models the case manager had authority for the procurement of the services deemed most useful for the individual client, combining the skills of "counsellor, salesperson and accountant."[8] Where such a role included responsibility for the assessment of client needs, together with the purchase of services from supplier organisations, the potential for *both* improved service for the client *and* greater cost effectiveness.

The enrolment of clients in the new system involved far more than simply appointing internal bureaucratic advocates to work on their behalf. The co-responsibility and self-governance elements of these reforms made greater demands upon clients and their families to contribute extra effort, reduce their use of social assistance, adopt compliant behaviours, and meet raised expectations concerning life style change.[9] It was also at this point that an organisational transformation away from so-called Fordist ideals of universal consumption towards greater individuality of services and a focus upon co-responsibility was evident to some observers and critics.[10] In other words the new model promised an interesting new form of "governance at ground level" in which clients were to be called upon to help produce their own program effects, rather than being consumers of pre-existing, or "finished" services. As Hasenfeld and Weaver have pointed out, this mix of both intensive support and increased obligation creates "unique organisational pressures" on clients and staff in these programs and organisational factors therefore dominate evaluations of success and failure.[11]

Service Delivery Dynamics

The new program established first by Labor and then substantially reformed by the Coalition had to answer questions which had not been a concern for the Commonwealth Employment Service. How would clients find their way to the 300 or more contractors? How would different types of client be "priced" so that contractors invested an appropriate amount of effort in getting them jobs? What incentives would guarantee that contractors gave clients the right interventions?

To establish a common system of service delivery the Labor government established case management as the required methodology to be used by all providers and created an independent regulator, ESRA, to license and allocate work loads to each of them. Each client would be classified by the CES when they reached twelve months unemployment and according to their "degree of difficulty." They would then attract a different payment for the contractor. For their part the clients would be entitled to select the case management agency they wished to work with, and would then be obliged to enter into a formal, signed, Case Management Activity Agreement (CMAA) with this agency. They would attend all interviews and courses prescribed by the agency and undertake all other activities deemed by the case manager to be helpful to re-employment. Case managers were also authorized to recommend that the client have his or her social security payment suspended or terminated for any non-compliance with the case management process. In fact it was made mandatory for contractors to sanction clients in this way, providing the strongest possible incentive for clients to participate in the new arrangements. In the government's view this formed part of a "reciprocal obligation," (later "mutual obligation"), in which they were providing more than a billion dollars worth of new programs and for their part the long term unemployed would be required to answer the call from contractors and trainers.

The contractors were to be paid a fee per client, which was composed of an up-front amount to begin the case management process, and then a further payment when the client obtained work or was in an approved training program. A final payment was made when the job seeker completed 13 weeks of work or training.

Not everyone greeted the new system with enthusiasm. Unions representing the staff of the CES fought doggedly to defend declining opportunities for their members. The non-profit sector also approached the new order with some alarm. For example the Catholic agencies warned that "people who are long term unemployed must not be forced into inappropriate labour market programs, or job placements." Their leadership also expressed the view that devolving the responsibility for "breaching" clients "is highly problematic" and that case management "should not have any policing component in it." [12] They and other community service providers indicated that they would seek to establish a network of service deliverers who would cooperate rather than compete with one another.

The system Labor had established succeeded in privatising the employment services sector, and the percentage of business conducted by non-government case managers grew steadily under ESRA's careful cultivation of the new industry. However, the new system was far from stable. The government provider, EAA, remained outside ESRA's purview thanks to successful lobbying by the CES and its head office, the Department of Education, Employment and Youth Affairs (DEETYA). They had used their superior bureaucratic influence to convince the Labour and Industry minister that he would do better to keep direct control over the government owned service, rather than have ESRA begin rationing its activities or altering its expectations. Predictably this state of affairs left the new "market" some distance short of achieving the departure from bureaucracy that advocates and ideologues desired. That might not have mattered if a further problem had not emerged.

As the 300 or so new contractors took up their new businesses a decision had to be made in DEETYA concerning the method to select clients from the existing list of long-term unemployed. Not all could immediately line up at the doors of contractors because there were simply too many. For reasons that all the parties would later deny and dispute, the decision was made to fill the contractors' lists with clients from the back of the unemployment roll. That is, those longest on the roll would be first to get the new service. Although this could be viewed as compassionate when viewed from the job seeker's perspective, the effect of the decision was to deluge the new contractors with the most difficult clients and those most likely to resist the easier forms of interventions. Contractors complained that they were being sabotaged by a department that had a vested interest in protecting the CES and its subsidiary, EAA. They had a point. ESRA was equally appalled since its mandate was being openly subverted by the DEETYA hierarchy. So Labor's scheme was built on an institutional foundation in which it was inevitable that the private and public sectors would fall into conflict. This was bound to create a strong incentive for the contractors to see their interests as one against the government and, even worse, would give the regulator an incentive to become both supporter of the private industry and competitor to the system's bureaucratic master, DEETYA.

On its own this pressure would almost certainly have forced the government to further reform these arrangements, either in the direction of bringing EAA under ESRA's purview or by removing ESRA and managing all the contractors on equal terms in a "tender and supply" system. However these probable changes might have taken four or five years to become necessary had another problem not undermined the Labor scheme.

The key to the Jobs Compact was a commitment that all those 18 months or more out of work would receive case management and consequent to this would get either a job or training. Labor funded the training part of this commitment with a major increase in the budget for employment. At first it appeared that a significant part of these funds would be used to finance a high quality case management relationship with each client. The expectation raised by the new program was one in which regular interviews and phone calls would form the basis of an intensive relationship with each client and that this would result in "barriers to employment" being addressed.

In fact most of the funds were devoted to short term training programs and the funds spent on case management were so low that many clients never received any more than a brief, routine interview and assessment. Furthermore, the intention to create a large number of in-work subsidies to enable job seekers to gain valuable on-the-job experience could not be achieved as employers and unions remained sceptical and in some cases were openly opposed[13]. Although much publicised as a new form of service, staff actually received very little training in case management and found themselves forced to work out how to meet the new expectations with few new resources.

Instead the funds flowed to hundreds of New Work Opportunity programs (NWOs), which helped satisfy the 13-week requirement for payment to contractors. Within weeks the entire system became consumed by the pressure to create and fill these programs. While many of the actual programs were undoubtedly successful and valued by those who participated, the effect on the dynamics of the service delivery system was often destructive. Case managers and agencies became recruitment points for whatever program DEETYA was funding in the local area. These pressures were irresistible, since failure to refer one's clients not only meant missing a payment but also gave one's competitors an opportunity to oblige DEETYA and improve their profits.

The Second Revolution - Job Network and the Howard Government

The second set of changes began in March 1996 when the recently elected conservative Coalition government under John Howard abolished the training programs that Labor had established and announced that Working Nation had been a failure because less that one third of those undertaking Labor's training programs had found real jobs afterwards. While there certainly had been problems with many of the training programs, the results overall were more promising than this suggested. The Howard government, however, preferred partisan attack to incremental adjustment. It announced a desire to make labour market assistance both more limited and more clearly linked to the client's "capacity to benefit." The revised "Vanstone"[14] scheme included

- Increase of private provider role from 30% to almost 50% of the market
- Closing of brokered training programs
- Delegation ("cashing out") of remaining program funds to providers
- Payments driven only by exits to jobs
- Termination of the role of the independent regulator[15]

The new Howard government had ample ammunition with which to attack Labor's reforms and they did not stint. Their less sympathetic view of the unemployed was in neat coincidence with the desire to cut public expenditure. They removed more than three billion from the DEETYA appropriation and closed most of the training programs that had provided contractors with many of their outcomes.

The new system put in place by the Coalition was announced as part of the budget preparations in 1996 and later enshrined in the *Reform of Employment Services Bill 1996*. In the budget paper, *Reforming Employment Assistance*, Senator Amanda Vanstone indicated that the Government wished to "concentrate intensive labour market assistance on the long-term unemployed" and to base such assistance on individual needs and upon the unemployed person's "capacity to benefit." The "radical and comprehensive" changes would come into effect in 1998, following a public tender round in May 1997.[16] In the meantime existing contractors would continue under ESRA direction but without training programs. After the new tender round ESRA would be closed and the government itself would become the purchaser of services. That is, DEETYA would be separated from the public employment contractor (a renamed EAA) and would act as supreme policy maker, regulator and banker for the new system. This was put forward as a commitment to "competitive neutrality" (Vanstone, pp.8-13).[17]

In addition to further strengthening the private sector role, this model provided for the development of a new public agency, first called the Service Delivery Agency (SDA) and later known as CentreLink. Legislation for this new agency was provided in the *Commonwealth Services Delivery Agency Act 1996* which gave this organisation control over all social security payments, not only those to unemployed clients but also those to pensioners, single parents and veterans. The Department of Social Security (DSS) and DEETYA would "purchase" these payment services from CentreLink and would also appoint representatives to the CentreLink Board of Directors, therefore becoming both customers and shareholders. For job seekers the new arrangement would see a "basic service" provided by CentreLink and an "elaborated service" provided by the new industry of contractors. Basic services included access to electronic job vacancy lists in CentreLink offices and registration for income support.[18]

But while the contractors had their access to training programs cut, they did not gain extra resources to spend on intensive work with job seekers. Their new role was to include finding and filling job vacancies. The government created a new National Vacancy Data Base that each contractor (including the public agency) was required to use. Gaining a job for a client was now the only way to complete the payment requirements and contractors were now required both to help job seekers prepare for work and also to get employers to lodge vacancies with them. This approach reflected the new government's belief that jobs were available but that long term job seekers were either not looking in the right places or were being overlooked by conventional recruitment agencies.

The form of employment counselling to be provided by the new contractors was defined as the "most intensive form of assistance" and described by the minister as "similar to, but more flexible than, the current case management system."[19] The government said that it expected that there would be fewer places available than there were eligible clients, and therefore expected the "capacity to benefit" principle to govern a rationing process. What this meant in practice was that not all the long-term unemployed would be referred to a contractor. Instead DEETYA would set in place criteria to determine which clients had the capacity to benefit from extra attention.

To critics this looked like a more blatant form of creaming in which only those clients already close to meeting employer expectations would be referred for help and the others would effectively be warehoused, or "parked," as front line staff described it. The government responded by pointing to a new program called the Community Support Program (CSP), which was to give assistance to those too far from the labour market to benefit from the intensive assistance system. However, the levels of funding for CSP would remain so low over the coming four years that its contribution to the overall system was soon widely devalued.

Because the senate remained hostile to key aspects of these plans the government was unable to enact legislation authorizing anything but the CentreLink part of the scheme. Instead it set about establishing the system using delegated authority held by the secretary of DEETYA. The new contractors would, in effect, be agents of a now disembodied CES. The public provider, now to be called Employment National, was established as a private corporation wholly owned by the government. The provisions of Labor's Employment Services Act – which required that all eligible clients receive case management, training or jobs – were to be put aside. To render that Act irrelevant and cover itself against possible litigation, the government chose to consign the term "case management" to the past and to describe its own approach as "intensive assistance."

According to the government this methodology was to be directed at "getting job seekers into real jobs,"[20] with higher payments to be made for more disadvantaged clients. According to the Minister each contractor would "be free to decide with the participant the optimal kinds and mix of assistance needed to get the participant a job."[21] Each job seeker would receive an intensive service that was tailored to their particular needs and abilities. These decisions would be made at the local level and not through program standardisation determined in Canberra. It was here that the two key thrusts of the new system – client-focus and competition – came together. Freed of bureaucratic regulation the adviser and the job seeker would have stronger incentives to achieve positive results, it was hoped.

The only other matter that remained to be clarified was the awkward question of sanctioning, or breaching as it was called in Australia. As we saw above, Labor had used new legislation to empower and oblige contractors to report breaches to the CES so that a stronger penalty regime could be imposed. This legislation was still in force but the new government had chosen to work around it using administrative and regulatory devices to build the revised system. Sanctioning now fell somewhere between two stools. If job seekers selected a private agency to receive their intensive assistance they would be asked to sign an activity agreement. This would become the basis of any future sanctioning by the private contractor. But by law only CentreLink could breach job seekers and thus only they could require job seekers to perform activities at threat of sanctioning. This left the contractors with incentives to "bark but not bite." It also left job seekers with confused obligations to the public and private elements of the new system.[22] The then leader of the Democrats, Cheryl Kernot, complained that under the legislation proposed by the Coalition job seekers were to be given no rights of appeal against penalties imposed on them by private contractors. Nor were they protected against any decision to exclude them from participation in the intensive employment assistance parts of the scheme.[23]

During early 1997 a transition system was put in place to allow Employment National, the CES and existing contractors to begin their new roles. These arrangements fuelled resentment in the private sector where it was believed that Employment National was already receiving special treatment in its preparations for the first tender round. The other concern was the fear among contractors that the new requirement to become a job vacancy agent as well as a placement agency would create advantages for private recruitment companies and allow them to dominate the new market.

Non-profit contractors and some for-profit companies not involved in recruitment saw the new demand for vacancies as a threat to their job seeker focus. They also believed it would now be easy for recruitment companies to churn job seekers through vacancies kept on their own books and never made available to the market as a whole. At its worst, this promised a new level of fraud in a system already open to abuse. And at the very least it seemed to promise a new segmentation into one sector oriented to recruitment and vacancy management, and another stuck with old commitments to skill development and other forms of job seeker enhancement. Critics inside and outside pointed out that there was no obvious way for contractors to integrate these competing priorities without a loss of focus upon the most disadvantaged job seekers.

Tender Politics

The tender for all the new contracts to deliver the Coalition scheme was planned to be finalised by the beginning of 1997 but had to be put back until May. Existing contracts with the old agencies therefore were extended from January to May, prolonging the atmosphere of uncertainty among the already alarmed contractor industry. The delay also forced the government to contract with the new public provider Employment National to take over many of the functions of the CES during this interregnum. This in turn led to the emergence of a world of Chinese walls and whispers inside the government sector in order to preserve the idea that Employment National was in fact an independent contractor rather than a part of the public sector. One measure widely publicised in the industry at large was that Employment National staff assigned to CES work would be limited in the access they would have to clients and to case files. This was intended to prevent them gaining an inside running with job seekers who would soon have to choose between competing agencies. But while this was taking place Employment National was also using its access to existing government building stock to make sure that its own premises were conveniently located near the new CentreLink offices and doing so well before other contractors were in a position to make their own real estate decisions.

Once under way, the tender process was itself a heavily regulated and highly selective institution. Watched by an independent probity adviser, between September 1997 and the end of December teams of assessors met in DEETYA's head office in Canberra to consider the bids of the many hundreds of would-be contractors, including most of the existing industry. Each local region had a three-person panel and a probity overseer. One of the members in every case was a DEETYA official from the state in question.[24]

The procedure required that no issue could be raised in the panel discussion unless it related explicitly to the tender specification. This, coupled with the fact that panels were not to exchange information about their deliberations, meant that every region was treated as a completely separate mini-tender. Each panel considered each bid and checked off its strengths against the tender specification. Those deemed unsuccessful at this stage were the ones in which one or more specification was deemed not to have been adequately addressed. This could include a too-high bid for the price sensitive vacancy-matching part of the new scheme (called Flex I) or an insufficiently compelling explanation of how "intensive assistance" would be delivered (this Flex 3 service having a stipulated price and thus being subject to more qualitative judgments).

Unsuccessful bids were then reviewed by a separate panel; if they disagreed with the first panel they were then sent to an adjudication panel composed of the most senior DEETYA officers. Insiders later acknowledged that while this approach followed a standard, verified pathway and met probity requirements, it was lop-sided. Unsuccessful bids received far more attention than those passed as adequate in the first round. It meant that the selection process was often weighted towards the need to justify exclusions, rather than defend selections. When some of the more controversial contracts given to newcomers became public, the weakness of this negative selectivity would become more obvious. But at the time bureaucrats believed they were keeping prejudice at arm's length, were assessing objectively, and were shielded from complaints of favouritism.

When the more positive aspects of the tender judgments were discussed after the event another weakness also emerged. Because none of the panel members were experienced providers of these services, qualitative judgments had to be defended textually. That is by reference to the level of professionalism and "polish" evident in the business strategy outlined in the bid documents. Panels were permitted to take account of previous performance, and officials later insisted that they had access to the performance data gathered by the previous regulator, ESRA. However, the very strong message given to panels was that this new tender was not searching for case managers and they should therefore be prepared to discount previous performance where it was mostly based on claims about case management proficiency. This served as a strong signal to panels to look elsewhere and mix their recommendations with old and new contractors.

There were also a number of other problems for tender assessment panels to resolve. For instance in at least one case a firm bid zero dollars for the training part of its proposed operations, clearly hoping this would attract a high volume of this form of business and a high volume of the more attractive work with intensive assistance. This threw the panel into confusion. Is a contract still a contract if no payment is being made? Could the government extract high quality service if it was in fact paying no fee for one part of the service?

Although the process precluded any negotiation with the bidders, the department was not required to take the lowest bid for any service. Averaging and balancing of cost and quality objectives was permitted. What this meant in practice was that some contractors were offered business at rates lower than they had submitted, the department's defence being that others in their region had submitted lower bids and had thus pulled the whole price structure downwards.

This was an impossible situation for contractors. They could not see what others were bidding and could not negotiate with government. Once offered a contract they had to say either yes or no. If they said no there was no guarantee and little likelihood that the department would make a second, better offer. As one contractor put it:

> We were being told it was just like the Vic Market and we were the banana
> sellers. What price would we put on our best stock? At what price would we be
> prepared to sell if the customer offered a lower bid? But we couldn't see the
> other sellers . . . couldn't see what price they had on their bananas. Worse still
> there was one customer in the whole market and he wasn't talking to us or
> giving us any kind of feedback.

The on-going problem of setting payments for the most lucrative part of the system, the intensive assistance work (Flex 3), had been decided using a three-part classification and a three-stage payment regime (Table One). The department acknowledged this fee structure left it entirely to the contractor to decide what, if anything, from these fees would be invested in either the job seeker or the employer. If contractors chose to pay employers a "subsidy" to accept a very disadvantaged person into a job for at least six months, that was their business. Or if the contractor simply chose to absorb the entire fee as profit to the firm, that too was up to them. The new policy would remain agnostic in regard to the local strategies used. Of course this also meant that evaluation would prove to be almost impossible since every site would be different and every recipe would remain the private property of the contractor.

Table One: Job Seeker Classification & Payment Schedule for Intensive Assistance

Client Classification	Share of total places	Maximum duration of activity	Payment at start	Interim payment	Payment at 26 weeks in a job.
1. Least disadvantaged ('3.1')	67 %	12	$1,500	$1,500	$ 1,200
2. Medium Disadvantage ('3.2)	26 %	12	$2,250	$ 2,250	$ 2,200
3. Most disadvantaged ('3.3')	7 %	18	$ 3,000	$3,200	$ 3,000

In addition to the rate of payment for each client, the other method for government control over contractors was the total number of clients flowing through the system. Not only would the Department monitor assessments made by CentreLink to be sure that not too many clients were classified in to the expensive (3.3) category, they would also be able to ration the flow of clients through the system by squeezing CentreLink resources. Shortly after it was established CentreLink was required by its Board to begin a program of severe cuts to its labour force, resulting in a major slowdown in the movement of clients through to the contractors.

The contractors were therefore dependent upon an administrative system that was both complex and ambiguous. DEETYA contracted for their services but CentreLink controlled their immediate fate. But they had no direct claim on CentreLink. The same pattern of ambiguity existed with regard to legal accountability. As we have already seen, without legislation the government was forced to resort to inferior regulatory powers. Different parts of the delivery system were thus subject to different forms of accountability. The federal Ombudsman's Office could inquire into the actions of DEETYA, CentreLink and Employment National, but not the other contractors.

Job seekers and contractors could also use the provisions of the Trade Practices Act to force DEETYA to act fairly with regard to its "trading" functions, but these were not clearly defined and thus would have first to be tested in court. It was not clear at the time and remains unclear to this day whether conducting a tender would be considered a form of trading and if so, which aspects of it were covered by the Trade Practices Act admonition against "anti-competitive conduct." Perhaps the very fact that these contractors had only one purchaser to which to tender made DEETYA itself a monopolist? Answers to these questions were prone to provoke discord and so soon were pushed to the background of relations between the participants without ever being resolved.

The Job Network

A new cast of contractors operating from several hundred sites was licensed and put to work in May 1998. Within days the controversies surrounding the tender outcomes began to emerge in the media. Many well-performing organisations from the case management period were not offered contracts, or were offered work that was not likely to be attractive. Many new agencies were given contracts even though they had no track record, no facilities and little obvious claim to expertise. With the code of silence imposed on contractors by the tender process the department was able to muffle most of these criticisms. It required successful contractors to sign agreements that prevented them from divulging details of their contracts. This left the public debate to languish in the hands of those easily scorned as the "sore losers" and inevitable casualties of a competitive process.

Had these been the only problems the new scheme might have survived its tortured first months unscathed. However the second wave of discontent came from the two groups most able to win sympathetic attention from the press. Jobs seekers found the system confusing and arbitrary and employers complained that it was difficult to use and apt to be expensive. For job seekers the biggest problem was gaining eligibility to use the new system. Many recipients of income support were not eligible to use the services of the contractors because they were not long enough unemployed, had not been classified by CentreLink, or were part of the new group which the government had decided lacked the "capacity to benefit" from anything more than basic services provided at CentreLink. Not understanding their status, or not accepting it, many of these job seekers began approaching contractors to seek the jobs they were advertising. Contractors turned to government and pressed to be permitted to provide this group with services. In refusing, the government appeared both callous and confused about what it wanted from the new system.

This bad start flowed over into relations with the government's natural ally, the business community. Because contractors were now approaching their roles in a business-like manner, many sought to charge employers a fee for finding them a suitable job applicant. Accustomed to the free assistance formerly provided by the CES, firms complained that the government's new scheme was creating a new inflexibility, particularly for casual and low paid jobs where turnover or transition costs were apt to be most painful. Nor were they pleased to have to deal with the profusion of new agencies seeking their help to place job seekers, satisfy job search demands, and gain practice at "cold canvassing" potential clients.

Flex One – Getting and Filling Job Vacancies

Undoubtedly the most difficult part of the implementation of the new order concerned the contracting-out of the labour exchange function of the CES. In the new system this was defined as the "Flex One" service where contractors would gather and fill their own vacancies. Every contractor was required to become a labour exchange and this forced them to invent new strategies inside their organisations to solicit vacancies from employers and then to fill them. Most began by copying the practices of the recruitment companies. The developed telephone "call centres" and employed staff to contact prospective employers. This also led to the development of new minimal-cost services for job seekers who were only eligible for this service. Since the price for Flex One was variable, each agency had to guess the likely cost of finding and filling these vacancies. The department had indicated that bids around $250 per vacancy were expected. Most were awarded at rates between $245 and $400. At this price even minimal efforts using call centres were unlikely to produce high returns. What would make the service profitable was the ability of the agency to win both this Flex One business and a good quota of higher value "intensive assistance" work of the kind outlined in Table One. In this case the job-matching functions would simply become an opportunity structure for placing high-return clients. Some agencies received such a mix of clients in their contracts and others did not.

Once the "call centre" method was in place some larger agencies had incentives to use it for managing job seekers as well as employers. This placed further pressure on job seekers to accept a new and more limited service. In place of attendance at the CES they now waited at home for a call from any one of the agencies with whom they had registered. Only in the intensive assistance cases would the relationship with a single contractor be binding. Contractors wanting to raise their profiles in the new job-matching business soon developed a variety of dubious tactics. For example, in occupations where there were known to be labour shortages, agencies would advertise positions that did not exist. Qualified applicants were then told the job was filled and were asked to supply their details so that they could be contacted when "the next position becomes available." Armed with a reserve of qualified applicants in a valued field, the agency would then begin approaching employers with offers to guarantee same-day filling of vacancies for employers willing to sign an agency agreement or place other vacancies with the contractor.

In order to pacify agitated job seekers, annoyed employers, and anxious contractors the government made several changes to the new system. During 1998 the job-matching restrictions were relaxed a little to allow a larger number of job seekers to use this service. The restrictions on asking job seekers for payments for assistance were also relaxed to help contractors find new ways to earn income. Perhaps most indicative of the political vulnerability of the Job Network arrangements was the decision of the Minister David Kemp to pay contractors an extra $10,000 for each site they operated as a means to soften the criticisms about the job-matching part of the service and the imminent collapse of several contractors operating in the worst labour markets.

Against this negative picture of the job-matching requirements imposed by the Coalition reforms was the frequent comment by interviewees who were impressed that this function had actually worked well and created a beneficial focus upon employers. It was indicative of these larger problems that in more than twenty interviews undertaken in this study in the period after Job Network had been in operation for twelve months, of the six managers who saw job matching as a good function to have devolved to contractors, five were from private sector firms and the sixth came from a larger non-profit organisation. Those with the most negative experiences were leaders of church and smaller non-profit agencies.[25]

Flex Three – Intensive Assistance

The intensive assistance function, which had previously been termed "case management," was now classified as the Flex 3 service and as Table One shows, this was the lucrative part of the contract. Most agencies did their planning on the basis that only twenty to forty percent of this group would actually reach the job outcome stage and so their viability was very much built upon the commencement payments provided by the government. And herein lay the problem. With the government ideology moving away from close attention to job seeker employment barriers and towards self-motivated search, the signals being sent to front line staff in the agencies seemed to be very different to those of the Labor government period. Job seekers still had to sign an activity agreement and were still at risk of sanctioning if they failed to comply. But the notion that all of them should receive regular interviews or any other particular intervention was now widely abandoned. It would be up to the agency to decide what it expected of job seekers. If some form of training appeared likely to result in a job, some funds from the commencement payments could be diverted. And if the job seeker was judged as unlikely to find work the agency could "park," or warehouse their file at the back of the queue and have no further contact until the twelve months elapsed and they were reclassified as no longer having a "capacity to benefit" from intensive assistance. This would take them off the contractors list and allow someone new to be referred from CentreLink.

The Politics of "Choice"

The formal part of the relationship between job seeker and agency was thus less structured than before. The signing of an activity agreement was no longer the trigger for the commencement payment, leaving the agency free to negotiate this at a later stage, after the job seeker had agreed to be assigned to the agency. Interviewees indicated that they did not rush to complete the agreement in the first session.

Because job seekers retained some element of choice regarding their referral to a particular contractor, this first meeting was considered as an important screening opportunity for many agencies. By indicating interest, hostility, sympathy or toughness the contractors could influence the job seeker's decision to accept to be registered with them. Once past this stage a decision to withdraw would cost the job seeker a sanction unless they could convince CentreLink that they had been severely mistreated.

In practice, the choices exercised by job seekers were little different to those available under the Labor government scheme. CentreLink was obliged to inform job seekers of all the agencies in the area able to offer intensive assistance. However, because of the unpredictable nature of the client flows through the CentreLink assessment and referral process combined with uneven rates of exit by job seekers finding work, some contractors might have a full list while others had space for many more referrals. Job seekers were only permitted to maintain a particular preference for 28 days, after which CentreLink had the power to compulsorily refer them to any available contractor. Perhaps more problematic even than these cumbersome referral arrangements was the fact that job seekers were to be given no information concerning the performance of the various contractors, the number of vacancies they had listed, nor the success in finding job seekers a job. The department said it hoped to resolve data verification problems and certain legal impediments in order to ultimately be able to provide these data. However, since to do so would also grant the public direct information on the performance of the Job Network as a whole, it had common cause with contractors nervous about this kind of exposé. Job seeker empowerment, therefore, remained one of the least successful parts of the new order.

And here finally was the most serious weakness of the new scheme. What occurred inside the contractor's office was not only driven by the vastly unequal relationship between the job seeker and the contractor, it was also hidden from the department's gaze under the commercial-in-confidence protocols accepted at the time of the tender. While the department could view performance outcomes from every site and could monitor information it required contractors to lodge on the national information system, it could not require contractors to reveal the methods they used to obtain results. Known as the "black box" among many agencies and described as the "eleven different herbs and spices" by others, these methods had replaced the protocols of case management when that model fell into political disrepute. Understanding what was actually happening at the front line of the service was therefore both more interesting and more obscure.

Conclusions

As one might expect with a study based on a comparative method, the Australian experience makes most sense when it is seen in the context of other reform pathways. Although they were clearly different in many ways, the two Australian schemes, "Working Nation" and "Job Network," look almost identical when placed beside the Dutch experience or that of the United Kingdom under the conservatives. But compared to each other they also show major differences, not least of which is the increase in systematic creaming over this period. Those issues of performance will need to be addressed by independent evaluation and in the meantime it is perhaps most relevant to review four crucial governance issues which characterize the Australian experiment and offer important insights into reforms being contemplated elsewhere in the OECD.

1. Competition among contractors. What was really achieved by requiring this multitude of small and medium sized agencies to behave as if they were in a commodities market? The main advantage has been to increase the authority of government purchasers at tender time, but to make the system very hard to steer the rest of the time. Unemployed people get no benefit from the competitive part of the system; indeed it might be argued that they suffer as a result of all the boundaries and trip-wires between these many agencies. According to Centrelink staff, only 40 percent of job seekers exercise their right to choose which agency they go to, and even in these cases the choice is most often based upon the convenience of location, proximity to train stations or to the CentreLink office itself.

2. The Role of Employment National. One of the obvious consequences of both versions of the Australian system has been to make the public provider almost irrelevant. In the EAA case this was because the organisation could not free itself of CES obligations and routines. In the Employment National case it was because it could not resist the temptation to be more rabidly entrepreneurial than even the most committed for-profit agencies. As a senior official in the UK Employment Service put it, "They seemed to want to be more catholic than the Pope." The fact that the government of the day could allow such a wanton disregard for the public

interest is testimony to the poor leverage available to decision makers in these quasi-market arrangements.

3. Regulating in the Public Interest. Although ESRA did a creditable job in supporting the first contractors, at no time has the Australian system been subject to effective regulation. In particular it is difficult to see how citizens can hold anyone to account for what is done with their tax dollars when the path from government department, via confidential tender, through an arm's length service delivery agency, to independent contractors motivated by paid outcomes, and out to highly vulnerable clients is so complex and obscure. A simple example of the problem is the prevalence of both creaming and parking. How can either of these problems be addressed when those making public policy have no direct influence over those delivering tax-funded programs?

4. The Senior Public Service. It is most noticeable in this case that one of the key governance effects of the quasi-market is to politicize the senior public service. Because ministers are formerly precluded from having any direct role in the tender process, senior public servants become the principle "program champions." It is their decisions that need to be defended publicly. As a result they lose any semblance of independence from the party political regime of the day. The government's political enemies become their enemies, evaluation issues become subsumed beneath questions of political damage control, and it becomes inevitable that any change of government will also occasion a major change in public service leadership. What this suggests for policy and program development is a severe form of alternation in which both public servants and their political masters must seek to build careers upon the destruction of the previous regime's achievements, the dismantling of significant parts of the program architecture, and conscious acts of memory loss designed to separate the virtues of the past from the proposed values of some new set of changes.

The Australian Working Nation and Job Network reforms are a remarkable achievement in any terms. They show a degree of pliability in public programs that would have seemed impossible even ten years ago. Their effects upon job seekers remain to be independently evaluated but it appears that the most disadvantaged have gained least, and may have become even more disadvantaged, particularly under Job Network. The effects upon governance are also complex with greater flexibility and the use of contractor skills being somewhat offset by significant loss of steering capacity by government and a serious loss of accountability of programs to parliament and other audit institutions.

The next iteration of reform, if there is to be one, will need to harness the competitive elements of the system and create a more genuine partnership between government and its agents. The goal of a seamless service, which is a core requirement of the case management system and a key objective of governance reform more generally, is no closer now than it was when Working Nation was first announced. In fact the quasi-market has created some new obstacles to this outcome. The awkward role of CentreLink will certainly need to be addressed if an integrated process for assisting very disadvantaged job seekers into work is to be achieved. And a model for a public agency that seeks to foster system-wide innovation and provide a guarantee of service for all those in need is also still to be achieved. If these things can be done with a little less attention to questions of ideological purity and greater willingness to acknowledge problems, this remarkable experiment may yet mature beyond its first years of controversy.

Notes

[1] Mark Considine, *Enterprising States: The Public Management of Welfare to Work* (Cambridge University Press, 2001). Full details of the interview and survey methodology are to be found in the book and are not repeated here in the interests of brevity.

[2] Australia, *Working Nation: Policies and Programs*, Government White Paper (Canberra: Australian Government Publishing Service, 1994), p. 127.

[3] Australia, *Working Nation*, p. 127.

[4] Chris Robinson, *Employment Case Management and Public Sector Reform*, Department of Prime Minister and Cabinet (PMC), 10 July, 1995 (Canberra: PMC, 1995).

[5] Paul Keating, *Launch of the Employment Services Regulatory Authority*, William Angliss College, Melbourne, 4 May 1995, E&OE Proof Copy.

[6] Government officials involved in policy development accept that field staff have become cynical of policy change. Most offices of CES and EAA contain staff who were involved in the first major reforms in 1989. At this point a special program for older and disabled workers was introduced in which CES staff, selected Skillshare officers and some disability service organisations were appointed as "Brokers." Their job was to work one-on-one with target clients and assist them back to work.

In 1990-91 the Newstart initiative included a division of CES staff into Jobcentres and Special Service Centres, the latter being defined as places where "at risk" clients or those already long term would receive regular interviews by specialist staff. This initiative built upon the "broker" role that was piloted in the 1989 scheme.

[7] C.D. Austin, "Developing Case Management: A Systems Perspective," *Journal of Contemporary Human Services* (October 1993), p. 452.

[8] Barbara Hammond, *Foundations of Case Management* (Waurn Ponds, DHSA: Deakin University Press, 1997), p.34.

[9] Nikolas Rose, "Governing 'Advanced' Liberal Democracies," in Andrew Barry, Thomas Osborne and Nikolas Rose, eds., *Foucault and Political Reason: Liberalism, Neo-Liberalism and Rationalities of Government* (Londo: UCL Press, 1996), pp. 37-65.

[10] J. Brudney and R. England, "Toward a Definition of the Co-Production Concept," *Public Administration Review* 43 no. 1 (1983), pp.59-71.

[11] Yeheskel Hasenfeld and Dale Weaver, "Enforcement, Compliance, and Disputes in Return-to-Work Programs," *Social Services Review* (June1996), p. 236.

[12] Fr.David Cappo, National Director, Australian Catholic Social Welfare Commission, *Our Values and Our Skills: An Ideal Combination for Case Management*, National Summit on Employment Opportunities and Case Management, Parkroyal Plaza Hotel, Sydney, 14-15 March, 1995.

[13] CEDA evaluation, 1999.

[14] While no official name was given to this amended scheme, it was largely associated in the public mind with the minister responsible, Senator Amanda Vanstone.

[15] The Howard government has continued this regime through 1996 and 1997 but had foreshadowed a further development of this market to commence in 1998. This is known as the "Flex Program" and imposes further change upon the various participants. The government will close its own Commonwealth Employment Service and merge these functions with the social security office, now to operate as a service delivery agency (called CentreLink) for all recipients of income assistance. This new bureaucracy will undertake the basic registration and referral functions found in all public employment agencies. Those deemed likely to benefit (and subject to available funds) will then be referred to three levels of assistance (Flex 1,2, & 3) to be provided by either the new public agency, or by one of the contracted agencies.

[16] Australia, Parliament, Senate, Reform of Employment Services Bill 1996, Second Reading Speech, Senator Amanda Vanstone, 1996, p. 10.

[17] Senator Amanda Vanstone, "Reforming Employment Services" (Canberra: Office of the Minister for Employment, Education and Training, 1997)" pp. 8-13.

[18] Australia, Parliament, Senate, Reform of Employment Services Bill 1996, Second Reading Speech, Senator Amanda Vanstone, 1996.

[19] Australia, Reform of Employment Services Bill, p.4.

[20] Australia, Reform of Employment Services Bill, p.4.

[21] Australia, Reform of Employment Services Bill, p.5.

[22] Former DEETYA legal adviser Tom Brennan of Coors, Chambers, Wesgarth argued that breaches initiated by private contractors were unlikely to survive appeal to the Administrative Appeals tribunal or the Federal Court for this reason. This was especially the case where the breach was based only on evidence supplied to CentreLink by the contractor. See Background Briefing, ABC Radio National, 28 March 1999.

[23] *Sydney Morning Herald*, 18 March 1997, p.4.

[24] This meant that local knowledge of labour markets could be drawn upon. It also meant an enormous Travel Allowance (TA) cost for the department and a boon for these state staff who spent three months working weeks in Canberra and being flown home for weekends. Senior staff freely acknowledged that this extra work enabled officials to "pay off houses," buy new cars, and "stack up considerable reserves," and certainly helped explain why those involved remained highly committed to the process.

[25] Twenty-two interviews were conducted with eleven for-profit and eleven non-profit managers from Victoria and NSW. They were asked, "How would you rate the Flex 1 arrangements now that you have had a chance to see them in operation? Generally good? Mixed? Generally bad? Further comment?"

Public, Private and Voluntary Sector Partnerships in Employment Programs: What are the Practical Boundaries?

Professor David A. Good, School of Public Administration, University of Victoria, Canada

---

Whenever we get into partnerships, we get into trouble and particularly because we lose control. I never know who is in charge. For example, if a businessman puts in three quarters of the investment and we put in one quarter and then he decides to move, how could we possibly stop him when three quarters of the money is his?

Member of Parliament

. . . there are many complexities to the accountability process. The partnership that the honourable member refers to adds to that complexity. That is not a call to go back to simple federal delivery of programs because I think we are potentially much more powerful and effective when we work in partnership.

Secretary to the Cabinet and Clerk of the Privy Council

What are the practical boundaries to partnerships between the public sector and the private and voluntary sectors in the area of employment programs? Are they broad and seemingly endless in scope, limited only by the creativity of public servants and private and voluntary sector providers? Or are they more limited and circumscribed by forces that shape the government's role in the development and delivery of employment programs? What is the capacity of government and the private and voluntary sectors to actually do partnerships in employment programs? How are these new partnership programs actually developed and how are they implemented? Why have these programs been so difficult to deliver? Why has there been (at least in Canada) so much interest in these programs in the media and at the political level? What is the appropriate role for members of Parliament in the delivery of these programs?

There clearly are limits in the private sector concerning what jobs get created, where and for how long, and who gets trained and with what results. There are limits in the voluntary sector especially when the over-extended delivery capacity of its diverse organizations is compared to the increasing expectations from government and the private sector. There are limits in the public sector associated with where employment activities take place, who gets helped and how much, and how public money is spent.

There are benefits to be achieved through public, private and voluntary sector partnerships in the delivery of employment programs. No one sector can do it all, especially in addressing chronic unemployment. The private sector creates the jobs and in the knowledge-based economy has an increasing demand for a skilled and innovative workforce. The voluntary sector with its diverse and autonomous organizations can provide a level of flexibility and on-the-ground responsiveness that governments can rarely match. Governments have the capacity to redistribute public resources and to help ensure that the needs of the unemployed and the excluded are addressed.

A better understanding of some of the limits should give a clearer appreciation of the potential for innovative partnerships in employment programs. One place to start is by focusing on the partner that is generally recognized to be operating under the most constraints, that is, the public sector. One way, but not the only way, to appreciate better the constraints on government is to examine what happens when things go wrong. We will therefore examine the public reaction (many would say over-reaction) to the release of an internal audit of the administration of grants and contributions programs of Human Resources Development Canada (HRDC), which included a number of employment programs. We will describe the management and program context of the department in terms of how and why employment and other programs were developed and delivered to engage partners, ensure flexibility, and improve results. While this case may be seen by some as extreme, it is useful for our purposes because it can better indicate how, in the real world, various institutions are likely to react when things do not go as well as initially expected. This should help us to more fully understand those aspects of partnership associated with employment programs that will need special attention in order to make partnerships work better and to improve results.

This paper examines two HRDC employment programs, the Transitional Jobs Fund (TJF) and its successor, the Canada Jobs Fund (CJF). TJF/CJF was implemented through collaborative arrangements with small and medium size enterprises in the private sector and, in a number of cases, through various local voluntary organizations. In addition to the sponsors of projects there was extensive consultation with local community partners on the project proposals. The program also had various partnership arrangements with other federal government departments and provincial governments. Members of Parliament played a unique role in providing advice on projects as part of the decision-making process. We will trace the development, implementation and eventual demise of the TJF/CJF program. We will also examine the program in relation to the internal HRDC audit of the administration of its grants and contributions program and the reaction to the release of that audit. We will then consider some lessons learned about the use of public, private and voluntary sector partnerships in the delivery of employment programs. The high public profile that was associated with the grants and contributions audit provides a large base of detailed public information that is normally not the case for most government programs. This public information includes the internal audit, the extensive media reaction to its release, countless questions in the House of Commons, media briefings and press releases, extensive parliamentary committee hearings including interim and final reports by the committee, and a separate report of the auditor general.

There are many different kinds of partnership arrangements. In this paper the focus will be on what some have called "collaborative arrangements"1 in which a government shares policy and program development, risk and operational planning, and design and management of the program with another party or parties who deliver the program or service. This can be distinguished from "delegated arrangements" in which a government, within a broad policy framework, has delegated key planning and operational decisions to the discretion of another party such as a provincial government or a private or voluntary sector organization.

TJF/CJF: partnerships in flexibility

Most new programs are designed and implemented against the backdrop of the prevailing public management philosophy of the day. TJF was no exception. Most employment programs are developed in response to external pressure. TJF was no exception. TJF was developed by HRDC in the context of the new public management and as an integral part of the reform to Employment Insurance (EI) in December 1995. In the face of longstanding concerns about the impact of Unemployment Insurance in undermining incentives to work, especially in Atlantic Canada, program eligibility to EI income benefits for seasonal workers and repeat users was significantly tightened through legislative and regulatory change. As a consequence there were significant income loses to both workers and unemployed individuals in Atlantic Canada and significant portions of Quebec. Pressure mounted from government caucus members and some Atlantic Canada MPs and provincial premiers to provide assistance in those regions of the country where individuals would be losing benefits as a result of EI reform. At the same time many members of the Liberal caucus were also concerned that the federal government was becoming more distant from Canadians and losing its ability to directly touch citizens as it downsized government, eliminated programs, transferred training programs to the provinces, and privatized a number of its functions.

It was in this context that TJF was developed and announced as a three year, $300 million program to encourage small and medium businesses to create sustainable jobs in areas of high unemployment. The areas of the country where projects would be funded were primarily in Atlantic Canada and Quebec in those areas hardest hit by Employment Insurance reform. The projects to be funded would be those proposed by small enterprises and included the creation of new startup businesses or the expansion and diversification of existing ones. The projects funded ranged across the broad spectrum of industrial sectors including aquaculture, tourism infrastructure, silviculture, manufacturing and light industry, food processing, retail and many others.

There had been a long and sordid history with direct job creation programs by the federal government. Because there had been such limited success with many of these programs the department was particularly attentive to how any new program could best be designed. As the department went about designing the new program it drew upon its experience with previous job creation programs. An immediate reading of the seemingly unending stream of program evaluations and reviews of previous programs provided the general answer to the often asked question of "what works and why?" In short, the answer was "not much and there are lots of problems."

To the experienced program designer this immediately suggested three things. One, any new program had to recognize the inherent skepticism concerning the effectiveness of direct job creation programs undertaken by a remote federal government especially in the absence of locally developed initiatives as part of a broader regional economic development scheme.[2] Second, any new program, if it was to be successful, had to be limited in scope, restricted to small projects, focus on results, engage partners, lever private sector funding, ensure clarity and transparency in the approval process, and minimize administrative processes and maximize flexibility to deal effectively with the private and voluntary sector partners. Third, any design needed to recognize the perception on the part of some critics that job creation programs can be prone to excessive political influence by ministers and members of Parliament in the development and approval of projects.

The program was developed with few objectives. Experience had indicated the greater the number of objectives the greater the likelihood that there would be conflicts among them and the more difficulties with successful implementation. TJF was designed with one objective: "to create long term sustainable jobs for individuals in high unemployment regions affected by EI reform."[3] It is a tall order to create sustainable jobs in areas of high unemployment, but by limiting the program to one objective and by maximizing flexibility in its implementation there was a better chance of some success. The program explicitly emphasized collaboration through "partnership initiatives with the private sector, provincial and municipal governments, other federal departments, community groups and other organizations".[4] Four specific program criteria were set out publicly:

- "Proposals must clearly demonstrate that they will lead to the creation of sustainable jobs,

- Other partners must contribute at least 50 per cent of the total project costs,

- Proposals should be consistent with the strategic plan for local/regional economic development, and

- Proposals must have the support of the province/territory in which the activity will take place."[5]

In addition, two other guidelines were established as part of the Treasury Board approved terms and conditions, namely, "flexibility to allow activities to reflect and respond to local and/or regional needs" and "implementation of TJF activities within a framework for evaluating their success in creating sustainable jobs and leveraging funds from other partners."[6]

The program was also designed with minimum constraints and maximum flexibility. To ensure maximum flexibility and to increase the likelihood of creating sustainable jobs there was a need for flexibility in delivery. The department did not establish a criterion or strict rule for defining a high unemployment region. Instead it established a guideline that allowed considerable flexibility for interpretation by HRDC regional managers in determining a high unemployment region and hence eligible projects. This meant that regional managers could respond to local needs, partners and circumstances. There were four definitions for high unemployment regions. The first was straightforward and open to little interpretation. It involved EI economic regions where the unemployment rate in 1995 was above 12%. This amounted to 20 of the 54 EI economic regions in the country, all of which had comparable unemployment data. Two thirds of the nearly 1100 projects were approved on this basis. The second case allowed projects within EI regions with unemployment rates less than 12%, but only in a specific sub-region or "pocket of high unemployment" above 12% as derived from labour market information calculated by the department and statistical data from Statistics Canada surveys. These projects were open to more local interpretation and involved about one third of the projects. Less than a handful of projects took place in the last two categories.

These involved considerably more discretion, where projects were approved on the basis of "community needs" such as high unemployment rates in communities of aboriginals or persons with disabilities, or "spin-off benefits" where projects could be eligible in low unemployment areas (less than 12%) if they provided jobs in surrounding areas of high unemployment (greater than 12%).

The program emphasized local partnerships and collaboration. This meant that HRDC employees worked at the local level with private sector sponsors, community and business groups, provincial and municipal governments, other federal departments, and the local members of Parliament. This was based on the view that local needs were best defined locally and that flexibility was required in order to ensure projects would have a positive impact on the community and create sustainable jobs. To ensure timely decisions on projects so that opportunities would not be missed, a decentralized, streamlined project approval process was put in place. Projects were reviewed and negotiated by HRDC officials at the local and regional level with recommendations flowing directly from the Regional Executive to the Minister for approval. HRDC headquarters provided a limited overview function, intervening only on a limited number of contentious proposals when, for example, the cost per job was considered too high.

Cutting administration while maintaining service

TJF was developed and implemented within the constraints and opportunities faced by the department at the time. This meant that TJF was designed to minimize its draw on internal HRDC resources, to maximize (or lever) the resources of other partners and to secure results through flexible partnerships in delivery. At the same time the department was launching its new TJF program it was also dramatically cutting its operating expenditures as part of the government's overall Program Review exercise. Faced with the immediate need to reduce departmental staff by 25% (5,000 FTEs) and achieve $200 million in annual savings, the department launched a series of mutually reinforcing initiatives to restructure and improve service delivery, increase productivity, improve and measure performance, streamline administration and reduce overhead, eliminate "red-tape," and empower employees. The principles underlying these initiatives were incorporated into the design of TJF.

Because of overall fiscal restraint across government and the operating reductions in HRDC, Treasury Board provided no new resources to the department for the administration and delivery of TJF. This meant that some limited implementation resources were squeezed from other programs and that staff responsible for other programs were multi-tasked in order to support the delivery of TJF. It also meant that partners where expected to assist in delivering the program and in measuring its results.

TJF was developed in the context of new approaches to service delivery. The department's service delivery network was completely re-engineered through the creation of a new service delivery network that involved the replacement of 450 Canada Employment Centres with 100 "parent" Human Resource Centres Canada (HRCC's) and 200 satellites.[7] Maintaining service levels required a number of things – one-stop, single-window service, extensive use of electronic service through the use of kiosks, strengthening and expanded telephone call centres, partnerships with service providers, and contracting with private sector delivery partners in the more remote areas of the country where offices were being closed. One-stop service required cross-training among the staff so that those employees responsible for the delivery of employment and training programs could also help those with an increasing workload of employment insurance claims. Kiosks and call centres required capital investments and more private sector partnerships meant more complicated accountability in service delivery arrangements.

Departmental field operations were strengthened by putting in place 100 HRCC directors in executive level positions. They were delegated increased responsibility for program approval and budgets and were encouraged to be innovative and responsive to citizen and client needs. Against the backdrop of a tradition of rigid program and administrative criteria, managers were encouraged to be flexible within the parameters of the legislation and regulations, and the reduced number of program and administrative policies and procedures. It was recognized that partnerships with business and voluntary sector organizations in the diverse communities across the country were critical to the delivery of quality service to citizens. A new level and scale of local partnership arrangements began not just in TJF but also in many other programs in the department.

The department accelerated its efforts to develop and publish service standards. The department launched "A Quality Services Journey" which emphasized "innovative changes in service delivery, advanced technology and an empowered and more autonomous local management with greater authority and maximum flexibility."[8] Speedy service was important to TJF partners to ensure that decisions could be made in light of commercial opportunities and financial deadlines. In 1997 the department committed to publishing service standards in all points of service by 1998. The high priority that the employees attached to this initiative was demonstrated in the approving words of the Auditor General in his April 2000 report, noting that the department "has made considerable progress in addressing service quality."[9]

Empowering staff while achieving results

TJF was developed against the backdrop of a new leadership profile for employees within the department. With a history of limited success of government-wide performance-based pay reforms in Canada and elsewhere,[10] the department turned its efforts to developing a new leadership profile for executives, managers and front line employees. Not only did the leadership profile set the tone for executive and employee behaviour, but it also formed the basis for executive compensation.

The one-page profile contained five central statements of prescribed behaviour that quickly resonated with employees responsible for TJF. These were: "taking ownership of change, supporting people, breaking constraints, making it happen, and investing in partnerships." The profile elaborated the expectations with expressions like:

- "driving change with courage and confidence so ideas, events and processes are challenged and people feel supported"

- "enable and show support for people to question the status quo and take risks"

- "promoting and trying new ideas and accepting the responsibility when things go wrong"

- "unleashing people to think boldly and implement new ways of doing business, letting go of control oriented processes so teams take initiatives and accept accountability for results"

- "building relationships with internal and external partners based on mutually acceptable conditions to improve client service"

- "setting personal agendas aside to deal with issues in an objective manner and act on inputs from clients, partners and colleagues"[11]

As the department encouraged its employees to question process constraints and procedural controls, it asked that they give more attention to the achievement of results. In 1996 the department completely revamped its program results and performance system, putting in place a new "Results-Based Accountability Framework." In the place of an antiquated system of a multiplicity of overlapping and little-used indicators of program performance, it established 12 key measures for its 4 major program areas. Fewer indicators meant that program performance could be measured and that the results could be reported to, and actually used by senior managers to monitor performance and make needed improvements and adjustments. The key measure for TJF was the number of sustainable jobs created.

These measures were quickly made operational throughout the department and were reported quarterly on a regional and program basis to the department's management board chaired by the deputy minister. In setting its new "Results-Based Accountability Framework," the department was explicit about how its employees should now operate:

> Human Resource Centres of Canada (HRCCs) will operate in an environment that is characterized by: decentralized service delivery, relaxed bureaucratic controls, and increased flexibility for managing resource and programs to optimize service to the public.[12]

Even if managers and employees only believed half of what they read, there was little doubt that emphasis would now be placed on achieving agreed results with a de-emphasis on administrative processes and procedures.

Breaking barriers to achieve results

Encouraging managers to focus on and to be accountable for program results was balanced with the need to provide them with more flexibility to actually achieve these results. If managers were to achieve results from TJF employment projects they needed to minimize the paper burden on themselves and the private and voluntary sector sponsors. In streamlining its administration and operations and in facilitating local flexibility in program delivery, the department launched a high-profile initiative entitled "Breaking the Barriers." The initiative was closely linked to the focus on the achievement of program results. The initiative was presented to staff and partners not as an initiative to break rules but rather to identify unnecessary procedures and processes that stood in the way of achieving results. The initiative was particularly well received by administrative and service delivery staff, including those responsible for TJF. It produced 7 reports in rapid succession that were widely distributed to employees. Within a short time, 43 separate barriers were eliminated, such as simplifying youth employment program approvals, eliminating 250 financial codes, streamlining financial allotments, increasing local office purchase authorities, simplifying government employee travel policy, and greater use of direct deposit of training allowance for clients.[13]

The role of members of Parliament

The role and involvement of members of Parliament in TJF projects was an important feature of the program. TJF program guidelines required that as part of the project assessment process the local HRCC manager receive input from community partners, provincial/territorial governments, regional development agencies, and members of Parliament. Members of Parliament were involved similarly in the student summer employment program. At the time HRDC noted that by involving members of Parliament there was a greater assurance that the project proposals take into account regional and local needs. Members of Parliament did not approve projects, nor could they veto projects, as was the case for provincial governments whose explicit approval was required before a project could proceed.

Although the role of members of Parliament in TJF was clearly advisory, as it became clear in the aftermath of the release of the grants and contributions audit, this was not fully understood by the public, the media and the opposition. A criminal investigation in 1997 of a Liberal party organizer who approached at least five proponents of TJF projects seeking political contributions in exchange for promise of project approval only added to the confusion. A 1998 evaluation report of the program that clumsily referred to "the presence of political factors" in the approval process without any elaboration added more confusion. The involvement of members of Parliament in an advisory capacity to the government in the development and implementation of programs is not new. Members of Parliament are there to serve the interest of their constituents. In direct job creation programs like TJF, where the benefits are geographically concentrated, members of Parliament will take a great interest in those projects in their own constituencies and will find ways to express their views.

Assessment and evaluation

Throughout the course of implementing TJF, officials placed considerable emphasis on program assessment and evaluation. An early external review noted that:

> The partnering model of federal, provincial, and non-profit and private sector organizations should continue to be encouraged. The model enables the efficient use of resources, expertise and knowledge, provides for one-window approach to clients, and ensures that proper skills are applied to the analyses of proposals.[14]

A separate independent evaluation[15] was undertaken that gathered information through interviews with 300 of the nearly 1100 project sponsors. The formative evaluation noted that the "vast majority of key informants" indicated that partnerships were "an important component of effective delivery." They approvingly cited the "extensive use of formal and informal partnerships at the local and regional levels, particularly in the review process." They noted that "the partnership approach brings increased scrutiny to the proposal review process, and tends to lead to the approval of projects which are most likely to succeed." They emphasized that "a good mix of partners helps sponsors identify and leverage funds from other sources."

The evaluation suggested that the program was doing reasonably well by standards associated with previous direct job creation projects in areas of chronic high unemployment. During the period (1996-98) the program helped to create 30,000 jobs with 22,000 considered to be incremental. Comparing jobs expected to jobs created, 79% of the jobs expected were actually created. The evaluation concluded that without the program one half the projects would not have been pursued and the program accelerated the jobs in one quarter of the projects. Over nine in ten of the private sector sponsors were satisfied with the program emphasizing its flexibility and partnership. The average cost per job of just over $8,000 was less than past experience.

A subsequent analysis undertaken by HRDC in May 2000 supported the generally positive results of the program. A regression analysis of TJF data found that several variables were important in influencing the number of jobs created. For example, smaller projects (less than $500,000) did better than larger projects, the larger the TJF contribution the greater the number of jobs created, projects in Montreal in designated "pockets" of unemployment did better than those in the rest of the country and projects created more jobs as time went on.

The research organizations and the senior analysts responsible for both the external review and the independent evaluation were sharply questioned by members of the Parliamentary Committee during the course of its hearings into the administrative audit of HRDC grants and contributions programs. The independent analysts defended their findings emphasizing that the number of jobs should be considered "short-term" since there was insufficient history with the program to know if the jobs were sustainable. The auditor general in his subsequent audit in October 2000 noted the limitations of the formative evaluation and concluded that the incremental job creation effect of 22,000 was "overstated" but did not question the total number of 30,000.

On the basis of the apparent success of the three year TJF program and its broad support from MPs and provincial governments (especially the Atlantic and Quebec), the federal government implemented an ongoing $110 million Canada Jobs Fund (CJF) in April 1999. The program was very similar to TJF with a continued heavy emphasis on collaborative partnerships. There were however three key differences between the programs, two of which were:

- eligibility for CJF was EI economic regions of over 10% unemployment as compared to 12% under TJF given the decline in the overall rate of unemployment

- closer coordination between HRDC and the federal regional development agencies in the delivery of the program to ensure CJF funding was "last resort" to avoid competition with repayable loans from the agencies

Unlike TJF, which had minimal program guidelines, CJF had a two-inch thick set of national guidelines covering areas of program administration such as eligibility, performance and accountability, partnership, planning and consultation, assessment and recommendation, project contracting, and monitoring. One of the most significant guidelines was greater clarity and hence less discretion concerning the eligibility of projects in sub-regions (the so-called "pockets" of unemployment) within economic regions. In reaction to concerns about the flexible administration of TJF, the department significantly "tightened up" the administration of CJF. Two very significant features remained, however: the advisory role of MPs in the approval process and the flexibility to use sub-regions for eligibility.

Despite the positive program evaluations, the achievement of job results, the support of effective partnerships, and the replacement of TJF by CJF, the TJF program came under increasingly sharp criticism from the media and the opposition. The *National Post* and the opposition Reform party focused their attack almost exclusively on the 17 projects in the prime minister's riding. Through the concerted use of access to information requests the National Post and the opposition mounted a sustained public campaign that began to put into question a number of the TJF projects. The concerns ranged across a wide spectrum of issues including allegations of jobs not being created, financial mismanagement, the inappropriate use of trust funds and political interference in the approval of projects. It was in this environment that the department released its internal audit of the administration of HRDC grants and contributions in January 2000.

Release of the internal audit of the administration of grants and contributions programs

One noted Canadian academic has described the audit and the political and public reaction to it as a "textbook case in public administration."[16] If it is indeed a textbook case, it is hardly surprising since the audit and the reaction to it dominated media, parliamentary, and public attention over a lengthy and sustained period, leaping into the public's consciousness in the early days of 2000 and remaining in the public eye into the federal election campaign at the end of that same year. The issue, although largely contained to one government department, touched the central features of the administrative and political apparatus of government, dominated the entire department and its minister, became of the focus of attention of the opposition and the media, took centre stage in question period from February until June, and was a significant preoccupation for the prime minister. The audit triggered more than 800 questions directed to the minister in question period, 17,000 pages of information about specific grants and contributions posted on the HRDC website, 100,000 pages released to the media and opposition under access-to-information legislation, several internal and external reviews, taskforces and reports, and a separate examination by the auditor general. While the audit focused on internal departmental administration, the reaction to it called into question the role and accountability of third parties in the delivery of government programs. Never before had an audit of any type, let alone an internal audit of the administration of government programs, triggered such a visible and sustained political and public reaction.

TJF was at the centre of attention in much of the reaction to the release of the audit. To understand better some of the perceived limitations on government in engaging the private and voluntary sectors as partners in the delivery of employment programs we will review briefly the highly critical reports by the media that touched on TJF and CJF following the release of the audit.

On January 19, 2000, HRDC released a 34-page internal audit of the department's administration of its grants and contribution programs undertaken by its own Internal Audit Bureau. The audit, perhaps better called a file review, looked at a purportedly random sample of 459 project files from eight grants and contributions programs.[17] These programs, "representing approximately $1 billion in annual federal spending," were delivered through regional offices and headquarters, often in partnership with the private and voluntary sector organizations. Most of these programs were labour market training programs designed to meet the needs of particular Canadians such as persons with disabilities, aboriginals, youth, new entrants to the workforce, women, or low-skilled workers. Only a small portion, 10%, were employment or job creation programs in the form of TJF. Others were social development and learning and literacy programs.

The audit was not a financial audit of the projects. Instead, it was a paper review of the extent and nature of the documentation contained in 459 project files. The audit purported to "assess the management and delivery of the grants and contributions." Accompanying the audit was a press release that noted the audit had revealed "a number of areas requiring improvement . . . including project monitoring, contracting procedures and general financial practices."

The press release emphasized that HRDC had "already taken action to improve the administrative standards," had put in place "a comprehensive Action Plan" and "will be working hand in hand with the auditor general as he conducts his government-wide review of grants and contributions . . . ." The press release highlighted the actions being taken, which included the establishment within the department of a new national grants and contributions performance tracking directorate, clear direction to employees on proper management, supplemental training sessions for staff, holding managers accountable for ensuring proper procedures are followed and the development of new management information systems. Coupled with the release of the audit on January 19th was a "technical briefing" of the media by senior officials of HRDC, a media scrum by the minister, and follow-up interviews with the minister by the national media.

The media (over)reaction

That night the national electronic media gave the item top billing. *CBC National* referred in its lead story to "stunning revelations about government mismanagement on a monumental scale." A reporter indicated that, "opposition critics are demanding that (the minister) resign." The assistant auditor-general of the Office of the Auditor General for Canada warned that, "once that kind of paperwork isn't there, anything can happen. There could be abuse, or there could be no abuse. You have no way of knowing." Local Ottawa television summed up by saying "government officials are admitting they basically lost track of roughly a billion dollars." The opposition Reform MP and HRDC critic declared that TJF "is so deeply flawed; it is so corrupt. It's being used as a political slush-fund, with no accountability at all. I think it should be scrapped."

The next morning the entire print media across the country was seized with the issue. The headlines to their stories read:

- "Audit finds Ottawa sloppy with job grants: 80% of projects that received money were never reviewed" *National Post*

- "Department loses track of $1 billion: sloppy records preclude monitoring of federal grants" *Ottawa Citizen*

- "Un monumental fouillis administratif" *La Presse*

- "Ottawa admits huge flaws in job grant programs" *Halifax Chronicle Herald*

- "Sloppy records keep public from knowing if $1 billion in federal grants wrongly spent" *Vancouver Sun*

Within 24 hours the key concerns around which the issue of the grants and contributions audit would revolve for the next year were beginning to set. These first impressions, whether accurate or not, immediately took hold. These first media impressions would become the lasting impressions despite the constant efforts of the minister, her department, the prime minister, and others to explain otherwise. As events surrounding the audit crisis unfolded over the course of the next eight weeks and subsequently into June when CJF was finally terminated, the media spotlight focused on many issues but it constantly returned to TJF/CJF.

Media reports, although not always accurate, provide a perspective on those features of the TJF program and its delivery by partners that the opposition and media perceived to be of greatest concern. For example, in early February the *Ottawa Citizen* carried detailed accusations by opposition MPs that TJF and CJF contained "qualification loopholes" such as "pockets of unemployment regulations." The article went on to state that these details were "kept secret" and were "custom-made for ministers" for their benefit. The article contrasted treatment in one MP's riding of Winnipeg Centre with the HRDC minister's riding in Brant. A *Globe and Mail* columnist drew attention to a "maverick" liberal MP's "discovery" of the HRDC minister's "special representations" and "fiddling criteria" and the subsequent $1 million TJF contribution "to attract" an American-owned telephone call centre to her riding, which was originally slated for his riding. A *National Post* journalist questioned the government's report showing that opposition ridings got more TJF money than government ridings. He noted that the *Post*'s own "computer-assisted analysis" of 1,082 TJF grants provided "clear evidence of election-style pork-barrelling," particularly in Quebec ridings where the strategy appeared to have involved luring voters away from the Bloc Party.

The *Globe and Mail* headlined a story with "Stewart's attack falls flat, Minister backtracks as job grants uproar continues in Commons." Journalists reported that the minister's strategy of accusing three Reform MPs who had denounced TJF and then sought job-creation grants for their constituencies had "backfired" when the minister subsequently had to clarify her statement that one MP "did not personally" call the minister, but the MP's office did.

On February 22 the *Toronto Star* reported that the minister "unleashed a paper blizzard yesterday, dumping more than 10,000 pages of job grant documents on the opposition." The *National Post* claimed that this new information "provided further problems" since "HRDC officials admitted that the figure that Liberal ministers had quoted as fact for months (that TJF had contributed to 30,000 jobs) was merely a consultant's estimate." The next day the *National Post* reported that in response to opposition demands for evidence on the jobs created, the minister "would only say that an evaluation by an Ottawa-headquartered consulting firm, based on a sample survey, showed that 'an estimated 30,000 jobs were created.'"

With respect to TJF projects in the minister's riding the *Globe and Mail* reported that "she has always claimed that 'no rules were broken' when $1.8 million in TJF grants went into here riding from 1996 to 1999 (and) it became clear yesterday that there were few rules to break." A *Vancouver Sun* columnist wrote that, "Stewart has explained her riding had 'pockets of unemployment,' but why didn't the same pocket criteria qualify Vancouver East."

Explaining publicly the administration of a job creation program in the midst of a government crisis is not an easy task. During the crisis there were no outside partners who were prepared to publicly defend the program. Throughout the crisis the minister and the HRDC officials attempted to explain why some MPs, including some ministers, were eligible for TJF and CJF projects and why other were not. In particular, attention was drawn to the minister's riding of Brant. In 1995 the city of Brantford was eligible for projects under TJF because the unemployment rate in the Brantford sub-region or "pocket" was 11.8% with peaks of up to 14.5%. In 1997, Brantford was eligible for projects under CJF because it was located in the EI region of Niagara that had an unemployment rate of 10.3%. It was especially difficult for the government to explain publicly how sub-regions of unemployment permitted eligibility to the program. The administrative flexibility that had been a source of strength in the delivery of these programs was a significance source of weakness when it came to matters of public accountability explanation in the face of a hostile media.

During a time of crisis third party partners are most unlikely to provide public support for the program or the government. In testimony before the Parliamentary Committee a respected leader from the voluntary sector explains why:

> We remained relatively silent on this issue because for us, this has become a major political problem . . . . A lot of (voluntary) groups said we don't want to go near that. We are based in the community. We don't want to be in the front pages of the *National Post*, the *Globe and Mail* or the local newspaper . . . . The way the story has been so often reported – very seldom has the good work of HRDC and the government been highlighted.[18]

The department put in place further changes to the administration of CJF and at the same time explored options for significant reform and possible termination of the program. The department tightened up program assessments and program approvals by requiring that all projects be recommended to the minister for approval by the national headquarters rather than by the regional executive heads. It also implemented a thorough system of checklists and forms for project approval and monitoring. More significant changes were considered which included eliminating sub-regions or "pockets" as a basis for eligibility, a more transparent method for calculating the number of jobs created and eliminating the advisory and consultative role of local MPs in the decision-making process.

Finally on June 22 the federal government announced the termination of CJF, transferring the funds to the four regional agencies that, according to the minister of industry, would be used to focus on "innovation and the new economy." The HRDC minister emphasized that the program was being scrapped because "the national unemployment rate dropped to 6.6% from 9.4% in 1995, when TJF was being devised." Looking back over the program and the ensuing crisis associated with the release of the grants and contributions audit, what are the lessons learned about the limits to public, private and voluntary sector partnerships in employment programs?

Learning the right lessons

There are a number of lessons that can be learned about collaborative partnership arrangements in employment programs that flow from the experience of TJF/CJF and the grants and contributions audit. One of the difficulties, however, with "lessons learned" is that they are often so general as to appear to be motherhood statements. The other is that they usually appear rather conventional, often a restatement of what should be done in an unconstrained ideal world but rarely if ever totally achievable. The lessons learned usually focus on what was not done and then prescribe what should have been done. This is usually cast under the general dictum of greater clarity for almost everything: clear program objectives, clear and focused accountability, clear roles and responsibilities of partners, clear and reliable results information, etc. The reality is that the objectives in partnerships, as they are in most government programs, are usually multiple, conflicting and vague. Accountabilities among partners are always multiple, inevitably complex and often fuzzy. The roles and responsibilities are often both contradictory and complementary at the same time. And the results information is rarely totally accurate and often incomplete. TJF/CJF was no exception.

The reality is that getting more clarity on one dimension – be it objectives, accountability, or results – will invariably come at cost. That cost might be rigidity, paper burden, slow responsiveness, missed opportunity, or increased resources. The lessons learned therefore for partnerships become not just what should be done, but also what should be sacrificed. Invariably there will be a need to balance seemingly conflicting values. Getting the balance right means learning the right lessons.

Employment programs, whether delivered directly through conventional government machinery or through innovative collaborative arrangements, are of intense interest to members of Parliament. The benefits as well as the costs of such programs are geographically specific. Those who benefit are often different from those who pay. Some MPs strongly support these programs while others strongly oppose them. Even among the supporters there is invariably competition for projects. This means that even if the explicit objectives of the program are singular, non-conflicting and clear (e.g., to create sustainable jobs) and are shared by most partners, there will be other implicit objectives that will be important to other partners. For example, any MP, particularly those representing areas of high unemployment, all too quickly comes to see that attracting employment projects to his/her riding is a part of doing the job as well as keeping the job. All this leads to an opposition and a media that are highly attentive and critical of the way these programs are delivered. Partnerships need to be prepared for this.

Partnership arrangements can be helpful in providing public support for projects. They can help develop a broader consensus for the program and increase the likelihood that better projects will be selected. For example, TJF/CJF project proposals involved a great deal of consultation among all the partners: the private or voluntary sector sponsor, the local community, the province, HRDC, other federal departments, and the local MP. The approval of both the province and the minister was required. Explicit provincial approval was important not only because it helped to ensure that the project was consistent with the regional development plan but also because it provided broader political support for the enterprise. However, as we have seen, partnership support for a project will not materialize into public support for an employment program when it is under strong opposition and media attack.

There are sharp limits on the extent to which flexibility for partners can be built into the delivery of employment programs. For example, when it comes to defining those geographic regions of eligibility the TJF experience suggests there is little room for flexibility. The flexibility that is provided should be spelled out publicly in advance through explicit rules and guidelines and communicated to all potential partners, including MPs. It would also be important that there be public documentation supporting this process. The Standing Committee report, prepared after hearing from an extensive list of witnesses, was particularly explicit on this latter point. It noted that, although "HRDC officials assured the Committee that regional offices informed MPs of these selection sub-criteria, we cannot support this claim because the Committee found no evidence that HRDC was able to apply the eligibility criteria for the Transitional Jobs Fund equitably across the country."[19] The TJF/CJF case suggests that in the absence of communicating explicit rules and guidelines at the outset of an employment program, subsequent explanations about program eligibility provided at a time of intensive probing and questioning, no matter how logical, are likely to lack credibility.

On the important matter of accountability for the results of employment programs, this case suggests that partners are under considerable pressure to provide both independent and detailed documentation of the results achieved. For example, while the auditor general approvingly concluded that the project results of TJF were "defined in measurable terms," he was sharply critical for what he considered to be "a lack of follow-through in their measurement and reporting."[20] An MP during the lengthy Parliamentary committees hearings expressed skepticism with the findings of the independent evaluation. He argued that the survey of project sponsors was inadequate since it included only 58% of the total and concluded that the 42% who did not respond "were embarrassed at the negligible or zero jobs (they) created." The media adopted an even higher standard for determining the number of jobs created by concluding that the independent evaluators could not rely upon the information provided by sponsors but had to speak individually to those actually employed. While no one would deny that the determination of the number of incremental jobs actually created is tricky business, it would appear that all outside critics are proposing standards of accountability that even the most trusting of partners in a collaborative arrangement would not, given reasonable capacity, be able to meet.

It can be argued that the media spotlight has made TJF/CJF an extreme case and that in more normal circumstances the requirements for accountability and results reporting would be more realistic and considerably less onerous. Perhaps, but if we assume, for example, that the accountability critics are even "half right," then it is still the case that in collaborate partnership arrangements the public expectations for accountability of results will be significant. The challenge is made considerably more difficult because the benefits for decision-making of flexibility and decentralization that come from partnerships demand that information on results be standardization and centralization. This will require a large investment by all partners in results information, in the systems that can generate the information, in the independent external evaluators that can assess and assemble the information, and the independent cross-checking that will be required. Most important perhaps, governments, as the principal partners in these collaborate arrangements, must be prepared to make the investments with their private and voluntary sector partners to increase overall capacity to secure reliable, timely and credible results information.

One question that dominated much of the controversy surrounding the TJF/CJF partnership centred on the extensive debate around the appropriate role of MPs in the review and approval process. At the one extreme there are those who argue that MPs should have no formal role in the decision-making process. The auditor general in his testimony before the Parliamentary Committee and in his report concluded that "written recommendations from the member of Parliament for the area as one of the inputs for the project approval process . . . confuses traditional accountability relationships."[21] On the other hand, parliamentarians in the report of the Parliamentary Committee cautioned that, "direct political involvement in HRDC's project selection can potentially create a conflict for parliamentarians, whose role is to hold the government accountable" but concluded that "MPs' involvement in the project selection process should remain advisory."[22]

If no formal role is provided to MPs in the approval process of employment programs our analysis suggests that MPs are likely to find and create an informal and unstructured role for themselves primarily because they care deeply about the employability of their constituents. Indeed, evidence suggests that even when there is a formal and visible advisory role, less formal and more invisible parallel ways for MPs to provide additional representation can also emerge.[23] One of the realities of involving MPs in an advisory capacity in TJF projects was the inability to consistently and credibly explain and defend that role in the face of a suspicious media and skeptical public. Indeed partners themselves, who were uncertain and confused about the role of MPs, expressed concern about the "presence of political factors" in the approval process. All this suggests that if MPs are to be involved in an advisory capacity in the project approval process then several conditions must be met. The role of MPs must be clearly defined both in terms of what is expected from them and how they relate to others in the advisory process. Second, the process must be open, transparent and understandable to all parties. Third, the political neutrality of public servants must not be, nor be seen to be, compromised. Fourth, the accountabilities of partners must be sufficiently clear.

Let's start with accountability. The formal involvement of MPs in an advisory capacity requires that it be clearly understood who makes the final decisions on the projects and who is accountable. In theory it is always the minister who makes the decision in the sense that the minister can over-rule a decision that has been delegated to officials. In practice, however, in a number of programs the responsibility for the approval is often delegated to officials because of the sheer volume of project proposals and the need for quick responses. Under TJF/CJF the minister approved the projects except for those in the minister's riding which in all cases were delegated to the deputy minister. With an average of over 300 projects requiring approval each year, there was considerable criticism from partners, provinces, proponents and MPs concerning the delays in the approval process and missed opportunities. The involvement of MPs in the advisory process would require that the minister, and not an official, have and be seen to have final approval, otherwise it could put undue political pressure on public servants. This, in turn, means that the minister be held accountable for the project decision. This also suggests that if MPs are to be involved as advisors in the process then no one should expect the timely approval of projects.

Just how to involve MPs speaks to the important need for transparency, openness and understandability of the decision-making process and the political neutrality of public servants. All MPs, whether government or opposition, must be and be seen to be treated the same. Some MPs will not want to be involved, others will be personally involved in the details of every project, and still others will leave it to staff in their offices. All these and other possibilities will need to be handled and explained to all partners in an open and transparent manner. Throughout the entire process public servants must be and be seen to be politically neutral. There is considerable evidence from the recent experience with TJF/CJF to suggest that the involvement of MPs in providing separate advice directly to the local HRCC director is flawed. First, it is not open and transparent since the advice of the MP is available only to the HRCC director and the minister and not to the community partners. Second, by providing the advice directly from an MP to the HRCC director it can create a perception of compromising the political neutrality of the public servant.

One way of meeting these important requirements, as suggested by the Parliamentary Committee in its report, would be to create project selection advisory groups consisting of the community partners and to include MPs in these groups. This has the advantage of ensuring a broad representation within the community for the review of the project. It also facilitates a more open and transparent process.

Concluding Comments

We began by asking what are the practical limits to partnerships between the public sector and the private and voluntary sectors. By focusing on a situation and a program where things went wrong – the administrative audit and the employment programs – we have seen that there are likely to be significant and real limits to such partnerships. This case does not foreshadow "a public sector without boundaries," as some might advocate, but rather a public sector under pressure. This case suggests that if the boundaries are not skilfully determined by governments and their partners, they will be clumsily drawn by opposition parties, the media, and internal and external auditors.

Determining new boundaries is hardly an easy task. Like any matter that involves limits, it will require not only the balancing of competing objectives and interests but also some hard trade-offs. That there will continue to be confusion over where the new boundaries should be is not surprising. As this case indicates, determining the new boundaries for "new governance" arrangements touches on some basic tensions across important values: accountability and quality service, political responsiveness and political neutrality, resource efficiency and building capacity, engaging citizens and political representativeness.

If some of the promises of partnerships are to be realized while avoiding the worst pitfalls, then the capacities of governments and their partners will need to be increased. Doing partnerships without capacity is risky business. Having capacity means that both governments and their private and voluntary sector partners be "partnership ready."[24] This will require adjusting traditional concepts of accountability, underwriting the costs for improved information and evaluation strategies, investing in public servants who can deal publicly with outside partners and outside critics, recognizing the limits to flexibility for public sector organizations, calibrating and sharing risks across the sectors, and strengthening the human resource capacity of the voluntary sector.

It will also require that those outside the partnership – the media, the opposition, the auditors, and the public – be "partnership tolerant." If the outcomes of partnerships continue to be judged only by the traditional standards that have been applied to public administration – have the processes and procedures been followed, have mistakes been avoided, have benefits been equitably distributed, and have public servants remained completely anonymous – then we are unlikely to move the boundaries.

Notes

[1] Canada, Report of the Auditor General of Canada, *Involving Others in Governing: Accountability at Risk*, Chapter 23, November 1999.

[2] For one perspective on the evolution of regional economic development approaches and programs and the illusive search for solutions see, Donald Savoie, *Regional Economic Development: Canada's Search for Solutions* 2nd ed. (Toronto: University of Toronto Press, 1992) and *Rethinking Canada's Regional Development Policy* (The Canadian Institute for Research on Regional Development, 1997).

[3] Canada, Human Resources Development Canada, *Terms and Conditions: Transitional Jobs Fund*, 1996.

[4] Canada, Human Resources Development Canada, *Transitional Jobs Fund*, 1996.

[5] Ibid.

[6] Canada, *Terms and Conditions: Transitional Jobs Fund.*

[7] F. Leslie Seidle, *Rethinking the Delivery of Public Services to Citizens* (Montreal: The Institute for Research on Public Policy, 1995), pp. 129-131.

[8] Canada, Human Resources Development Canada. *A Quality Services Journey,* 1996.

[9] Canada, Report of the Auditor General of Canada, *Human Resources Development Canada: Service Quality at the Local Level* (April 2000), pp. 2-5.

[10] Hal G. Rainey, "Assessing Past and Current Personnel Reforms," in B. Guy Peters and Donald J. Savoie, eds., *Taking Stock: Assessing Public Sector Reforms* (Montreal and Kingston: McGill-Queen's University Press), pp. 187-220.

[11] Canada, Human Resources Development Canada, *The HRDC Leadership Profile*, 1995.

[12] Canada, Human Resource Development Canada, *Results-Based Accountability Framework,* 1996.

[13] The initiative was so successful that it was immediately duplicated government-wide by the Treasury Board Secretariat through the publication and dissemination of a major document. The Clerk of the Privy Council, Jocelyn Bourgon, in the introduction to the document *Breaking Barriers: Innovation in the Public Interest,* challenged public servants to "relentlessly pursue the elimination of self-inflicted impediments to improved service delivery – such as bureaucratic red tape, turf protection and fear of change."

[14] Canada, Consulting and Audit Canada. *Review of the Transitional Jobs Fund,* (Ottawa: August 1997) v.

[15] Canada, Human Resource Development Canada, *Evaluation of the Transitional Jobs Fund (Phase 1)* (An evaluation study conducted by Ekos Research Associates under the direction of the Evaluation and Data Development Branch of HRDC), 1998.

[16] Savoie, *Ottawa Citizen* February 15, 2000.

[17] The eight grants and contribution program areas included: Labour Market Training, most notably Employment Benefits and Support Measures including targeted wage subsidies, self employment initiatives, job creation partnerships, skills development, employment assistance

services, labour market partnerships, research and innovation, and the opportunities fund for persons with disabilities; Transitional Jobs Fund, to encourage the creation of sustainable jobs in areas of high unemployment; Youth Programs, to give young Canadians work experience, skills and information in making the transition from school to work; Aboriginal Training Programs, in the form of 54 agreements with aboriginal organizations to deliver training to aboriginals under the Aboriginal Human Resources Development Strategy; Human Resource Partnerships in the form of agreements with sector councils representing business, labour, and educators to develop human resource strategies in such sectors as the steel industry, tourism, automotive repair, information technology, etc.; Social Development, including research, development and demonstration projects to test out best practices in childcare delivery and partnerships and innovations with the voluntary sector; Learning and Literacy, including grants to organizations to promote literacy by increasing public awareness and developing innovative practices, demonstration projects to adopt new learning technologies, and partnership arrangements with provinces and national learning organizations to promote lifelong learning; and Labour programs, including contributions to labour and other organizations to promote a safe and productive work environment.

[18] Canada, The House of Commons Standing Committee on Human Resources Development and the Status of Persons with Disabilities, May 16, 2000.

[19] Canada, The House of Commons Standing Committee on Human Resources Development and the Status of Persons with Disabilities, *Seeking a Balance: Final Report on Human Resources Development Grants and Contributions,* June 2000.

[20] Canada, Report of the Auditor-General of Canada. *Human Resources Development Canada: Grants and Contributions,* October 2000.

[21] Ibid.

[22] *Seeking a Balance.*

[23] An October 1997 internal memorandum prepared by an officer in the Office of the Ethics Counsellor and released under Access to Information described a process involving consultation on TJF projects with the regional minister for the province of Quebec and "other liberal members in the field."

[24] John Langford "Managing Public-Private Partnerships in Canada." Paper for conference on "New Players, Partners and Processes: A Public Sector without Boundaries." Canberra, April 5, 2001.

Commentary

Dr Peter Shergold AM, Secretary, Department of Employment, Workplace Relations and Small Business, Government of Australia

I am very pleased indeed to provide a commentary on these two stimulating papers on the issue of engaging the private sector in service delivery. Professors Good and Considine focus their attention on the delivery of publicly funded employment services through outsourced providers. The papers introduce us to the complex and often tense relationship between government, parliament, public service and private provider, which emerges in this new world of public sector governance; a relationship increasingly played out, as we have just heard, in the full glare of media scrutiny.

My commentary reflects the perspective of a practitioner. Perhaps for that reason I found myself empathically sharing the traumas of my Canadian colleagues who bore responsibility for the administration of the transitional job fund and its successor, the Canada Jobs Fund. And neatly, to round out my emotions, I found myself righteously indignant at the conclusions on Australian employment services in the last decade, many of which, in my view, are both unsubstantiated and unsustainable.

"Unemployed people get no benefit from the competitive part of the delivery system." "The role of providing best quality service to the least well-off job seekers plainly requires the active contribution of a public agency." Well, I do not think Professor Considine's thoughtful paper argues these bold statements. Rather, with the appendage of the word "discuss" behind them, I think they provide useful questions for an examination in "Public Policy 1." And I would have to say that if I had to answer those questions I think I could sustain an argument that would resolve both essay topics in the negative.

I was going to let my concerns go unremarked until Professor Considine's final comment to us this morning, namely that we had in Job Network created a system in which there were high levels of "creaming," that is, providing services only to the best, most well-off job seekers. This statement is simply not supported by factual evidence. The statistical evidence does not show that to be the case. Nor is there evidence from more disadvantaged job seekers that they are being "parked."

Indeed people who are from non-English speaking backgrounds and sole parents – traditionally "least well-off job seekers" – get above average outcomes from the Job Network. And I must say that the assertions of parking seem to me totally and utterly at odds with what I know to be the management ethos of the Salvation Army, the Catholic church, Mission Australia, Baptist Community Services and other not-for-profit organisations which together comprise 50 per cent of the providers delivering publicly-funded employment services.

To return to the papers, my direct responsibility is for Job Network, the outcome of the Coalition government's reforms, which Professor Considine argues are superior to those attempted by the previous Labor government. As an apolitical public servant I note this particular conclusion without comment. But I can certainly attest that Job Network is an astounding creation, a revolution in public administration.

As Meredith Edwards suggested in her opening remarks this morning, Job Network does take us into uncharted waters in terms of governance. Nowhere else in a developed country, to my knowledge, has the delivery of public employment services been placed entirely in the hands of a competitive network of providers: 200 public, private and not-for-profit providers delivering five programs worth a billion dollars annually from 2000 sites; in which most elements are price competitive; and in which the public provider, Employment National, is responsible for less than 5 per cent of the market.

The IT system that supports Job Network represents the cutting edge of electronic government. Its touch screen network is now winning substantial exports around the world. Its Internet site, Australian Job Search, is not only the government's number one site but also the employment industry's most frequented site. And this creation, I assert on the basis of extensive evaluation, is already delivering employment outcomes better than earlier systems at a very much lower cost with greater support both from employers and job seekers. Importantly, its program and its performance, particularly over the last 12 months, have continued to improve.

Now, those simple facts do not mean that the Job Network is uncontroversial. Bipartisan support for the continuation of Job Network does not imply a lack of political contest. The contest is fierce. And it is fierce precisely because of the two related governance issues which Professors Considine and Good explore so well.

First, what limits are there to collaborative partnerships between government purchaser and outsourced provider in the delivery of publicly funded programs? Second, is the chain of accountability weakened by the contracting out of delivery? This is not easy terrain philosophically or pragmatically. The issue I have to address on a day-to-day basis is how best to strike a balance between administrative flexibility, which generates greatest competitive activity and probably ensures the most cost effective outcomes, and prescriptive regulation, which is demanded to ensure accountability for public funds but which may, in effect, constrain innovation.

This is difficult when, as Professor Good so neatly characterises, program objectives are usually multiple, conflicting and vague, and accountabilities are always multiple, inevitably complex and fuzzy. The lesson I have learned on the job, but which these two papers have helped me to articulate, is that there are five distinct components to ensure effective governance in an outsourced environment.

- First, **probity**, which is vitally important, particularly in the tender process and in the allocation of business.

- Second, **audit**, which needs to be undertaken continuously, both by one's own contract managers and auditors on a prudent and transparent risk management basis and externally by the Australian National Audit Office.

- Third, **evaluation**, in order to assess on an ongoing basis the performance of programs and the cost effectiveness of their delivery so as to make improvements on an iterative basis.

- Fourth, **accountability** through ministers to parliament. There are at present two major unreconciled tensions in this regard. There is the parliamentary desire to monitor, indeed regulate, process rather than just assess outcomes – in other words, to say "You must spend this amount of your money on training of jobseekers. You must do the following things on their behalf " – and the parliamentary wish to be provided with confidential documents on the price charged by individual providers for delivering services in a competitive market. Now, both of these are understandable demands, but if they are acceded to it may result in many providers not entering the market, particularly small business and not-for-profit organisations, who shy away from red tape; and is likely to reduce outcomes and increase the cost to the taxpayer of their delivery of those outcomes.

- Fifth, **public scrutiny**, usually by a media that is (paradoxically) as ideologically opposed to outsourcing as it is disposed to stereotype public servants as bureaucratic paper pushers, and for whom a newsworthy story generally has to be simple, negative and preferably linked to wider issues of political contest.

So let me conclude in as provocative a manner as Professor Considine. It seems to me that to address these five aspects of 21st century governance requires a new breed of public servant. It requires senior public servants who are as committed to the delivery of programs on behalf of the government of the day as they are to providing robust policy advice on the development of those programs. It requires public servants who cannot always be traditionally self-effacing if they are to promote public programs effectively, work in partnership with outsourced providers, stand up to pressure in the very unequal balance of power that is the parliamentary committee, and be willing to respond publicly to press articles that inaccurately portray the departmental management of programs. In other words, it requires public servants with a bias for action, even a passion that can be too readily mistaken for partisanship.

That, along with all the other issues for governance identified and analysed so well by Professor Good and Professor Considine, represents, in my view, a new challenge for governance and for public administration.

Discussion

Chair: Professor Sue Vardon, Adjunct Professor, National Institute for Governance, and CEO, Centrelink Australia

---

SUE VARDON: Are there any comments? Would either member of the panel like to comment on the commentator? I thought Mark might have a view he wanted, in fairness, to debate.

MARK CONSIDINE: Well, thank you, Peter. There were no surprises there, but I should at least respond to the two leading criticisms, and obviously you can't do much in a 20-minute paper. As I indicated, the study itself is an empirical study of the dynamics of the front end of this service, not only in Australia but elsewhere. So the statement that the unemployed are not better serviced is based on looking at the caseloads and the case management process of a randomly selected group of for-profit, non-profit and government service delivery agencies in Australia under Labor, under the Vanstone period and under the first contract. I can see there have been some changes in the second contract, which is the one we are now in, but that was the context.

In that survey material it is absolutely unmistakable that the caseloads of frontline staff have moved from averages around 90 to well over 250 in many organisations, and that the effect of that is to park a significant number of clients. When you look at the interview and the survey responses from managers and frontline workers, the criteria that is used is the program's own criteria, which is capacity to benefit. The explanation of that is that "we are under pressure to get outcomes in this year to meet this target, and the closest somebody is to employability the more likely it is that we'll get those results."

We did not have time to talk about the incentives structure. There are some ifs and buts about that. But the caseload data and the strategies of these organisations are pretty straightforward factual empirical issues, not something that the government or the department has been researching, or at least they are not publicising the research if they are.

The least well-off need a public agency. This question of what the ambition and purpose of public programs should be in a results-orientated world is really the provocation or the issue that I was trying to raise. If there was a longer period of time we could talk about how some of the subgroups within this long-term unemployed cohort fare under the system. But in regard to the choice issue, in neither the Labor government program nor the current program is it, to say the least, very easy for an unemployed client or customer to make a reasoned or rational choice on the agency they would like to go to based on their performance.

We do now have a star rating. Most of the unemployed people that I have spoken to do not know about the star rating. The stars themselves do not reflect detailed measured performance by site, which is where the service is delivered and consumed.

It is difficult even for the advocacy agencies, and certainly for the service delivery agencies, to come to terms with whether or not they should openly compete with one another on the basis of performance in trying to communicate with clients. That is, should the Salvation Army advertise in a local area that they had more job placements in the last month, are better with more disadvantaged people than others, and go head to head with other agencies? This is a highly controversial issue for them in both their business and ethical frameworks. For the most part, the so-called choice factor for unemployed people is near to zero.

I should leave time for people to discuss the other things in the open forum. The details of the larger study are available and I am happy to talk about that, if we need to.

JOHN LANGFORD: I did a study for the OECD on value clashes between public and private sectors in the context of the emerging world for service delivery - private service delivery. The study was done almost four years ago, so there were not the data around that you were describing. The combination of the anecdotal and shallow empirical data at that point suggested a number of interesting challenges that add on to the issues that have been raised by speakers and commentators today.

A fundamental one that struck me was the degree to which you were going to expect private sector delivery agencies to simply import public sector values into the way they did business. The area that was interesting was that the most basic public service value was fairness. And fairness comes in the idea that you treat each file – I know that is not a very service oriented word to use – but each file the same.

There was certainly in the literature up until late 1997 some very significant evidence of creaming, essentially, by private sector agencies. They would simply disperse or hold back or park the hardest case. They were facing standards and evaluation criteria with respect to performance evaluations of what the agency had done that encouraged them to do that. Most of the data that I was looking at came from American sources.

There also were some other very interesting issues with essentially religious organisations. I notice that Dr Shergold mentioned this, so I just raised that with no attempt to make a definitive comment. There was a lot of concern being raised in the United States, particularly in inner cities, about the proselytising aspect that went along with the delivery of social services in the context of religious organisations. Under the new compassionate conservatism in the US we are going to see a lot more debate on that.

Finally the other point I would raise, and these are all in the context of standard public service values, is the issue of political neutrality. This was a very interesting issue because there you found – and we certainly experienced this in Canada – that you may be providing organisations with vast amounts of money. In fact you become their major provider of funds, in many cases, for the services they provide. But that does not alter their ideological mindset where they have a very strong set of charitable principles, whatever they happen to be. They were very, very commonly in the past involved in advocacy work with respect to government policy, and they wanted to continue that work.

Some studies found that, even at that point, they were using some of the money provided by governments to enhance the advocacy work they were doing. They would get together in associations to continue to press government for changes in policy.

You had this very odd situation that you would never get in the public sector, obviously, of people who were your partners in the provision of social services advocating against the policies that they were at that point themselves implementing. That obviously raises some very interesting and troubling questions for people who expect fair and politically neutral public policy.

On the private side the only other point I would make is that there was some very clear evidence that the for-profit participants did not have a clue about the culture of information use and privacy protection in the private sector, and were often packaging information to use in other ways. So they were seeing information fundamentally as a commercial product that they could exploit. There were some very clear difficulties here, not obviously on the social services side so much, but certainly on the medical side.

I raise those just simply because they are extensions of some of the points that have been raised by earlier speakers.

SUE VARDON: I am sure that Peter wants to comment and others may wish to comment. Is there anybody else in the audience, along those same lines, who just wants to respond to what John has said?

JIM CARLTON: For those of us in the audience who are not totally familiar with the field, the interesting thing that emerges is a complete clash, it seems. The research evidence of Professor Considine would seem to indicate measured outcomes totally different from those indicated by Dr Shergold. Now that great gap between the research and the actual positive outcomes on all the performance criteria one would, if you were coming in from outside, want to see resolved.

MICHAEL KEATING: I wanted to make the same point that Jim Carlton has just made. I always have some difficulties with surveys. I feel the question often determines the answer. On the other hand, there is quite a lot of data in terms of outcomes, which, Mark, you did not mention. You know, in the end just what is the employment experience and subsequent experience of people in different classes of disadvantage? I just wondered why you did not refer to that?

Can I just make two other points? One is that you are constantly iterating and changing employment programs in the light of experience. That is possibly true of all government policy, but especially true of employment programs. I think really the question that we ought to be looking at is not necessarily what is the state of play at any point in time, but which has got the best prospects of moving ahead? In effect, is a quasi-monopoly government provider likely to provide a better service than we would hope to get to in working in a partnership with other groups?

As a person who once had responsibility for the so-called "quasi-monopoly," the CES, let me say it, at best only ever filled 18 percent of vacancies, which is hardly a monopoly. In fact, most people did not get a job through the CES; they got it some other way. I think I am right in saying, Peter, that the present service fills a larger portion of vacancies. But that monopoly in fact had a lot of competition within itself, individual offices competed like mad.

So there was creaming in the old days. We should not fool ourselves on that. There certainly was. In fact, there was rather less good protection against the creaming, partly because we were not as sophisticated as now. We did not have the information systems and also, quite frankly, the statistics were falsified by the officers.

SUE VARDON: That is a big confession, Michael.

MICHAEL KEATING: Oh, that was before my time.

RICHARD MULLIGAN: I wanted to make a comment on the Canadian experience, which is new to me and very interesting. From the point of view of accountability, which arises also with what Peter Shergold is saying, the main drivers for accountability tend to be centralised. In other words, they are parliament, the ministers, and the national media. This always is driving accountability to the centre. Yet Meredith is saying that we won't get further with partnership unless we can devolve partnership.

The other comment that you made, which related to this, was on the other side from the charities, who are saying, "Well, we do not want to be on the front page of the paper." You could argue that if they are taking public money, providing a public service, they should be prepared to front up if things go wrong in their territory. Ministers should also be prepared to say, "Do not ask me, ask the Salvation Army. Put them on the 7:30 Report." Until we are prepared to do that we won't actually be into true partnership, because we won't have partnered accountability.

I am not sure what the answer to this is. The public seems quite happy with the division of responsibility as it is now. When things go badly wrong everything congregates on the centre. The ministers feel obliged to pick it up. Everybody else feels obliged to duck for cover.

If we are going to have any major changes there has to be some pretty profound changes at all levels. It seems to me that ministers and senior public servants are the ones to start and say, "Do not ask us" until they can you get a much better answer from somewhere else further down the line.

DENIS IVES: I wanted to flag this point that has been mentioned a couple of times about the role of members of parliament. It is quite a dilemma with job programs and, indeed, other programs that have a locational basis. I am just wondering if any further comment can be made on that.

It always seems appropriate members of parliament should take an interest in these matters. I think members of parliament in Australia always knew not only where the CES office was but who the top 10 officers in that office in their electorate were. I assume that is continuing with the Job Network, but it must be rather more difficult.

It is quite a dilemma that, on the one hand the community might like to see members of parliament interested in these issues, but if behind the scenes they are exerting undue influence and accountability is not clear, then there can be a problem. We have had a number of problems identified in Australia. I am interested if there are any further ideas on what is a proper role and how it could be better defined to allow members of parliament to be involved, but in a more transparent accountable way.

JENNY STEWART: The question is for David Good. I was wondering to what extent you would say that the problems with the TJF resulted from program design faults. In other words, was it that there was too much flexibility at the local managerial level or was it rather the information systems were lacking, so that when questions were raised the answers simply were not there?

DAVID GOOD: Let me make comments on the last question and talk about the role of members of parliament. I also want to pick up on one or two of the other comments as well.

With respect to the question of whether there is too much flexibility or lack of information, it is probably the case it was a bit of each. What one needs to appreciate is that if there is to be flexibility it must be circumscribed and bounded in some fashion quite clearly. To leave the concept of "pockets of unemployment" to the discretion of officials in my view is not adequate in the end. The hard lesson is that decisions about what the roles are and what flexibility there should be have to be open and transparent. It is also important that there be centralised information systems.

Back on the question of the accountability coming back to the centre, it tends to flow back that way. As much as one can say "wouldn't it be nice if the other partners would come out and take their view?" in many respects it will tend to flow just in the nature of democracy and in the nature of accountability of officials to ministers and the democratic process back in that fashion. This leads one, then, to the conclusion that what is extremely important is a much better understanding of the nature of the accountability process. What is needed is much better discussion with all parties – with public service, with the voluntary sector and with the private sector – to be able to understand what they are getting into. This leads one to the question of the role of members of parliament.

Our sense was that yes, members of parliament do want to be involved in these programs. They are part of the community. And the question becomes: How can you do that in a more open and transparent manner? Some ideas put forward by the parliamentary committee were to formalise the structure with community advisory groups on which members of parliament would sit. Our experience was if you do not have an open and visible process then one will be created which will not be open and will be invisible just by the sheer nature of these projects. Therefore, I would go on the side of the angels – at least I think it is on the side of the angels – and argue that being open and more transparent in these processes is important. They will by nature be political in the best sense of the word because they are questions of values; they are questions of whether we are going to do it here or over there. I would argue that the role would be very important.

I want to say one last thing on the information. The centralisation of information and the ability to have that information at your disposal very quickly, not on the general stuff but on precisely what is in the project, precisely who is involved, precisely how many jobs are there and exactly what happened, is not an insignificant task. You need that information if you are going to do these things. Therefore, do not underestimate the costs of providing the links, the capacity building and everything else you need with the parkers so they can engage themselves in the process. Because one of the dilemmas, if you are too late on the process, if you do not have the information at your disposal immediately, is that you will then not be able to deal with the media in an effective way.

SUE VARDON: I go now to the panel to talk about the information, the issues that were raised about data or the issues relating to values, which I thought was an interesting one because it is a big issue in Australia.

PETER SHERGOLD: I would like to touch on that and discuss the points that have been raised in a stimulating discussion. First, briefly, the issue of creaming: Mike Keating is absolutely right. In any system there is the danger that whatever the disadvantaged group you define, for a variety of dynamic reasons some members will get better service than others, either because there is a conscious choice or because there is "self-parking." Some people are much more assertive in what they want done for them and better able to make use of the assistance provided. Other people, frankly, do not mind if they disappear from the radar screen.

But if we are trying to find out if and how it occurs, do not go inside the "black box." Do not focus on how much training has been provided or the case management load. What do we want to know? What are we seeking? We are seeking to get people into jobs. Look, then, at the job outcomes rather than input measures. That is the key way to tell whether there is creaming going on.

There are two key things you need to look at. First, compare disadvantaged groups and examine how they are being served by the system. The particularly disadvantaged groups, with one exception, are doing very well from the outcomes of Job Network. The one exception is indigenous clients, and that is not to do with creaming, it is to do with a whole series of cultural, educational and geographic reasons. This is being addressed by the government in different ways, such as by providing wage assistance that is not available to other clients. But based on outcomes they are the only group that seems to be losing out through Job Network.

Second, there are statistical ways you can test for creaming. One of the things you would expect, if there is a substantial amount of creaming going on, is that when clients enter the Job Network member you would get very significant outcomes in the first few months and that performance would quickly drop away. You would get outcomes quickly (for those that can easily be helped) and for the others (the hard cases that are parked) you would not see outcomes recorded.

In fact the evidence is completely the reverse. Look at what happens to Intensive Assistance clients in the first 10 months and you will find that the outcomes being achieved increase progressively across that 10-month period. It is just the opposite pattern of what you would expect if there was creaming occurring. That outcome pattern, together with continued audit and job seeker surveys, helps to assure us that there is not significant evidence of creaming.

Let me now address the issue of choice. I have got to say it is a pretty courageous political decision to issue performance ratings on individual providers in 19 different regions so that providers are awarded from half a star to five stars. It is only just been done. It does not surprise me that at the moment not many clients are looking at the list and saying, "Well, I want to be sent to the five star provider."

Does that mean people are not asserting their choice? No, of course it does not. People are already using their choice with Job Network in just the same way as most Australians assert their choice with respect to doctors. They do not do an analysis of how good the doctor is. The first things they look at are: Is he or she conveniently located? What do my friends tell me? I can tell you, and Sue will confirm this, that jobseekers do that all the time. They look at the six Job Network providers in the region and they say, "Well, those are the two most conveniently located for me to visit. Those are the two my mates have recommended. I want to choose one of those two." Choice is a reality.

Finally, there is the issue of comment. It is a really fascinating issue, and one I have faced. It is a key issue of governance. The fact is, as David has said, that on the whole outsourced providers, when there is media and political controversy, will duck for cover. They will not wish to be visible. And it is for the most sensible of reasons. These are providers that have to work with governments of different political persuasions, and they will want to take a low profile when political debate rages. But let us remember that the minister, too, may not only want to take a low profile but almost certainly is required to because of the governance arrangements. The minister is usually not the decision-maker on contractual arrangements. Increasingly, if we want effective outsourced provision, it is the public servant, not the minister, who has to make and defend decisions.

When the second Job Network tender was finalised it was not the minister who decided on the outcomes. Rather it was myself, the public servant. Therefore, when a major political debate occurred on the outcomes of the Job Network tender the minister was necessarily constrained in what he could say. The providers were, quite understandably, reluctant to put their heads up. The focus, far more than in the past, was on the public servant who made the decisions. It is the public servant who, in this new world, has to be far more willing to comment publicly in an environment of political contest. That is a very difficult issue of governance to deal with.

SUE VARDON: Well, it is, first, an interesting debate because we have two different views of the role of the minister. It is not being resolved today, but at least both arguments have been put on the table. Mark, any quick comments before we go back for one last question?

MARK CONSIDINE: A couple of things that have been raised. Starting with Jim Carlton's question about the data, part of the difference arises from exactly what Peter was referring to, this question of the black box versus data about the overall performance of the system in the context of the business cycle and everything else that contributes to employment outcomes. Clearly the governance issues that I am raising are precisely to do with what contractors actually do. And this, in the Australian case, is referred to as a "black box issue" or the "11 different herbs and spices." The contractors do not want anybody to discuss that. They certainly are not in a big hurry to talk to one another about it, except in the most general terms. They are not happy to have the department look at it closely, in spite of the excellent audit efforts. Yet the attempt to both explain effects, such as they are, and then to learn from them is built upon some understanding of what is in the black box, what are they doing with public money, with public clients, with the mandate of policy that the government's established.

So that is what I have been looking at. There are profound governance issues and dilemmas and severe contradictions. I do not think the system is in any way going to resolve those in its current form, but it provides a backdrop for a bigger debate in a group like this.

Whether survey data, Michael, is better than the data that government departments give us is an arguable point. All I would say in defence of that, very briefly, is that the survey instruments we have been using for this are test and re-test. These are reliable survey instruments, going back 10 or 20 years. I am happy to go through that in more detail. Whether people answering anonymously or giving testimony about their own job in their own workplace are capable of delivering reasonably reliable data is an issue that really goes to whether you think people in those circumstances are going to tell you anything worth knowing. I think they are going to moderate the effect of the critical material they give you, and that makes some of the findings in the Australian case all the more concerning if even half of them are true.

Finally, the point about the NGOs: we really could have had a discussion about this as an issue in itself. It is absolutely important that we do at some point. In the work I have done there are two things I would mention. Firstly, after an initial period of reticence the NGO strategies have converged around the same priorities and strategies of the for-profits and so too ultimately between Working Nation and the first Job Network tender and Employment National. In fact, Employment National went out the other side. As one English observer told me last year, they regard Employment National as more Catholic than the Pope. That is, they intended to exceed even the private sector ethos.

What it means for the NGOs is that they have enormous problems now with the advocacy issue here. When they sign the tender document as a successful tenderer they are prohibited from engaging in all sorts of things to do with discussion of their results, their relationship with the department, and so on.

Some of that is unavoidable in a tendering contracting process that has the probity requirements that Peter referred to. Others are systemic to this quasi-market arrangement, and we now would be very surprised to hear a big religious organisation like the Salvos launch a major critique of the program from which they derive so much money and to which they are so committed. That, quite frankly, is a civil society question mark about whether the effect of having these people work for government is overall of benefit to the clients for whom they are supposed to be advocating.

SUE VARDON: Thank you. Just one very last question, comment.

RICHARD CURTAIN: I am an independent consultant specialising in public policy. One of the important difficulties about partnerships is the fact that it does not recognise the inequalities that exist between the parties. One of the major difficulties that exists looking at employment services arrangement as a governance or public policy issue is how to ensure that the contractors have a degree of power that is equivalent to the other side. From the work I have done looking at the new deal in the UK and comparing it to Australian arrangements, two features are different. One is the existence of a business-led new deal taskforce that operates to promote innovation and change in the employment services arrangements that operate there. There does not seem to be an equivalent arrangement here. The other thing is the use of an innovations fund where employment service providers can apply for funds to set up innovation in the delivery of services. It would seem to me that that would be one way of addressing this problem of confidentiality: it is that people who received moneys under that fund would do so on the basis that they would provide public information about the innovation that they are seeking funding for.

So until you can achieve a more equal balance between the parties you end up with a lot of the governance and policy problems that we have had discussions about this morning.

SUE VARDON: Thank you. That concludes the session. Meredith, we went into your uncharted waters a bit and had a look at some very important issues. We certainly put more issues on the table than we resolved, but I think we gave them a very good airing. So would you please thank Mark, David and Peter for a very stimulating morning.

PART 2

MANAGING PUBLIC-PRIVATE PARTNERSHIPS

Managing Public-Private Partnerships in Canada

Professor John Langford, School of Public Administration, University of Victoria, Canada

Overview of the Argument

It is ironic that as we gather to contemplate the complexities of managing in a public sector "without boundaries," there are already signs in Canada that border guards are being re-installed and governments are rethinking their involvement in many of the public management reforms of the past two decades. Besieged by exposés of misuse of public funds, inadequate results, risks to public health and safety, time and cost overruns, conflict of interest, partisan manipulation, and accountability shortcomings, politicians and senior officials are heading for the exits. One seasoned player in Ottawa recently anguished that "[W]hat is happening in government is a major shift from seeking partnerships and innovation to a rules-based approach." [1] At a meeting with academics at the University of Victoria, the Secretary to the Federal Cabinet left no doubt that his plan for recruitment and retention of public servants was based on a traditional vision of the public service as the key service provider. All of this is a long way from Treasury Board Minister Massé's confident prediction a mere three years ago that "[T]he future of governance is partnership and shared responsibility." [2]

But governments are not monolithic structures. Therefore, retrenchment and rebureaucratization are only part of the story. Many agencies in Ottawa, provincial capitals, and big Canadian cities are too committed to new ways of engaging citizens and groups, managing people and resources, and producing services to turn back to traditional models. For example, chief information officers, tasked with conceiving and implementing e-government, all proceed from the assumption that major initiatives in this area can only be undertaken through long term collaborative partnerships with private sector firms at the leading edge of innovation. [3] Similarly, many managers responsible for the delivery of social and health services cannot contemplate any way back from the complex web of operational partnerships with private and third sector organizations that have become the everyday reality of these agencies.

Interestingly enough, it is experiences with rather modest variations on the partnership theme that have created the anxiety felt by some politicians and senior officials. The reality is that, in Canada, there has been relatively little experimentation to date with more robust forms of public-private partnership. One reason for this is the enormous governance and management challenges which such initiatives pose to public sector agencies.

The governance challenges are daunting enough. Introducing public-private partnerships into the mix of instruments available to policymakers in a Westminster model of government raises difficult questions about the sharing of decision-making power with non-governmental organizations, the direction and coordination of ministerial portfolios containing partnerships, the application of public sector values and standards to private and third sector partners, the relevance of public sector audit and performance measurement techniques, and appropriate flow of information and accountability from partnering bodies to democratic legislatures.[4]

Having reviewed the governance challenges in an earlier writings, it is the management challenge of collaborative partnership that I would like to turn to in this paper. I will proceed by briefly clarifying what a more robust public-private partnership looks like, lay out the nature of the partnership management problem as it can be understood from the extensive literature on private sector strategic alliances, contrast private sector approaches to alliance management with the evidence of government efforts to meet the management challenge of public-private partnerships, then set out some steps which might be taken to make Canadian public sector organizations more "partnership ready." My intention is that this analysis provoke a useful exchange of views on the capacity of public sector organizations to meet the difficult challenges of managing collaborative public-private partnerships across what Donald Kettl refers to as "fuzzy boundaries."[5]

Collaborative Public-Private Partnerships

Partnership is undoubtedly one of the most abused words in the contemporary administrative lexicon. The term is now commonly used to dress up any working relationship between organizations no matter how prosaic the connection or oppressively lopsided the power imbalance among the parties. A very limited funding arrangement between the Department of Indian Affairs and a poor, small native band in the hinterlands of Canada can be proudly described by public officials as a partnership when not one element of any common sense definition of the word is present in the relationship. Similarly, we are all familiar with the overnight linguistic upgrade of straightforward contract-for-service relationships into partnerships. While such hyperbole may momentarily warm the hearts of the participants, it doesn't alter the strict principal-agent relationship that most governments establish with their contractors.

What then are the features of a public-private partnership that make this concept a key factor in the erosion of the boundaries between the public and private or third sectors? The central feature is multi-year collaboration between a public agency and one or more private or third sector organizations in the concurrent fulfillment of public policy objectives and the goals of the private or third sector organizations. Collaboration implies sharing and in the case of partners this means shared vision, authority, information, planning, decision making, financial risk, responsibility and accountability. A collaborative partnership may be legally legitimized by a contract, but it is not a client-contractor relationship in which the government simply specifies the service or product it wants and the partner delivers it to the dictated standards. [6]

There would be no point in portraying collaborative partnership as a pure type and, therefore, a null category by insisting that a partnership have high, measurable quotients of all of the afore-mentioned characteristics before it could qualify as collaborative. There obviously is a continuum of privatization in which public enterprise, contracting for services, and weaker and stronger partnerships with for-profit or not-for-profit organizations are key milestones on the road to a significantly restructured state. But I do subscribe to the views of those Canadian authors who distinguish collaborative from consultative (information seeking and sharing), contributory (financial support and sponsorship) and operational (work sharing) partnerships.[7] The focus of this paper is in line with the theme of our symposium. It is robust collaborative partnerships with private and third sector organizations which have the potential to truly wear away the boundaries of the public sector by creating relationships in the gray area between public and private or public and third sector organizations which test many of the values, structures, processes and skills associated with traditional public management.

While I have no intention of wasting your time on a null category, the fact is, that despite all the ideologically induced excitement about partnership, there are not many examples of collaborative public-private partnerships in Canada or elsewhere. A recent comprehensive study of public-private partnerships in the United States, concluded that "[f]ew authentic, fully integrated, co-accountable examples of partnering were observed."[8] The most prominent cases in both jurisdictions to date appear to be in the area of infrastructure construction and operation (roads, bridges, public transit, energy generation and distribution) and community facilities construction (schools, libraries, convention and community centres) where the fiscal constraints on governments in the 1990s forced them to seek out private financing. Canada's most widely known (in some cases, infamous) collaborative public-private partnerships would include the Confederation Bridge joining Prince Edward Island to the mainland; the Charleswood Bridge in Winnipeg; Highway 407 outside of Toronto; Teranet, a high technology joint venture land registry system in Ontario; CANARIE, the Canadian Network for the Advancement of Research and Education; and a licensing arrangement between the RCMP and Walt Disney to market RCMP-related merchandise.[9]

An emerging area of collaborative partnership is information and communications technology, especially in the development of e-government. Here the major rationale for partnering is the inability of government to recruit and retain the expertise to make information, databases, interactive opportunities and services for citizens and organizations available electronically. Although there are grounds for supposing that robust collaborative partnerships with private and third sector organizations would flourish in the social policy area, few governments have gone much beyond performance contract relationships (i.e. contributory or operational partnerships) designed to substitute such organizations for state agencies as operators of welfare functions.

My point here is not to diminish the significance of consultative, contributory or operational partnerships, but rather to suggest that the promise of collaborative public-private partnerships – one of the brightest stars in the business-driven administrative reform constellation – remains to be achieved. One reason for this curious reality is that governments have not successfully addressed the management challenges that truly collaborative partnerships present. To get some sense of the dimension of that challenge, I turn first to the extensive literature on the management of strategic alliances among private sector organizations.

Lessons from the Private Sector

The literature on private sector partnering is more sophisticated than its public and third sector counterparts. While the latter have barely emerged from normative rhetoric about the benefits of public-private partnerships, the former has added a significant body of empirical case studies and a tougher, more critical analysis of the conditions under which organizations can make partnerships work for them. This is hardly surprising in view of the fact that collaborative partnerships or strategic alliances have emerged from the relative obscurity of supply chain management to become a key tool to ensure survival and build value in a globalized economy. Airlines, drug companies, "convergence" enterprises in the telecommunications, internet, e-business and biotech sectors, and even petroleum companies have all embraced strategic alliances and alliance blocks as vehicles for creating extra value out of complementarity, raising cash, sharing risks, gaining access to new customers and markets, competing more effectively with larger rivals, accessing technology or expertise, setting standards in a new industry and bridging cultural divides.

Contemporary strategic alliances allow a firm to avoid the complexities of vertical integration, merger and, more recently, even the formal establishment of separate joint ventures or licensing arrangements. But the business administration literature makes it clear that the successful creation and maintenance of alliances that add value make tough demands on the managers of the partnering organizations. In fact, the literature is replete with case studies of alliance failure with the general consensus being that managing alliances is as difficult as "stirring concrete with eyelashes."

Nevertheless, it is possible to discern in this literature and its distillation of the experiences of private sector firms, a degree of convergence on the organizational culture, structures and processes, and managerial capacity which must be present if an "alliance manager" – a term intended to include all managers working on an alliance – is to have a reasonable chance of making a success of a partnership opportunity. It is noteworthy that many of these features would be found within organizations which attach a high priority to eradicating the "silo" mentality and structures which foster intra-organization competition and territoriality in large bureaucratic enterprises – a thought I will resurrect towards the end of the paper.

The Culture of Partnering

From the cultural perspective, the key message from the literature is that successful partnering organizations must have a high tolerance for risk and uncertainty. On a more positive note, the organizational culture of an alliance candidate should foster the values of trust, collaboration, information sharing, horizontality, networking, negotiation, consensus, and flexibility. These are not just a "wet dream" collection of post-modern corporate attributes, but rather characteristics dictated by the very nature of alliances. The argument made in the literature is that if these value foundations are not evident in the partnering organizations, there is little chance that appropriate managerial structures, processes or skills will be enough to make the alliance a success.

The significance of the tolerance for uncertainty and risk emerges from the reality that

> alliances are complex organizational forms that are usefully viewed as incomplete contracts. They typically involve the transfer of know-how between firms, a process that is fraught with ambiguity . . . [i]t is difficult to prespecify the contingencies that arise in their management. For example, unanticipated changes in the environment may alter the incentives of the contracting parties; intangible personal, organizational and cultural attributes may affect the ongoing relationship between firms in important ways as well.[10]

Risk and uncertainty, then, are implicit in all aspects of an alliance. At the most obvious level, most partnerships require large investments of funds and often of technological and human resources. Often key resources have to be shared with partners. In addition, the success of these interdependent and, consequently, complex arrangements depends on the performance of a partner organization which you do not control.

While some eschew the notion of "trust" in favour of "enlightened self- and mutual interest,"[11] the former is generally portrayed in the literature as the most basic and significant value building block. Trust is obviously mutually reinforcing and, therefore, very difficult to sustain in partnerships in which managers in one organization sense a lack of trust in the other partner. Organizations built on a "dog eat dog" competitive internal culture will make poor partners. Niederkofler observes that

> Goodwill and trust were found to have a stabilizing effect on the relationship at all development stages. They increased the partners' tolerance for each others' behaviour and helped avoid conflicts. Goodwill and trust also raised the general level of communication between the partners and thereby increased the chances for uncovering and dealing with operating misfit.[12]

A further premium attached to the value of trust relates to the need for "extra value," creating synergy that in turn "demands a true partnership in which the partners are willing to discuss their perceptions and goals in a search for new solutions." Trust is essential to this exchange as "partners are not likely to cooperate in a search for new solutions if they do not have the assurance that the outcomes will not hurt them."[13]

Without trust, other key values such as collaboration and information sharing are likely to be weak. Collaboration is stressed in the literature because it provides a clear counterpoint to the ethos of competition that is the foundation value of market-based organizations. Where the complementarity that adds value in contemporary strategic alliances is often based on the sharing of the very information that creates competitive advantage, it is easy to see why sustaining and operationalizing the value of collaboration through information sharing is one of the hardest tasks facing an alliance manager. The degree of difficulty is obviously considerably higher in the private sector where it is common to be involved in strategic alliances with competitor organizations.

The collaboration and interdependency that blur the boundaries between organizations also accompany the displacement of both market and hierarchical bureaucratic values and the infiltration of the idea of the horizontal network.[14] Where every partner in an alliance brings resources necessary to the common goal of creating extra value, then competition and opportunistic behaviour within the alliance must be muted and no one partner can be in charge.[15] Valuing the idea of the network makes it possible for partners to rationalize behaviour that sustains an incomplete alliance contract with informal rules rather than behaviour that simply exploits a "hole" in the contract.

Building further on trust and the network, it is easy to understand the significance placed on the values of negotiation and consensus. If no one partner is in charge, then negotiation is the only reasonable way to create consensus among the partners. Decision-making takes on a very different character in an alliance than it does in a hierarchical bureaucracy where the focus is on leading and controlling subordinates rather than juggling constituencies.[16]

Finally, flexibility is obviously going to be a significant cultural asset in a setting in which the rules of engagement are not fully set down in the contract and it is impossible to know at the outset how the alliance might evolve. "[F]lexibility in response to change, particularly concerning partner objectives" combined with a strong orientation towards organizational learning are demonstrated by Faulkner and others to be key variables in the ultimate success of a strategic alliance.[17] Bleeke and Ernst support the link between flexibility and success: "nearly 40% of the alliances in our sample gradually broadened the scope of their initial charter . . . . Of those alliances that had evolved, 79% were successful and 89% are ongoing. In contrast, of the alliances whose scope remained unchanged, only 33% were successful and more than half have terminated."[18]

The focus of this discussion has been on the corporate culture of individual partnering organizations, but the success of an alliance ultimately depends on the boundary-spanning interaction of two or more corporate cultures within the partnership itself – what a recent study refers to as the "alliance spirit."[19] "Although cultural compatibility was rarely a major consideration in selecting a partner, sensitivity to culture at least was found to be a very important factor in predicting alliance effectiveness."[20]

> Acceptable alliance behavior is based on norms that typically emerge as partners interact. When partners share a basic understanding of what it means to a partner, governance becomes easier. Successful alliances are built on the premise that partners share similar views of acceptable alliance behavior. Norms encourage collaborative actions in pursuit of shared vision.[21]

The collaborative actions are not limited to the joint production of outputs which make the partners more competitive as a collective, but include the extension of joint competencies across the partnership through more intense forms of information sharing and transboundary learning.

Structures and Processes for Partnering

In the literature on private sector strategic alliances, considerable attention has been focused on the structures and processes the partners create singly and together to initiate, implement and end alliances. Not surprisingly, a good deal of this literature is replete with mechanisms designed to institutionalize within the partnership the key corporate values that make alliances work.

In the initiation phase of alliance making, one of the most significant management challenges within individual partnering organizations is the establishment of a future-oriented, organization-wide strategic architecture which incorporates a more tightly focused alliance strategy. Case studies demonstrate that alliance planning often is limited to individual business units within an enterprise, thereby divorcing the consideration of the alliance option from the creation of an overall vision and strategic plan for the organization. As a result the organization does not systematically consider what strengths it can employ to leverage growth through partnering, or pay attention at the corporate level to the full scope of firms with which it might potentially partner. Instead, it falls back on predictable, "no-brainer," defensive alliances that do no more than plug holes.[22]

Organizations with considerable alliance experience integrate partnering into their wider activities by creating structures such as a senior alliance management team, an alliance oriented senior executive position, and a committee of the board focused on creating alliance opportunities and overseeing their management and evaluation. In larger organizations with a strong commitment to partnering, specialized alliance managers, facilitators, database coordinators and auditors will be found in the corporate headquarters and the relevant business units. Such enterprises might have well developed alliance policies and procedures, including sample proposal forms and contracts; best practice guidelines for risk management, benchmarking, performance measurement and alliance breakup; case histories of successes and failures; contact lists of internal experts; standard tests to apply to potential partnering opportunities; an alliance data base or map of the organization; and finally, a comprehensive alliance management training program.

While there is little evidence to suggest that the selection of alliance form is crucial to its effectiveness,[23] sophisticated alliance firms focus considerable attention on boundary-spanning structures and processes designed to enhance the interorganizational bond with their partners. In the more rigid forms of partnering such as joint ventures, structures such as the board of directors and its various committees can be used to enhance the bond among the partners, make decisions, and resolve disputes. In the more contemporary and less structured strategic alliances, successful boundary spanning will depend more on the establishment of processes that operationalize the key partnering values. These would include processes for more open communication and information-sharing (e.g. joint task forces, collocation of activities, executive conferences), interest-driven consensual decision making, alliance learning (e.g. through secondment[24]), informal dispute resolution at the working level, and procedures for penalizing poor performance and negotiating a divorce if the alliance fails.

Alliance Management Skills

Even if the culture of an organization is oriented towards alliances, partnering is a key feature of strategic planning, and the organization has created appropriate structures and processes, the success of partnerships will still depend on the skills of those individuals tasked to manage the partnership over the course of what might be a considerable life span.[25] Effectively, the locus of power shifts from the traditional hierarchy to the "interface manager."[26] The skill set is obviously going to be closely related to the key alliance values, structures and processes outlined above. It is the fit among these three factors that creates the value-adding synergy that is the objective of the exercise.

The private sector literature generally groups the managerial capacity required around different phases of the alliance life span. At the front end of the cycle, the most critical tasks are the ability to identify alliance opportunities, calculate probabilities of success for the most promising opportunities, select strategically compatible partners, and design the alliance. Alliance managers must have the confidence to choose strong partners over those that are easily dominated. They must have broad knowledge of the players in the sector in order be able to identify opportunities that offer complementarity of strengths, and overall compatibility of information and problem-solving systems, styles and values.[27] Having identified a partner or partners, an alliance manager must be able to design the partnership. This involves clarifying the objectives of the partners, defining the strategic, economic and operational scope of the alliance, and calculating the worth of what potential partners bring to the alliance. This valuation process is usually complicated by the presence of hard-to-value assets, the shifting of contributions over time, the difficulties associated with measuring anticipated contributions, and the tendencies at the early stages of the relationship for potential partners to exaggerate their alliance costs and underrepresent potential benefits. Cutting the deal also involves making choices among institutional forms (e.g. joint venture, consortium, contract, memorandum of understanding) – choices which depend on calculations of the level of uncertainty of the joint enterprise, the amount of integration required to effectively perform the tasks defined, and the speed of decision making required.[28]

Especially at the deal making stage, alliance managers are most fundamentally risk managers. Risk management skills in a public sector setting tend to be focused negatively on the identification, assessment, prevention and mitigation of harm to the public, clients, the environment and – all too prominently – the reputation of a minister.[29] In the context of private sector alliance building, by contrast, the focus is more positively on finding opportunity within the complex tension between the potentially exponential return on joint activity and the substantial setback that would accompany the failure of a substantial alliance initiative. The alliance manager has to understand the goals of potential partners and be ready to give up some benefits for his/her organization in some areas to gain concessions in others and thereby create a win-win situation. The result may take the form of a contract, but the skills are those of a negotiator, not a lawyer.[30]

In the implementation phase of the partnering cycle, the key skill sets are those that support the maintenance and enhancement of boundary relationships within the partnership network and between the partnering business unit, its employees, and corporate headquarters. An alliance manager has to be first a network builder or a process manager,[31] able to create a web of relationships among stakeholders at all relevant levels of the partnering organizations.[32] Within the manager's own business unit this can be a particularly demanding task if the alliance is one which may lead to job rationalization and downsizing. Looking outward, the task is often complicated by the contemporary reality that multi-party alliances are becoming commonplace. Sustaining this portfolio of horizontal connections places a high premium on the communications, consensus decision making, and dispute resolution skills required to make a success of the partnering processes outlined in the previous section. Managing "horizontally" is a particular problem in alliances involving both large and small partners, where alliance managers from the larger partner can feel pressure from superiors to exercise control rather than negotiate towards a consensus.

Finally, as an alliance develops and matures, the alliance manager has to be able to move it to new levels. The core skill involved in renewing an alliance is building momentum by creating realistic benchmarks or milestones, delivering outcomes, and using the shared sense of progress to persuade partners and superiors to pool more resources and move on to the next set of goals. In the event that periodic evaluation processes indicate that the alliance is floundering and can't be revived, exit management skills come into play. In the private sector setting, extraction from an alliance can be a delicate business especially where proprietary information has been shared.

This very brief overview provides some insight into the way in which the most sophisticated private sector organizations approach the partnership management challenge. As Canadian government agencies contemplate multi-party partnerships with large information technology firms to produce online services, they face the prospect of negotiating with organizations with extensive strategic alliance experience, a strong alliance culture, a wide array of alliance-oriented management structures and processes, and highly skilled alliance managers. Are public agencies ready for such encounters?

Management Challenge – the View from the Canadian Public Administration Community

By some estimates, management shortcomings account for as many failures of private sector strategic alliances as do problems inherent in the basic fit between the objectives of the partners or shortcomings in the outcomes the alliance produces. The management factor has not received much attention from the Canadian public administration community. A review of Canadian public administration literature, consultant's reports and government publications on collaborative partnerships – especially material produced following the first flush of the New Public Management reform movement in the late 1980s and early 1990s – could leave the reader with the impression that the management of collaborative partnerships was simply not going to present that great a problem.

Only a small proportion of the writing in Canada dealt with the management of partnerships at all. In a seminal article on partnerships, Ken Kernaghan mentioned the "desirability of consensus decision-making" and the need for "careful planning, implementation, and evaluation." But none of his hypotheses about the requirements for successful partnerships focused on their management.[33] In a deservedly well-known issue of the public sector management journal, *Optimum*, dedicated entirely to the partnership concept, Rodal and Mulder insisted that public sector managers who attempt to implement partnerships "discover that they face major challenges for which they have not been prepared." Curiously, the management challenges they set out later in the article (accountability, government leadership of P3s, power balancing within partnerships) are really governance questions about fitting robust partnerships into a traditional Westminster model of government.[34]

However, another article in the same issue of *Optimum* truly confronted the management challenges of partnerships and briefly sets down principles and best practices for each stage of the partnership cycle.[35] The article drew specific attention to:

- the need to enhance the capacity of government managers to coordinate government activities and activities across the partnership interface;

- the high premium placed on consultation, negotiation, consensual planning and decision making skills;

- the requirement for organizational paradigm shifts within an agency (from programs to projects, from vertical chains of command to horizontal team work);

- the relocation of management authority and responsibility to accommodate the need for joint decision making with private partners;

- the significance of more open communication within the government agency, across the partnership and among external stakeholders;

- the skills required to manage risk at all stages of a partnership;

- the training required to make managers more aware of the cultural difference among partnering organizations.

Rodal then went on briefly to discuss how these management challenges emerged at different stages of the partnering cycle. Highlights of this analysis are:

- a framework for analyzing when a partnership would work;

- the major questions that managers should ask at the planning stage;
- a list of barriers to successful implementation;
- suggestions concerning the design of performance evaluation instruments;
- thoughts on the management of transitions in and out of partnerships.

Although this article successfully outlined the significant management challenges facing government agencies contemplating collaborative partnerships, there was little evidence that Canadian governments in any systematic way picked up this challenge and began to prepare their managers for partnering. Since the federal government appeared to make the most substantial effort, the remainder of this section is focused on that effort.

A number of "how to" partnership guides were issued by federal government departments and central agencies in the mid-1990s.[36] In the most comprehensive and influential of these, the Treasury Board Secretariat set out "to develop a set of principles and best practices for collaborative arrangements in a federal government setting."[37] Drawing on the earlier writing of Rodal and others, the report sets out a six-step approach to promoting successful collaboration, and three of those steps drew specific attention to tasks that managers must perform. These tasks include:

- consulting a range of departmental and central agency specialists on legal, financial, contracting, risk and project management, human resources, official languages and communications issues;

- following a basic planning checklist including activities such as situational analysis, objective-setting, risk management, management of inputs, division of outputs, communications procedures, audit and evaluation, dispute resolution, and termination.

- building trust, respect for all parties' objectives and contributions, flexibility, open and regular communication and the ability to share responsibility, work and rewards.

While superficially this report suggested that the federal government was moving smartly to meet the management challenges of partnering, a closer analysis suggests caution. First, the report makes it clear that whatever the demands of partnering, no changes were being contemplated in the regime of rules and structures within which government managers regularly operate. Second, there was no indication that the management skills required for dealing with partnerships were going to be widely inculcated at the operating agency level. In short, managers were given lists of tasks but no plan to enhance their ability to take on those tasks.

In this context, consultants on the edge of the public administration community continued to draw attention to managerial shortcomings in public sector agencies considering partnerships. For example, a "Best Practice Guideline" from a major Canadian law firm advised that the process of identifying potential partners and choosing among them could not be reduced to the traditional request for hard bids to provide services specified in detailed plans. Governments were cautioned that the establishment of fair, open and accountable Requests for Qualifications and Proposal processes focused on what were usually poorly defined government "business units" required institutionalized procedures and negotiation, evaluation and risk management skills that were not available in most federal or provincial operating ministries.[38]

In 1997, four years after the original blossoming of public administration literature on partnerships, two of the early advocates of collaborative partnerships reflected on the progress to date at the federal level:

> . . . if the government wishes to rely increasingly on the private sector, it may have to devise institutional arrangements that are better suited to this mode of governance. Such arrangements would provide greater systemic support for partnering arrangements than is currently the case, in particular by enhancing the preparedness and augmenting the capacity of the public sector to take and manage risks.[39]

Individual federal agencies sent out mixed messages. For example, while admitting that "there remains much more to be done," the Canadian Heritage ministry insisted that its management philosophy was "evolving to meet the challenges and opportunities that come with the increased emphasis on partnering . . . . It is responsive and flexible . . . . Support for partnering is visible from all levels of management from the Deputy Minister to the line managers . . . ."[40]

This upbeat note is not reflected in a comprehensive consultant's report entitled "Impediments to Partnering and the Role of the Treasury Board," which was commissioned by the federal Treasury Board Secretariat in 1998. The report summarized the lack of progress in the federal system in equipping line managers to partner effectively:

> The government system of rewards and sanctions does little to encourage partnering, while the prevailing culture of risk aversion may actively discourage such arrangements. The skills needed to establish and manage partnering arrangements are inadequately recognized and there is a shortage of people with the needed skills in any case. Turf and jurisdictional protectionism, cultural differences and interpersonal conflicts create further difficulties. Care has to be taken to avoid creating a master/servant relationship, which is inconsistent with the concept of partnering. Other risks to the health of partnering arrangements cited by participants include the lack of audit or evaluation framework, system incompatibilities, lack of capacity of some partners to fulfill their responsibilities, inadequate representation in the arrangement of certain stakeholders and, last but not least, poor communications.[41]

When the auditor general of Canada weighed in on the issue of collaborative arrangements, he argued that "[t]here are risks that deserve attention. These include the risk of poorly defined arrangements, limiting the chances for success; partners not meeting commitments; insufficient attention to protecting the public interest: insufficient transparency; and inadequate accountability."[42] While the major foci of this report were accountability and reporting to Parliament, the auditor general also targeted federal government partnership management practices. In particular, the auditor general drew attention to the importance of leadership at the political and bureaucratic levels, the establishment of coordination mechanisms among the partners, and the need to establish trust in a partnership. In a subsequent report, the auditor general expressed concern about managers' preparedness to assess the capacity of potential partners to perform adequately, the absence of dispute resolution mechanisms, and shortcomings in arrangements for non-performance and partnership termination.[43]

Efforts to deal with these powerful critiques would appear to have been limited to the building of a locus for partnership development and guidance within the Alternative Service Delivery Division at the Treasury Board Secretariat and the generation by the Secretariat of guidelines around key issues such as risk management.[44] The last available word from the Treasury Board Secretariat on "partnership readiness" was a brief observation in a Powerpoint presentation on Alternative Service Delivery delivered by a senior Treasury Board official in October 2000. Referring to public-private partnerships, the single line reads: "Experience, expertise in government is limited."[45]

This brief and very incomplete survey suggests that the public administration community (government included) is continually being reminded – mostly by consultants with one eye on the private sector – that the management of partnerships requires significant cultural, capacity, procedural and structural change, but that little has actually been done to make Canadian public bureaucracies "partnership ready." My own personal observations, drawn from involvement in executive and senior management development programs at all three levels of government in Canada over the last decade, support that conclusion. Queried on the topic of their capacity, managers consistently record that they do not have access to the authorities, structures, or skills to initiate or manage complex collaborative relationships with private and third sector partners. While efforts to improve service quality, break down departmental "silos" and make public bureaucracies more "business-like" have implicitly addressed some of the partnership management challenges, no Canadian government has taken on the partnership capacity issue in any organized way. Both the government and academic communities continue to focus primarily on the significance of public-private partnerships as instruments of governance.[46]

Where Do We Go From Here?

In Canada at least, the "alliance management gap" is an imposing barrier to the widespread employment of collaborative public-private partnerships. In a 1998 survey, 50% of the public sector respondents to a Canadian Council for Public-Private Partnerships survey indicated that their organizations did not have "specialists who assist in planning and implementing partnerships," and were not likely to have them within two years.[47] I doubt that this situation has changed much over three years. Assuming that Canadian governments will want to rely more heavily on collaborative partnerships in the future, what can be done to reduce this gap?

Smaller governments (e.g. at the municipal and regional levels) have indicated a willingness to purchase consulting services to assist in the partnering process. While this approach may work for the start-up phase of an alliance, it does little to equip line managers with the capacity to sustain the relationship over the length of the partnership. For more senior governments, the most obvious solution would be to build managerial capacity incrementally on top of recent reforms in public management which have devolved more responsibility and latitude for experimentation on to managers, installed business practices and performance measurement, inclined central agencies towards system-wide leadership through the establishment of best practices, stressed the significance of learning, and fostered the notion of horizontal management of issues across the public service. The latter connection strikes me as being the most promising as there is a reasonably close fit between values, structures and skills required for horizontal management within government and those required for partnership management across sectors.

Some key steps – many of which are inspired by the U.K. experience with public-private partnerships – would include the following:

- Movement away from the traditional government procurement model, which keeps line agencies at arm's length from potential private partners, forces the latter into anachronistic tendering processes and transforms most production interactions with the private sector into principal/agent relationships tightly controlled by a central government purchasing agency. The new facilitative and flexible procurement regime being developed at the Office of Government Commerce in the U.K. shows promise in this respect.[48]

- Creating system-wide dialogue on the inherent tensions between traditional public service values and the values that provide the foundation for good alliance management. The auditor general recently opened up such a debate, drawing attention to the tension which public sector managers engaged in public-private partnerships perceived between trust creation and accountability, information sharing and confidentiality/ privacy protection, and risk tolerance and fiscal prudence.[49]

- Adoption of progressive risk management strategies. For example, recent German and Austrian government initiatives provide for "experimentation" or "flexibility" clauses to allow public sector agencies to try innovative arrangements such as multi-year collaborative partnerships in a setting that is more risk tolerant.[50]

- Further development of the guidance role of the treasury or management board in the establishment and management of partnerships involving one or more line agencies and private sector organizations. The Treasury Task Force in the U.K. is a useful model to consider. Its role has recently been divided between the Office of Government Commerce and Public Private Partnership UK, a public-private catalyst organization designed to help public agencies structure and negotiate the financial aspects of a partnership deal.[51]

- The establishment of public-private partnership units in major ministries and agencies to provide a focus for alliance management at the business unit level. While too narrowly focused, the Private Finance Units established in some UK ministries provide an interesting model.

- Focused training of alliance managers through "partnership boot camp" projects and the continuous teaching of a core "public-private partnership management" curriculum. An interesting model is the program provided by Price Waterhouse Coopers in the U.K. to familiarize public servants with all aspects of the Private Finance Initiative.[52]

Final Words

The focus of this paper has been on the management of public-private partnerships, so I have religiously steered away from ideological arguments about the appropriateness of privatizing the state through the use of such instruments. Equally, as noted at the outset, I have ignored the political and governance issues raised by extensive involvement in collaborative partnering with private and third sector organizations. At this point, however, it would be useful to acknowledge that some governments will be more inclined ideologically than others to put resources into making their managers "partnership ready." Similarly, some governments will be more willing than others to contemplate the political risks and governance complexities associated with experimentation with collaborative partnerships. Many governments seem to share to some degree the ambivalence now evident in Ottawa and other Canadian capitals about the privatization of state functions.

But even governments that are reluctant participants in collaborative partnering recognize that many governmental activities (such as the construction and operation of community facilities, transportation and communications infrastructure, remedial environmental projects, and e-government implementation) will only be sustained through alliances with the private sector. If this is the case, then governments will have to create and sustain capacity to manage these boundary-spanning activities. In my view, this represents a daunting challenge to even the largest and most sophisticated public services.

Notes

[1] Arthur Kroeger, "The HRD Affair: Reflections on Accountability in Government," Speech to the Canadian Club of Ottawa, December 12, 2000.

[2] Marcel Massé, "Governing for the Future," Quebec City, July 15, 1997.

[3] John W. Langford and Yvonne Harrison, "Partnering for E-government: Challenges for Public Administrators" *Canadian Public Administration*, forthcoming (2001).

[4] See John W. Langford, "Power Sharing in the Alternative Service Delivery World," in R. Ford and D. Zussman, *Alternative Service Delivery: Sharing Governance in Canada*, (Toronto: IPAC/KPMG, 1997; John W. Langford, "The Ethical Challenges of Alternative Service Delivery," paper prepared for the OECD Conference on Public Sector Ethics, Paris, November, 1997; John W. Langford, "The Governance Challenges of Public-Private Partnerships," in S. Delacourt and D.G. Lenihan, *Collaborative Government: Is there a Canadian Way?* (Toronto: IPAC, 1999).

[5] D.F. Kettl,. "Bridging Fuzzy Boundaries: Best Practices in Managing P3s," in *Shifting Involvements: Private and Public Roles in Canadian Health Care*, Proceedings of the CHEPA Conference, Hamilton, Ontario, 1998.

[6] G. Drewry, "Public-Private Partnerships: Rethinking the Boundary Between Public and Private Law," in S.P. Osborne, ed., *Public-Private Partnerships: Theory and Practice in International Perspective*, (London: Routledge, 2000), ch. 3.

[7] Kenneth Kernaghan, "Partnership and Public Administration: Conceptual and Practical Considerations," *Canadian Public Administration* (Spring 1993), pp.57-76; J.D. Wright and A.B. Rodal, "Partnerships and Alliances," in M. Charih and A. Daniels, eds., *New Public Management and Public Administration in Canada* (Toronto: IPAC, 1997), ch.12; J. Boase, "Beyond Government? The Appeal of Public-Private Partnerships," *Canadian Public Administration* (Spring 2000), pp.75-91.

[8] Pauline Vaillancourt Rosenau, "The Strengths and Weaknesses of Public-Private Partnerships," in Pauline Vaillancourt Rosenau, ed., *Public-Private Policy Partnerships* (Cambridge: MIT Press, 2000), ch.13.

[9] Boase, "The Appeal of Public-Private Partnerships," Canadian Council for Public-Private Partnerships, http://home.inforamp.net/~partners/ (2001); A. Daniels, "Taking Strategic Alliances to the World: Ontario's Teranet," in R. Ford and D. Zussman, *Alternative Service Delivery: Sharing Governance in Canada* (Toronto: IPAC/KPMG, 1997).

[10] B. Anand and T. Khanna, "Do Firms Learn to Create Value? The Case of Alliances," *Strategic Management Journal* 21 (2000), p.295.

[11] Y. Doz and G. Hamel, *Alliance Advantage: The Art of Creating Value Through Partnering* (Cambridge: Harvard Business School Press, 1998), p.28.

[12] M. Niederkofler, "The Evolution of Strategic Alliances: Opportunities for Managerial Influence," *Journal of Business Ventures* 6 (1991), pp. 237-57.

[13] E. Klijn and G. Teisman, "Governing Public-Private Partnerships: Analysing and Managing the Process and Institutional Characteristics of Public-Private Partnerships," in Osborne, ed., *Public-Private Partnerships: Theory and Practice in International Perspective*, p.92.

[14] M. Castells, *The Rise of the Network Society* (Cambridge: Blackwell, 1996).

[15] C. Alter, and J. Hage, *Organizations Working Together* (Newbury Park: Sage, 1993).

[16] D. Faulkner, *International Strategic Alliances: Cooperating to Compete* (New York: McGraw-Hill, 1995), p.91.

[17] Faulkner, p.186

[18] J. Bleeke, and D. Ernst, *Collaborating to Change* (New York: J. Wiley, 1993), p.25.

[19] R. Spekman, L. Isabella, and T. MacAvoy, *Alliance Competence: Maximizing the Value of Your Partnerships* (New York: Wiley, 2000), ch.4.

[20] Faulkner, p.185.

[21] Spekman, Isabella, and MacAvoy, p.6.

[22] Doz and Hamel, p.253.

[23] Faulkner, p.187.

[2424] R.P. Lynch, "Building Alliances to Penetrate European Markets," *Journal of Business* [24]

[24] *Strategy* (March/April 1990), pp. 4-8.

[25] Faulkner, p.185; Niederkofler, 1991.

[26] D. Limerick and B. Cunnington, *Managing the New Organization*, (San Francisco: Jossey-Bass, 1993), pp.83-4.

[27] Limerick and Cunnington, pp.96-7.

[28] Doz and Hamel, ch.5.

[29] Canada, Treasury Board Secretariat, Risk Management Policy, http://www.tbs-sct.gc.ca/pubs_pol/dcgpubs/RiskManagement/riskmanagpol_e.html, 1994.

[30] Faulkner, p. 187.

[31] Klijn and Teisman, p. 96.

[32] J. Botkin, and J. Matthews, *Winning Combinations* (New York: J. Wiley, 1992), pp.136-38.

[33] Kernaghan, "Partnership and Public Administration," pp.73-5.

[34] A.B. Rodal and N. Mulder, "Partnerships, Devolution and Power Sharing," *Optimum* 24, no. 3, (Winter 1993), pp.27-47.

[35] A.B. Rodal, "Managing Partnerships," *Optimum* 24, no. 3, (Winter 1993), pp.48-63.

[36] For a comprehensive list see: J.D. Wright and A.B. Rodal, "Partnerships and Alliances," in M. Charih and A. Daniels, *New Public Management and Public Administration in Canada*, (Toronto: IPAC, 1997), fn. 10, p.288.

[37] Canada, The Treasury Board Secretariat, *Stretching the Tax Dollar: The Federal Government as "Partner": Six Steps to Successful Collaboration*, (Ottawa: Supply and Services, Canada, 1995).

[38] G.B. Cowper-Smith, "Public-Private Partnerships: Initiating Contracts and Contracting with the Private Sector, Best Practices Guidelines." Paper presented to the Canadian Council for Public-Private Partnerships Third Annual Conference, November, 1995.

[39] Wright and Rodal (1997), p.277.

[40] Canada, Canadian Heritage, *Public Private Partnering Resource Kit*, (Ottawa: 1998).

[41] Canada, Consulting and Audit Canada, *Impediments to Partnering and the Role of Treasury Board*, May 13, 1998, p.4.

[42] Canada, Auditor General of Canada, *Report to the House of Commons* (Ottawa: Public Works and Government Services Canada, April, 1999), chapter 5, p.7.

[43] Canada, Auditor General of Canada, *Report to the House of Commons* (Ottawa: Public Works and Government Services Canada, November, 1999), chapter 23, p.20.

[44] Canada, Treasury Board Secretariat, *Annotated Bibliography for the Study on "Best Practices in Risk Management: Private and Public Sectors Internationally* (1999), http://www.tbs-sct.gc.ca/pubs_pol/dcgpubs/RiskManagement/siglist_e.html; *Best Practices in Risk Management:: Coordinated Conclusions from PMN and KPMG* (1999), http://www.tbs-sct.gc.ca/pubs_pol/dcgpubs/RiskManagement/siglist_e.html; *Best Practices in Risk Management: Private and Public Sectors Internationally* (1999), http://www.tbs-sct.gc.ca/pubs_pol/dcgpubs/RiskManagement/siglist_e.html; *Review of Canadian Best Practices in Risk Management*, 1999, http://www.tbs-sct.gc.ca/pubs_pol/dcgpubs/RiskManagement/siglist_e.html; *Risk, Innovation and Values - Examining the Tensions* (1999), http://www.tbs-sct.gc.ca/pubs_pol/dcgpubs/RiskManagement/siglist_e.html.

[45] Toby Fyfe, Director, ASD Division, Treasury Board Secretariat of Canada, "Public-Private Partnerships: An Alternative Service Delivery Perspective," Powerpoint presentation, October, 2000.

[46] Fyfe, "Public-Private Partnerships"; K. Kernaghan and D. Siegel, *Public Administration in Canada*, 4th ed., (Toronto: ITP Nelson, 1999), ch. 11.

[47] Canadian Council for Public-Private Partnerships, *Building Effective Partnerships*, (Toronto, 1998), p.21.

[48] U.K., Office of Government Commerce, 2001, http://www.ogc.gov.uk/ogc/isite.nsf/default.html.

[49] Canada, Office of the Auditor General, *Report to the House of Commons*, (Ottawa: Public Works and Government Services Canada, 2000), chapter 23, p.69; John Langford, "The Ethical Challenges of Alternative Service Delivery."

[50] Canada, Treasury Board Secretariat, *Best Practices in Risk Management: Private and Public Sectors Internationally* (1999); *Risk, Innovation and Values - Examining the Tensions* (1999).

[51] See Public Private Partnership UK, http://www.partnershipsuk.org.uk/ .

[52] Price Waterhouse Coopers, http://www.pwcglobal.com/extweb/uk/ctgems.nsf/Docs/ED300EAC936E27C08025697A005E71E9?OpenDocument.

Partnerships and Collaboration: Propositions from Experience

Associate Professor Alison McClelland, School of Social Work and Policy, La Trobe University and Adjunct Professor, National Institute for Governance

Introduction [1]

Significant external and internal forces mean that the role of government is being renegotiated in Australia and many other countries. "New deals are being struck"[2] and promoting partnerships between government and other sectors is often a key strategy in these "new deals." This may be especially so in the "liberal"[3] regimes of Canada, New Zealand and the United Kingdom, yet countries such as The Netherlands and Sweden are also experimenting with models of different inter-sectoral relationships in the provision of welfare (broadly defined). And there is also relevant discussion and activities in countries such as the transitional economies of Eastern Europe and in parts of Asia, where countries are exploring new relationships following the collapse of dictatorial governments.

This paper focuses on partnerships between government and community welfare organisations (CWOs)[4] in Australia. Partnerships are a special form of collaboration, sometimes involving a contract.[5] In Australia there is currently some interest in contractual arrangements, through compacts or partnership agreements, between peak welfare bodies and governments at both state and national levels. They are seen as a way of promoting improved collaborative action between the sectors. A critical contention of this paper is that the current debate about partnerships needs to be informed by a much sharper awareness of what we are trying to achieve before we develop such compacts or agreements. Why is there a renewed interest in partnerships and what problems are we trying to solve through partnerships? If we want improved collaboration, should the main emphasis be on formal partnership arrangements and what should accompany such arrangements?

Partnerships and the changing role of government.

The current interest in partnerships between government and CWOs is the result of a number of interlocking, not necessarily consistent, forces of change. External and internal forces mean that the role of government is changing. These changes are affecting the relationship between CWOs and government, giving rise to new problems and issues.

The significant forces leading to a reassessment of the role of government include globalisation, substantial internal economic and social pressures (such as more uncertain labour markets, more fragmented families and communities and growing spatial inequality) and a dominance of neo-liberal thinking. There is also a belief that the way government operated in the past is not effective in dealing with new problems and new risks. The new role of government aims to be:

- smaller or, at least more efficient government

- government that facilitates rather than provides – to "steer rather than to row" and to split the functions of purchaser and provider

- less rigid, with a preference for government action that builds community capacity and that is more responsive to local needs.

Changing roles and relationships

These changes have placed greater emphasis on the contribution of CWOs in fulfilling functions previously seen to be the role of government, especially service delivery functions. In doing so they have changed the relationship between the sectors – they are more dependent on each other. For CWOs it has meant an increased dependence on government for funding, and therefore sometimes for survival. For government, it has meant an increased dependence on the effectiveness of the actions of CWOs for the achievement of its critical welfare responsibilities. For both CWOs and government, it has also meant greater complexity in their relationships. More functional areas traditionally undertaken by government and more non-government organisations are potentially affected.

Changed funding relationships

One very significant aspect of the changed relationship is that the funding relationships between community organisations and governments are now more at "arms length," tightly specified in terms of required outputs and often the result of some form of competitive tendering. The increased dependence of government on the effectiveness of CWOs and the greater complexity of the relationships have been partly responsible for these changed funding arrangements. However, reduced resources, efficiency requirements and the dominance of promoting competition as the way to achieve responsive and effective service delivery have also contributed.

Problems with the form of the relationship and the funding models

There have been problems experienced with the funding models used and with other aspects of the relationship between CWOs and government. There is increased suspicion and some elements on frustration on both sides. Governments are suspicious that CWOs represent provider, rather than consumer, interests. CWOs are concerned that their relationships with government are not equal and fail to recognise the different ethos, values and functions of community organisations. Competitive funding arrangements are seen to act as a disincentive to collaboration and cooperation between CWOs. Output-based funding is seen to gear priority towards activities of doubtful long-term effectiveness.

The interest in promoting more formal overarching partnership compacts (or agreements) between government and CWOs partly arises from the need to deal with these problems. It is envisaged that partnership compacts could help by providing for the identification of common goals and interests, as well as formalising processes to protect the interests, and needs, of each sector. However, a key thrust of this paper is that a number of critical issues in relation to the effectiveness of CWOs, governments and the roles and relationships between the two sectors need to inform and to accompany such agreements. The paper will argue that if these issues are not dealt with, the pressure for partnerships will not necessarily promote improved collaboration on the ground and will have little impact on the quality of service delivery and planning. The paper develops this argument through a number of propositions that are informed by the author's personal experiences, mainly in the community sector, over the past 30 years.[6]

Propositions

Four propositions are developed from these experiences.

- First, we should not import partnership ideas from other countries until we have closely examined our distinctive Australian experience.

- Second, past experiences indicate that the development of effective partnerships depends on a number of critical factors. These include leadership, mutual understanding and respect, infrastructure and a sense of shared responsibility for service delivery and policy development.

- Third, if partnerships are to contribute to better services, they need to be accompanied by a much greater understanding about the determinants, or preconditions, for effective service delivery by CWOs and by government.

- And finally, partnerships need to recognise and foster the perspectives and understandings that CWOs can bring to government program and policy development.

We should not import partnership ideas from other countries until we have closely examined our distinctive Australian experience. Australia has had a distinctive tradition of involvement of CWOs in the delivery of welfare services.

The experience and interest by other countries (such as Canada and the United Kingdom) in partnerships and compacts has been partly responsible for the current interest in partnerships in Australia. But we need to take account of our distinctive experience before we also develop similar compacts. Historically, critical welfare functions of governments in Australia (especially in Victoria) have always been undertaken by CWOs, often in some form of loose contractual relationship with the state.[7] Such functions included care of families in distress and substitute care of children, care of people with disabilities, the accommodation needs of aged and homeless people and child protection and custodial training of young offenders (until the mid and late 1980s). In this respect Australia's welfare state history is distinctive as in other countries, such as the United Kingdom. Government, especially local government, was responsible for the delivery of such services. But when welfare services were being developed in Australia's early years, Australia lacked a developed system of local government, and thus the early state administrations turned to the charities to take this role.[8]

This distinctive system had advantages and disadvantages.[9] It had the disadvantage of limiting the direct accountability of government (by placing some of the risk on to welfare organisations) but also increased the diversity of organisations delivering services in Australia, providing some choice for clients. Over time the scope of services delivered by CWOs has increased, in parallel with an increase in the demand for the state to take action in new emerging areas of need. In the 1960s there had already been an expansion in the involvement of CWOs to encompass aged nursing home and hostel care, with legislation providing Commonwealth support for this role through the provision of capital grants. Again, the

Menzies Government chose to expand the welfare state through the activities of CWOs in this period, in contrast with other countries where the expansion involved direct state provision.[10] The 1970s and 1980s saw an extension of this role to new areas. Some examples are home and community care, women's refuges, and community-based child care. It also involved the growth of different types of organisations which were more community- based, self-help and participatory. This had been an approach supported by Professor Ronald Henderson in the Poverty Inquiry of the early 1970s.[11] As Henderson envisaged, the expanded role of CWOs has been critically accompanied by the development of a strong, broadly based constituency and capacity in the community welfare sector.

Thus, Australia has always had elements of the "third way" with an important historic role for CWOs in service delivery that has expanded alongside the expansion in government interest and responsibility for welfare. In a real sense therefore, Australia's welfare state has always contained some elements of partnership arrangements between state agencies and community organisations and there may be some critical lessons we can draw (and adapt to current circumstances) from past arrangements. Some of these lessons could be significant in identifying the critical preconditions for effective collaboration, and the actions that need to accompany collaboration to improve services delivery, planning and policy development. They are elaborated in the next three propositions.

Past experiences indicate that the development of effective partnerships depends on a number of critical factors. These include leadership, mutual understanding and respect infrastructure and a sense of shared responsibility for service delivery and policy development.

During the 1970s and early 1980s in Victoria, well-known individuals such as Marie Coleman, David Scott, David Green, Colin Benjamin, Jerry OudeVrielink and Barbara Spalding provided strong leadership in the development of cooperative relationships between the sectors and the different levels of government. Their commitment to something that was beyond the immediate interests of their organisations meant that they worked together from different sectors and developed an infrastructure that enabled the relationships between the sectors to be productive and sustained.

The development and operation of the Victorian Consultative Committee on Social Development (VCCSD) is a relevant case study of partnerships in action over this period. Indeed the Committee was formed following a partnership endeavour in Victoria in 1972, aimed at planning coordinated assistance to those affected by the Darwin cyclone. This post-cyclone planning involved VCOSS[12] (bringing together the relevant CWOs responsible for disaster relief) and the respective state and commonwealth welfare departments. Following this successful cooperative activity, it was decided to continue it on a broader scale. The VCCSD was formed and eventually had membership from all three levels of government, the peak welfare organisations in Victoria (such as the Youth Council of Victoria, the Children's Welfare Organisation and so on), as well as other relevant peak bodies, including the Municipal Association of Victoria. Located in VCOSS, the Committee was staffed by an officer seconded from the Commonwealth Department of Social Security with resources also from the Victorian Social Welfare Department. The VCCSD functioned as a forum for mutual exchange and planning about welfare related issues in Victoria and included the undertaking of specific areas of research and policy analysis. With very high-level representation from member organisations, it provided a non-threatening space to tackle issues such as youth homelessness, unemployment, aged-care services and the introduction of information technology.

According to a past director of VCOSS, in those days, in contrast with the present, when one talked about the "welfare sector" the focus was not only on the non-government organisations, but the term also included the different tiers of government as well. The salient point was that there was a sense of common endeavour and belonging, reinforced by close ties between key players and structures that brought people from different sectors together in a sense of mutual exploration, based at least in part on mutual respect and a sense of common goals. In some ways, it could be argued that it was no accident that such an organisation was formed in the 1970s, when participatory governance was being sought in a number of ways. There were initiatives such as the Australian Assistance Plan,[13] the introduction of advisory committees to government, and the regionalisation of the Victorian Social Welfare Department. It was also a time of expansion rather than contraction of government responsibility for welfare but critically also a time when it was considered that the organs of government did not have all the answers, but that policy and planning must have an input from different perspectives. Government staff were also mandated to spend time developing strong links outside of government.[14]

However, later experiences indicate that this sense of shared endeavour did not only apply to the golden period of the 1970s when there was a sense of all things being possible. A relevant example of the latter part of the 1980s is the Social Security Review (SSR) established by the minister for social security (Brian Howe) with an external consultant, Bettina Cass. The SSR was supported by staff from the research and policy unit of the Department of Social Security and was assisted by an Advisory Committee that had a diverse membership, including representatives from the Australian Council of Social Service (ACOSS) the peak national welfare organisation, as well as other CWOs. Through the SSR a great deal of information was shared between the departmental staff and Advisory Committee members and at least some common ownership of the issues and solutions was developed. This was furthered with the associated development of a Social Security Advisory Committee with some overlapping membership and operating over a similar period.

The SSR lasted for some time (between 1986 to 1989) and produced over 30 Background Papers and six Issues Papers. The Advisory Committee had to confront problems of contraction and generating greater efficiencies, as well as comment on proposals for growth. This was the time when increasingly new initiatives had to be financed out of savings generated by the departments pushing for the initiatives. While not all conflict was avoided, it is arguable that the SSR and associated committees had several distinctive and important attributes. First, there was a real commitment from the top (the minister, Brian Howe) to the gathering and sharing of information. Second, the length of time allowed people from the two sectors to develop trust and common understandings of the problems and possible solutions. Finally, the departmental staff had some familiarity with service delivery issues as at that time the department delivered services and gave policy advice.

If partnerships are to contribute to better services, they need to be accompanied by a much greater understanding about the effectiveness of service delivery by CWOs and by government.

It is now increasingly acknowledged that a problem with policy development in Australia has been a neglect of issues connected with implementation.[15] One of the contributing factors has been insufficient understanding about the effectiveness of different service delivery approaches. This lack of understanding has contributed to some of the problems connected with service agreements and output-based funding arrangements (for example, disagreements about what kind of outputs should be rewarded arise from an inability to be sure of the longer-term effectiveness of different interventions). Both CWOs and government organisations have a responsibility to develop a better capacity to research the effectiveness of service delivery.

In the period 1974-75, the author had been working on a Masters thesis on the application of cost-benefit analysis and program budgeting to welfare decision making. In the course of this exploration, work was undertaken with a group of CWOs in the Barwin region of Victoria, to see if it was possible to define and measure the objectives, outputs and outcomes of service delivery. In those days these were very new ideas in Australia and most welfare organisations had difficulty in thinking in these terms. Still the research showed that it was possible to achieve much greater clarity about what organisations were really wanting to achieve and how their particular interventions could contribute to an improvement in personal and social well being. There was a growing sense about the importance of service evaluation and experts were sometimes imported from the United States to show us how we could do it.

But twenty years on by the early 1990s, there had been insufficient development in the understanding of community organisations about how to measure the effectiveness of their services. And so, when output-based funding was introduced into service contracts, organisations did not have alternate measures to suggest in response to their often legitimate concerns that the defined outputs were too narrow and inadequate. In some ways this neglect, while problematic, was unsurprising. Most community- based organisations did not have the resources or the expertise in research and evaluation. And changes associated with the quality of personal functioning and the quality of personal relationships are not easy to assess, a point often overlooked by some due to the narrow economic thinking that has dominated this field. The need for improved funding for research and evaluation has been highlighted for improvement by a number of reports over the years including the Baume report of the late 1970s and the then Industry Commission in its draft report on charitable organisations in Australia in the mid 1990s.[16]

The neglect of an understanding of service effectiveness is not confined to the community welfare sector but also applies to government welfare-related activity more broadly. The recent report by the Reference Group on Welfare Reform illustrates this neglect.[17] In this report the Reference Group recommended a fundamental reorientation of the "social support system." The Reference Group wanted a much more individualised approach, in which social security recipients were to be given more active assistance based on their individual needs and circumstances, to participate economically and socially (in particular to engage in paid work).

But in some ways this was not new. The SSR had already acknowledged the importance of a more active approach to the assistance of unemployed people and sole parents in the 1980s.[18] Subsequently, the Hawke government introduced greater requirements for long-term unemployed people to take part in activities to improve their employability and the Jobs,

Education and Training (JET) program for sole parents was introduced. In the 1990s this approach was extended further through "Working Nation," introduced by the Keating government, which included more individualised assessment and assistance, introduced "reciprocal obligation" requirements and also provided a range of labour market programs.

These past attempts to provide more individual assessment and assistance to welfare recipients had many elements similar to those proposed by the Reference Group as new initiatives. Yet the report of the Reference Group was generally silent on these past changes and about the lessons from them in terms of what might have been effective and what needed to be done differently.

This neglect of the lessons from the past at least partly stems from a neglect of a thorough understanding of service effectiveness in Australia. McDonald has described community service delivery as an "almost 'knowledge-free' zone."[19] In a similar vein, Saunders identifies a lack of attention to issues of practicality as a serious defect of Australian social policy.[20] It continually compromises the capacity of policy to meet its intended objectives. According to McDonald, "ideology, or more mildly, explicitly normative orientations are regularly substituted for knowledge." The result is that the conditions for partners to disagree about required action according to their orientations, or the orientations or their superiors, is enhanced and mutual understanding is compromised.

Some elements of neo-liberalism and the "new managerialism" have implicitly sidestepped this issue by putting their faith in output-based funding to resolve the issue of understanding service effectiveness. This is not sufficient for two reasons. First, it places all the responsibility and risk for understanding service effectiveness on to the contracted agency, which may not have sufficient resources to develop a sound understanding or may not act to share this knowledge (as it may lose a competitive advantage). Secondly, the lack of knowledge about effectiveness compromises the capacity of the contracting organisation to be clear about the range of outputs that should be required.

Partnerships need to recognise and foster the perspectives and understandings that community welfare organisations can bring to government program and policy development

There is a danger that the development of partnerships may focus too heavily on the funding agreements between the sectors – on the role of CWOs as service providers primarily – and not sufficiently on the capacity of CWOs to contribute to good public policy. This policy development role needs to be reconsidered in partnership discussions and, most importantly, the capacity for CWOs to undertake this role needs to be further developed.

Around 1995 at the BSL, the prime minister's Social Policy adviser, Mary Ann O'Loughlin, was invited to speak to a gathering a staff from CWOs. In response to a question about how CWOs could be more effective in influencing the public policy process, her response was that they should be giving policy makers information they lacked. This information was intelligence about what was happening "on-the-ground." Such information included data about changing needs and the effectiveness of different interventions, particularly innovative methods of service delivery. But the capacity for CWOs to supply such needed information depends on some systematic collection of data about changing needs, the development of innovative services and the assessment of service effectiveness. And while a number of CWOs are attempting to collect and analyse such data, the attempts are still far too few and still too often based on limited anecdotal information. And even when they do, their efforts may still be dismissed as representing "provider interests." Also, the more general policy and planning usefulness of "on-the-ground" information depends on such information being located in a broader research and policy context. This broader context is frequently informed by information more readily available to government departments than to CWOs. But the sharing of such information with CWOs is often increasingly limited. The point is that good policy making requires a combination of broader statistical information and case material, which is best obtained by CWOs and government departments working together and sharing information as freely as possible.

Further, one of the historic functions of CWOs in Australia has been the development of innovative ways in meeting needs. In contrast with more rigid public bureaucracies, CWOs have been seen to be capable of the more flexible responses required for innovation. But this historic function is threatened by the increased reliance on government funding, alongside more rigid output requirements (usually with a short-term time frame), combined with a more complex environment that requires a more sophisticated research and development capacity to inform innovation.

Conclusion: Key Themes

Partnerships can have different objectives and can be pursued in different contexts. This paper has not attempted to define these differences but has attempted to inform the debate about partnerships by examining the interaction between CWOs and governments in terms of the functions of service delivery and program and policy development. A number of propositions have been outlined, based on personal experience with interactions between the two sectors over the past 30 or so years. These propositions have not been exhaustive nor have they covered the extensive work being undertaken on partnerships by different government in Australia, by the community sector and by academics.[21] However a number of themes or issues emerge from this work and from the material in this paper. These should inform the question of what we are trying to achieve from partnerships and how we should be going about it.

The first theme is that, in one sense, partnerships are not new in that historically the responsibility for service delivery has been shared between direct public provision and service delivery through CWOs. What is different is the extent of contracting out of service delivery to CWOs, the complexity of the interaction and the terms and conditions applied to the agreements between individual CWOs and the government. The current discussion of partnerships could be better informed by a careful examination of the strengths and weakness of past relationships and they way they have been managed.

Second, two of the key functions of CWOs could be undermined partly, but not only, as a result of changed funding relationships. The role of CWOs in developing innovative ways of meeting needs could be undermined by a requirement to meet rigid output measures that could mean they are less likely to be adventurous in their service delivery. And their useful role in public policy in terms of providing information based on their service delivery experience will have less currency if it is seen to only represent provider interests. CWOs have to take some responsibility for acting on these issues. They may have to seek some alternative sources of funds to support innovation and also ensure that they place greater priority on ensuring they have a strong consumer input that reflects in a systematic way the changing circumstances of their users and the value of the services to them. Many CWOs are acting in these areas but more could be done. Government can help by giving much greater priority to funding innovation and research. But we also need to explore the capacity of service agreements to support learning from mistakes. Supporting a more reflective culture on both CWOs and government departments is an essential part of improving service capacity and improving relationships.

Third, and related to the previous point, it is absolutely essential that both sectors give much higher priority to developing a sound body of information about service effectiveness. This should be regarded as a joint endeavour rather than through separate structures within government and within the community sector. Indeed the development of some structures, jointly managed by the community sector and government, with a brief to undertake detailed micro-research on service effectiveness in particular areas, at either state or national level, could meet a substantial knowledge gap and also promote closer relationships over the long term. Similarly, planning structures that are long term and involve both sectors should be encouraged.

Fourth, relationships are best developed and improved through long term contact on a mutually supportive and respectful basis. The emphasis should be on developing structures that are likely to last for some time and that perform functions of real value to both sectors. Priority should be given to these, rather than one-off meetings as a method of communication and liaison. In this way trust and a greater sharing of useful information is more likely to occur. But such long-term arrangements will only be sustained if participants are able to move to a focus beyond the immediate interests of their organisations. Leaders in government and in the community sector have a major responsibility for the development of a broader focus and sense of accountability in the respective sectors.

Fifth, there are clear tensions in these relationships that cannot be easily resolved and that need to be recognised and accepted by both sectors. One is the tension created by the accountability requirement of government. Public funding means some clear demonstration of public benefit has to be provided by the organisation receiving the funds. But the defining of these benefits must be broadened beyond a narrow technocratic approach and be informed by a range of perspectives. How to balance accountability in a way that allows for flexibility of action is the ongoing challenge of public policy in Australia. Community organisations need to be respectful of the need for accountability by government organisations and also ensure their own governance arrangements make them accountable to the various communities they directly serve.

Sixth, there is a danger that that the discussions about partnerships will focus on the structural relationships between the sectors (consistent with a history of searches for "structural fixes") without a clarification of the key functions of government and of community organisations in the changing welfare state. However if the debate about partnerships starts from a debate about the welfare responsibilities of government in a changing world then it could be extremely fruitful. This should include an examination of the changing nature of risk and the sharing of risk. There is a perception that, at a time of greater uncertainty about the future risks faced by individuals and organisations, the public policy approach has been to increasingly devolve risk away from government. As Mitchell says, it has meant a move away from government's use of "risk reduction" strategies and an over-emphasis on "risk coping" strategies, with risk-coping strategies more likely to be borne by individuals, the market and community organisations. Mitchell suggests the new role for government should be "social risk management" and that "a critical element in any renegotiation of a 'new deal' should include a reconfiguration of the balance between reduction, mitigation and coping strategies."[22]

Finally, we need the think carefully about the word "partnerships." The use of the word partnerships implies some equality of power and does not reflect the reality of difference in power relationships between government and CWOs. We need to go back to the question of what we are trying to achieve through partnerships. If the key goal is to encourage collaborative effort between the sectors on a more informed and respectful basis, the main response should aim to foster the situations and cultures in which such efforts take place. This means placing priority on conversations around shared goals and outcomes; joint activities in areas such as research, training, and service quality improvement; organised staff exchanges; and longer-term agreements that allow for stability and trust to develop.[23] This may be the more productive answer to the question of what we are trying to achieve through partnerships.

Notes

[1] This paper is derived from a presentation to the Canadian/Australian Symposium, *New Players, Partners and Process: A Public Sector Without Boundaries,* Canberra, National Institute for Governance, April 5, 2001. I would like to thank David Green and Monica Pfeffer for their comments and suggestions.

[2] See D. Mitchell, "Globalization and social cohesion. Risks and responsibilities." Paper delivered to the *International Research Conference on Social Security,* Helsinki, 25-27 September 2000, p.1.

[3] Using the Esping-Anderson typology of welfare states where liberal regimes are those with a dominant role for the market in the promotion of societal well being with the state having a more residual role. In contrast, conservative/corporatist and social democratic regimes have a more substantive role for the state. See G. Esping-Anderson, *The Three Worlds of Welfare Capitalism,* (Cambridge: Polity Press,1990).

[4] A number of terms are used to describe community welfare organisations including the third sector, voluntary organisations, not-for-profit organisations, non-government organisations and community organisations. The term community welfare organisations (CWOs) will be used in this paper. It applies to organisations that have a focus on welfare and do not have profit maximisation as the dominant motive, involve voluntary activity, and are governed by voluntary boards or committees of management and therefore are not directly responsible to the electorate for their continuation.

[5] M. Lyons, "Partnerships and Collaboration" Presentation to seminar, *Partnerships and collaboration and localism as the basis for organising service responses*, Victorian Department of Premiers and Cabinet and Victorian Department of Human Services, Melbourne, 12 July 2001.

[6] Over the past 30 years, these experiences have included working in the community sector, mainly in policy positions but with some experience in service delivery. Over this time there was close involvement in various roles with the Australian Council of Social Services (ACOSS), commencing in the mid 1980s and continuing to the late 1990s. In addition, the author has worked in the public sector for a short period and also was part of a major review undertaken through the office of the relevant minister but with strong links with the department. During much of the 1990s, the author was Director of Social Action and Research at the Brotherhood of St. Laurence (BSL) as CWO that combines service delivery with social research and policy development. Overall, this work has been substantially concerned with the interface between government and CWOs at both a service delivery and policy level.

[7] See the observation by P Weller, "Introduction: the institutions of governance," in M. Keating, J. Wanna, and P. Weller, eds., *Institutions On The Edge? Capacity For Governance*, (NSW: Allen & Unwin, 2000). Weller observes that Australia "has a long tradition of developing and determining policy through bodies held at arm's length" (p3) with a statist not a socialist tradition (p7).

[8] T Kewley, *Australia's welfare state: the development of social security benefits*, (South Melbourne: Macmillan of Australia,1969).

[9] This comment was made by Len Tierney in personal communication in 1969. At that time Tierney was Reader in Social Studies at Melboune University.

[10] J. Roe, "Perspectives on the Present Day: A Postscript," in J Roe, ed., *Social Policy In Australia. Some Perspectives 1901-1975*, (Cassell Australia, 1976), pp.311-325.

[11] Australian Government Commission of Inquiry into Poverty, *Poverty in Australia. First Main Report, April 1975*, (Canberra: Australian Government Publishing Service, 1975).

[12] VCOSS is the peak organisation representing a range of CWOs in Victoria.

[13] The Australian Assistance Plan (A.A.P.) was introduced by the Whitlam Labor Government in the early 1970s to assist with regional planning for welfare services. One of the objectives was "the involvement of 'local residents and welfare consumer groups' in planning and provision of welfare services," as noted by L Tierney, *Victorian Evaluation Of The Australian Assistance Plan* (Department of Social Studies, University of Melbourne, 1975), p24. It is interesting to note that Victoria was the only state to continue the A.A.P after the Fraser government abandoned the program in 1976. This was due to the strength of the partnerships between sectors and the participatory orientation of the Victorian premier, Dick Hamer. This orientation was also important for the development of the VCCSD. The importance of such leadership and orientation at the top is also mirrored in the later discussion in this paper about the role of Brian Howe as minister for social security.

[14] This section is informed by personal communication from David Maxwell, the executive officer of the VCCSD over much of its operation, as well as from David Green, at that time a senior staff member of the Victorian Social Welfare Department.

[15] See M. Edwards, *Social Policy, Public Policy. From Problem To Practice*, (NSW: Allen & Unwin, 2001) and P. Saunders, "Reflections on Social Security and the Welfare Review," *The Australian Economic Review*, 24, No.1 (2001), pp.100-108.

[16] See Australia, Senate Standing Committee on Social Welfare, *Through a glass, darkly: evaluation in Australian health and welfare services*, report from the Senate Standing Committee on Social Welfare, (Canberra: AGPS, 1979) and Industry Commission, *Charitable Organisations In Australia. An Inquiry into Community Social Welfare Organisations*. Draft Report. (Canberra: Industry Commission, 1994).

[17] Commonwealth of Australia, Reference Group on Welfare Reform, *Participation Support for a More Equitable Society: Final Report of the Reference Group on Welfare Reform*, (Canberra: Department of Family and Community Services, 2000).

[18] See B. Cass, *Income Support for the Unemployed in Australia: Towards a More Active System*, Issues Paper No. 4, Social Security Review, (Canberra: Australian Government Publishing Service, 1988) and J Raymond, *Bringing Up Children Alone: Policies for Sole Parents*. Issues Paper No. *3*, Social Security Review, (Canberra: Australian Government Publishing Service, 1987).

[19] See the comments by C. McDonald, "Building the evidence base: new research, new thinking", in ACOSS, ed., *Just policy, sound research, joint action. Selected papers from the 2000 ACOSS Congress*. ACOSS Paper 111, (NSW: Australian Council of Social Service, 2001), p78.

[20] See P. Saunders.

[21] For example, in Victoria the Department of Human Services is developing a DHS Partnership Charter and there is a Parliamentary Inquiry into DHS's Service Agreements.

[22] D. Mitchell, p.10. In her paper Mitchell develops the framework for risk management, which needs to be considers when renegotiating the role of government in the management of risk.

[23] P. Faulkner, "AGM Presentation," in *Victorian Social Work* (Summer 2000) p.12.

Commentary

Dr Glyn Davis, CEO, Premier's Department, Queensland Government.

Challenge One – Managerial Capacity

As Professor Langford argues, private industry is well experienced in forging collaborative partnerships, whilst on the other hand, "Experience and expertise in government is limited."

In forming partnerships, government will be forced to meet and negotiate with private parties that maintain strong alliance cultures and supporting people, systems and processes. Conversely, government and many community organizations have few of those developed tools in the arsenal.

The success of public-private partnerships will be highly contingent on the managerial capacity of those individuals tasked to manage the partnership. Senior public services executives have just recently added corporate management techniques, such as performance measurement and objective setting, to their basic regulator and adviser role.

With the onset of public-private collaborative partnerships yet another role, that of a diplomat and negotiator, will emerge. Public service managers must now combine three potentially conflicting roles: provide policy advice to the ministers, manage their own departments, and manage external relations with the many agencies now linked to departments through contacts, agreements, and partnerships.

Given that government has demonstrated a fairly unenviable record of retaining experienced contract management staff,[1] it is arguable that the real challenge lies not in developing managerial capacity, but in retaining the skill base.

Challenge Two – Fragmentation versus Integration

Fragmentation weakens coordination and the gaps between intention and outcomes become more apparent. Jurisdictional and implementation problems are almost inevitable when a range of departments, central agency specialists, and private parties all become involved in seeking a solution. Horizontal coordination between departments, across different levels of governments and with several participating organizations is a major task. The Queensland government's Cape York Partnership provides some idea of the magnitude of the horizontal management challenge.

Make no doubt about it – participatory governance is time consuming, resource intensive, difficult and, one could argue, selective with regards to who participates. But although difficult, the task is not impossible. Australia and Canada are perhaps better prepared for the challenges of horizontal management than many other nations due to the long-standing complex patterns of cooperation between levels of government created by federalism and experiences in employing alternative service delivery mechanisms, especially within the community sector.

Challenge Three – Accountability and Risk

It has been argued elsewhere that public sector organizations cannot delegate responsibility, even when no longer delivering the service.[2]

Will the same hypothesis hold as public-private partnerships become more and more "boundary-less"; i.e. when partners no longer just deliver services, but are instrumental to the fundamentals of policy design, management and decision-making?

If it is difficult now for consumers, and indeed the parties themselves, to identify those "in control," how much more difficult will it become when multiple agencies are responsible for designing, planning, delivering, and evaluating outputs? Indeed is it time, as suggested by our speakers, for government to reassess how it selects it is partners? Is the traditional procurement model forcing possible partners into bidding wars, with the winner nothing more than a government supplier?

Stemming from the problems associated with the tendering process, both speakers earmarked inflexible accountability requirements as partly responsible for the prevailing culture of risk aversion in the public sector. The accountability challenges for government become even more apparent when you lay the need for a more risk tolerant, flexible structure against three critical issues:

First, the public service's traditional view of risk management; i.e. identify, assess, and mitigate.

Second, financial prudence and government's fiscal responsibility to taxpayers.

And third, increasing political/ministerial control of the policy agenda, priority setting and decision making, with ministers making more use of private advisers and rejecting the counsel of their agencies.[3]

The preparedness of political actors to be flexible, to deal with media hysteria or public confusion, and to learn from mistakes of the past, rather than mitigate risk or shift blame on to private collaborators, greatly challenges the courage of individual and collective ministerial responsibility.

Challenge Four – Performance Measurement

Performance Management through objectives and targets presupposes a hierarchy.[4] It is an intra-organisational view.

Is this method appropriate for collaborative inter-organisational contexts or true partnerships? If organisations are partners does it not become inappropriate for one manager to impose objectives on the other?

Alternatively, the "simple" notion of independent actors agreeing on shared objectives, and clear and agreed expectations is not "simple" as it relies of many complex issues including full knowledge, access to information and the expertise to exercise choice. Yet both papers provide examples of the reality.

Professor Langford cited information and communications technology, especially e-government as one of the emerging areas of collaborative partnerships. Government entertains such partnerships because it does not otherwise have the capacity to recruit or retain the expertise to provide or develop the service itself.

Similarly, Alison explained many community-based organizations have neither the resources nor expertise for research and evaluation, and attempts to date to gather data have been based on anecdotal evidence.

Governments and private organizations have multiple objectives, creating difficulties of problem definition and objective settings difficulties even in isolation and with the most basic policy proposals.

Challenge Five – Trust and Respect

Both papers nominate organizational cultures rich in trust, mutual support and respect as critical to the success of collaborative partnerships.

If "hierarchies are characterised by authority and rules, the market by prices and competition, then trust and diplomacy are the most important attributes of collaborative networks."[5] But as Professor Langford reminds us, trust is mutually reinforcing and not easily attained.

This complication was well illustrated in the context of community welfare organizations. Alison cited increased levels of suspicion and frustration between the partners; with government on one hand suspicious that CWOs represent provider interest, rather than consumers; and CWOs concerned they remain an unequal to a partner who does not share their ethos, values or functions.

When trust is in short supply the tendency to slip into a master/servant relationship prevails. Paradoxically, trust building takes time and can only be developed on a strong foundation of the key management instruments identified by our speakers today:

- strong managerial capacity
- horizontal management and network building
- accountable and ethical behaviour
- a risk tolerant environment
- mutually developed objectives, targets and performance measures.

Conclusion

The difficulties of achieving policy goals are often overwhelming, even when government holds most of the cards. These challenges are exacerbated as government cedes operational control and enters into more complex private relationships.

In truth, not all public-private partnerships will or should move from contact service delivery arrangements to collaborative partnerships in the truest form. Types of public-private partnerships are, and will become increasingly more, numerous and diverse and their management will not lend itself to a single set of management techniques.

The challenge for the public service is twofold. First, to develop core skills for managing contracts, hierarchies and partnerships; and second to balance the ever-changing, diverging, intersecting and often conflicting demands of all three.[6]

Notes

[1] G. Davis and R.A.W. Rhodes. "From Hierarchy to Contracts and Back Again: reforming the Australian public sector," in M. Keating, J. Wanna and P. Weller, eds., *Institutions on the Edge: capacity for governance* (Sydney: Allen and Unwin, 2000), pp. 74-98.

[2] Moss (1997), in Davis and Rhodes.

[3] Davis and Rhodes.

[4] Davis and Rhodes, p. 96.

[5] Davis and Rhodes, p. 95.

[6] Davis and Rhodes, p. 98.

Discussion

Chair: Professor Paul Barratt, Consultant, former Head of the Department of Defence, and Adjunct Professor, National Institute for Governance

DIANA LEAT: While I was at DEMOS in London we did a number of studies of what Tony Blair called "joined up government," which is integrated government or holistic government. The issues that John Langford raised about people working on the boundaries, people we call "boundroids" for short, became hugely important. A lot of what you said resonated with what I remember they said. They talked about managing out of control, and sleeping soundly on the border. They also talked about the importance of career structures that recognise "boundroid skills", and they talked a lot about how they would be penalised in their careers for the choices that they had made to work on boundaries and across sectors and across silos in government.

The other thing that I wanted to raise was to be very clear about what sorts of partnership we are talking. I would say the same thing about accountability.

The different types of partnership can range from one-night stands to serial monogamy. One of the most important situations is extreme promiscuity. It seems to me that it makes a huge difference if you only have one partnership on the go or if you have half a dozen so.

The other thing that is important is distinguishing between partnerships between orphans, and partnerships between bits of organisations that have parents – parent organisations. Organisational theory has served us very, very badly in understanding the permeability of organisational boundaries and the sort of multiple relationships that go on across those boundaries. So I suppose I am saying I want lots of distinctions.

JIM CARLTON: I thought it might be useful just to draw attention to the fact, and this is drawing on Professor McClelland's remarks about there being quite a number of these partnerships in Australian experience, that until December of last year I was secretary general of the Red Cross here. We, of course, were in a major partnership with nine governments, federal, state and territory, in the running of the Australian Blood Service. There was also another partnership with what used to be the Commonwealth Serum Laboratories (CSL) which, oddly enough, I had ministerial responsibility for back in 1982-83. During my seven years with the Red Cross we had to, first of all, change the relationship with CSL to that of an NGO like us with a privatised company, and the government had to change its relationship with CSL from being one that ran the CSL – although I can tell you as the former minister-in-charge of it did not – to a much more satisfactory partnership. We also had to work with all the governments to bring about profound changes in the organisation of the blood service to make it more or less impregnable to legal attack and also viruses, and just about everything else.

There is quite considerable experience here in Australia that could be looked at. By sheer chance our friends and colleagues in the Canadian Red Cross have gone through, during the same period, the most appalling experiences because of a complete breakdown in the partnership between the Canadian Red Cross and the provincial and the federal governments. If anybody did want to have a look at case studies or research into this area, it is profoundly interesting.

The partnerships are of immense importance to the community in each of the countries. The work that is done within those organisations is very, very difficult, both from a litigious and from the medical scientific point of view. It is interesting because we have the Canadians with us, that a comparative study of the two happenings might be quite valuable.

RUSSELL AYRES: I wanted to be a bit of devil's advocate in this and ask what is there in these arrangements that is to stop collaboration declining into collusion? I was reflecting on this, particularly given I have had experience in the private sector.

PAUL BARRATT: I will give you an example from our own defence domain. Australia is now the only country that operates F-111 aircraft. We are in the process of outsourcing the servicing of those aircraft to a defence supply contracting company. So the people in the Bombay Bloomers will become civilians in overalls who will service these aircraft. Of course, what we are passing over with it is the unique skill of being able to service those aircraft. We can no longer call on the Americans or other operators of the aircraft if we start to develop skill gaps or shortages of personnel. We may, in the early years, be able to recruit some redundant US technicians, since they have now phased the aircraft out.

If you look at the flying life of the aircraft, can we be confident that whoever becomes a private provider will invest in the training of new personnel? How do we price this arrangement when they have a capability that is unique in the world? You want your F-111s to fly; we are the only people that can keep them in the air. At the same time they have to provide a level of service that provides the government with the interest in keeping those aircraft flying. So there is a nature of a partnership here. It could become a very tense partnership. There is a fair bit of risk in it and there will certainly need what you have both said as a foundation of the partnership, is trust. There is a fair bit riding on it.

Consider any of the higher risk areas of procurement, like we are about to embark on – the building of an airborne early warning and control aircraft. There has been, I know having made the decision on who was the preferred supplier, a very, very rigorous evaluation of the tenders and the selection process. Once that decision is made, whilst a layperson might regard that as a supply contract, it is very much more in the nature of a partnership for a number of reasons. You have a monopolistic situation certainly, because you cannot get three or four years into the project and decide you'll have the other brand.

Secondly, in my view you cannot have a situation where this project is a success for the Defence Department but not for the contractor, or it is a success for the contractor but not for the Defence Department. They either both win or they both lose. And the build time is long enough that circumstances change, requirements and specifications are going to evolve through the life of the project.

So while it looks like I have written a contract for you to provide me with some goods, the nature of the interaction is much more partnership-like. The oil industry got close to this a long time ago. They recognise that if you are building an offshore oil rig you cannot drive down the price at the tender stage and then try to extract maximum mileage out of your contract. There has to be some level of risk sharing where if you strike unexpected technical problems you have both got to reach into your pocket to solve them, and not just say, "You signed the contract, deal with it."

ALISON McCLELLAND: Just a comment on the collusion issue, which I think is an important one. It depends on where you see the balance of risk between the need for collaboration and the opportunity for collusion applying in a certain situation. At the moment, in terms of relationships between government and community welfare organisations, I would see the balance of risk not being that there is going to be too much collusion but that there is not going to be enough understanding and collaboration.

There are opportunities for collusion in the closed nature of some agreements. So it seems to me that close, collaborative relationships are to be encouraged where they are open and they are not confined. If it is only a relationship between the government and the one or two major organisations, at the expense of a number of other smaller local organisations, it seems to me that there are strong possibilities of collusion and that is very problematic. So I think it is a balance of risk and circumstances, such as transparency and diversity, that are critical.

ROD NETTLE: I'm working with the Centre for Regional and Local Government Studies on a number of areas, one of which is going to cross over this year into the public-private partnerships. My question is to you, John. It is really about the Canadian experience. I have been working in regional development here probably for about 10 years now, and in that time I have worked very closely in the private sector and particularly in the capital market sector. I found in Australia it is the capital market sector that is the driver, if you like, of the public-private partnership. So I was wondering whether that is much the same in Canada.

Working with them, the reason why they could pick up the ball in private-public partnerships was for profit. That is what they were there for. They could see an opportunity to create win-win situations between public sectors and private sectors by them taking over some particular functions.

In my time I have worked with the capital markets on developing and overseeing the complete and utter failure of two major private sector/public sector partnerships, not because the private sector could not do it or did not have the cash to do it, but we ran smack into the fact that the public sector just did not want to go there in the first place.

I go back to where I started. The question was about where are the drivers of the public-private partnerships? Where are they in Canada? In Australia, from what I have seen, it has been primarily the private sector rather than the public sector, and the public sector resistance has been as much out of ignorance of what the private sector had to offer, because they were not used to thinking like that. So what is the Canadian experience?

JOHN LANGFORD: Well, the experience with what I'm calling "partnerships," really robust collaborative partnerships, to start with has been fairly limited. As I pointed out, most of them have been infrastructure or development of community projects. The major driver has been lack of government financing. So we are like the UK. The major driver has been situations in which government is trying to find a way to provide capital finance without going into debt.

The classic kind of situation would be the building, operation and eventual return to government of a bridge joining New Brunswick and Prince Edward Island. This arrangement exhibits some of the key characteristics of large public-private partnerships. For instance, the bridge build/operate consortium remains deeply interested in the evolution of transport policy over the life of the partnership, particularly where policy making can create competition for the consortium. For example, the present premiers of the two provinces now want the ferry service re-installed. It is not going to happen because the whole approach to creating toll revenue from that bridge is based on a monopoly. That means that inherently the consortium has become a partner in policy making.

The other significant driver has been ideology. Some governments set out to show that you could do this; that you could demonstrate that your belief in new governance and public-private partnerships was actually going to operate. Those have turned out, in some ways, to be the worst of the experiences.

A third driver has been the need to access technology which you cannot access without partners. In the context that Paul described, it is impossible to consider many of these IT related procurements as a contract. They just do not work out that way. There are multi-year dimensions to them in which the goals are unspecified or they have to be renegotiated along the way. All of the elements that I described as being part of the strategic alliance approach to the management of partnerships are present in the points that Paul made.

ROD DOBELL: John's comment about the exhortations from the private sector to be just a little bit hardnosed and realistic about all this and put aside some of these public sector values which interfere a bit with getting on with the job – this problem of collusion is one that is been around a long time. Adam Smith warned us, if three or four business people get together the public interest is at risk. The incentives are all very clear, very understandable. We have had this exhortation or admonition, to look for relationships that are cordial but not cozy, relationships that are close but not closed, and a number of other recognitions that this problem is endemic to any kind of structure.

We also have to keep in mind that while we are talking about trust and respect and the forging of links within this new larger organisation we are talking about creating a stronger boundary between this new larger organisation and the rest of the world. The trust and social capital are defined within this larger organisation, but it does mean that there is the group excluded from this closer, more cohesive, more effective organisation. You have to keep in mind the consequences for those in the community who are not part of this potentially more effective organisation but possibly more distant from the public sector values.

MARIAN SIMS: My question or comment really follows on from the last speaker. I think we need to bring back the notion of power politics as being about who gets what, et cetera. I was really taken with Jim Carlton's comment earlier about the Red Cross. It seems to me that rather than the issue of the relationship between the Red Cross and government and the Commonwealth Serum Laboratories being seen as a kind of a partnership that works, I would pick up on the point about collusion. By having itself protected against litigation, hemophiliacs for example, about a third of whom actually have HIV and/or one of the many hepatitises, have been entirely excluded from the process. Whilst I think most medical practitioners are entirely sympathetic with the goals of the Red Cross, looking at different stakeholders and defining the question of who is involved more broadly, hemophiliacs, for example, would say that Canada has been much more generous in terms of recognising their situation, whereas Australia is seen as having a more secretive, collusive mode of decision-making.

So it would be interesting to have a more detailed study in a public health process in both countries.

JIM CARLTON: There was no denial of access to litigation for hemophiliacs at all. There were a very large number of cases. I was talking about whether there was a potential for the Red Cross to be totally wiped out as an organisation as a result of that, or whether governments would support the Red Cross financially to meet the costs of claims, which were in fact met. I just wanted to make that quite clear. There was no legislative denial of access to litigation on the part of hemophiliacs.

FRAN HINTON: I found this particularly interesting from the point of view of my agency, because right now we are engaged in a set of partnerships for a government contribution to build, own, and operate a capital facility. It involves purchasing a whole range of community services with the not-for-profits and the sorts of arrangements that apply, the IT outsourcing, to establishing a partnership with the NRMA for a long-term positive parenting campaign, which has delivered great outcomes for both partners.

The notion of distinguishing between the different types of partnerships that are involved and the issues that are involved are quite germane, from my perspective. It seems to me that, in terms of the managerial capacity and the skills, one of the areas in which we have perhaps fallen down across the public sector is that we have failed at the outset to articulate the policy objectives of partnerships - whether they are with Barnardos or Marymead or a whole range of other Salvation Army areas. Maybe we would do better to be thinking about that in a more explicit way at the outset.

PAUL BARRATT: Thanks very much for that. Could I ask if either of our panelists would like to make any concluding observations before we break?

ALISON McCLELLAND: Well, just a couple. On the issue of collusion that came up in the second last question, I think there is a concern about collusion if the relationships are closed. The comments before related to relatively closed relationships. There is a tension between our desire to develop long-term close relationships and the possibility of collusion. There is a tension there.

At the moment there is a tension in welfare delivery in terms of the power of a couple of very large welfare agencies and the lack of entry capacity, because of the terms and conditions of the agreements, of a lot of community-based organisations. There is a real issue about who is able to enter and who is not that we have to think about when we are looking at our agreements, and that is quite serious.

The concluding comment I would make is in relation to the last comment. In many cases we are talking about the relationship between community sector organisations and governments. We are not talking about partnerships in the sense that you were talking about, John. And that is what is worrying me. We are using the word "partnerships" in this debate quite loosely. We are getting into trouble and we need to think about what we are trying to achieve. From the community sector perspective many of those organisations are using the word "partnership." What they are wanting is a relationship that is more open, based on trust and collaborative, and that is not necessarily a partnership. That is a better dialogue and more respect.

JOHN LANGFORD: I would just like to say I appreciate the comments that people have made on the subject. I'm interested in the possibility that in the afternoon we'll pursue some of these themes as we go through the issue of horizontal management. There is a lot of resonance between those two areas.

I would be interested to hear more about how we build more managerial capacity in this area. It seems to me that there are obligations not just on government to do that but also obligations placed on schools of public administration, like my own, and other similar educational organisations. Overall, I do not see much evidence that these skills are really a significant feature of education or professional development programs.

So you raised the point at the end of the day about the kind of capacities and skills required. They are varied. Obviously Alison and I are not talking about the same kinds of partnerships, but we certainly are probably talking about some of the same skills. I would like us to be more forthright about whether or not we are thinking of building public services over time in which these skills are important, or is partnering just a fad. The next government comes in, they do not say so much about partnerships so we give up and go back to something else.

PAUL BARRATT: Thanks very much. Ladies and gentlemen, we have come to the end of what I think has been a very stimulating, high quality session.

PART 3

DEVOLUTION AND DISCRETION: BUILDING COMMUNITY BASED MANAGEMENT INTO CONTEMPORARY GOVERNANCE

Community Based Management in Complex Ecosystems[1]

Professor Rod Dobell, School of Public Administration, University of Victoria, Canada

Purpose of this paper

Increasingly, it is recognized that both the natural and the human components of ecosystems dynamics are complex, profoundly uncertain in structure, ceaselessly changing and intricately inter-related through the constraints of a "full world."

With respect to natural systems, one result is a rapidly growing body of international covenants and national legislation designed to regulate human activities with significant ecological impacts. With respect to social systems, one result is a rapidly growing (and globalizing) structure of civil society organizations and heightening expectations of individual opportunities for participation and influence in processes of decision-making in those organizations and institutions (ironically, just at the time of – or perhaps as a consequence of – the dramatic growth of institutions and tribunals intended to discipline and constrain the use of the regulatory powers of governments responding to such participation and influence in trade and commercial activity).

Both sets of influences demand that public servants modify their beliefs and their practices and that formal organizations modify their principles and cultures. Like corporations, public sector organizations are driven by changing mindsets and beliefs to amend fundamentally their modes of operation, both in application of industrial principles and in obligations to find reconciliation of strikingly different perspectives.

The goal of this paper is to examine some resulting problems of discretion, devolution and coordination in public management, using for illustration some recent history in the Clayoquot Sound Region, on the West Coast of Vancouver Island.

This is a strikingly attractive and substantially pristine region, on the extreme Western fringe of Canada (about as close to Australia as one can get in Canada without getting very wet). Like remote coastal communities everywhere, it has been hard hit by problems of economic structural adjustment, arising from transformation of the economy from a resource-dependent, logging and fishing community into something else (to know what else, is a big part of the problem).

The Commitment-Compliance Cycle

Before going on to talk about specific developments in this region, it will be helpful to review very briefly (in this section) some general questions of policy formation and implementation, and (in the next section) some recent developments in environmental governance in tiered systems.

It is hard to keep all the various strands in hand without some mental picture. With apologies, I am going to refer here to one version of a standard image of the policy cycle, what I call the commitment-compliance cycle, in order to emphasize the number of conceptually different links in the chain of policy development, program and process design, and service delivery or operational management.

Using the metaphor of the policy cycle for shorthand, I am going to argue that there are dramatically new and important developments associated with the formation of collective intent, and indeed throughout the whole mandate development process, or what has sometimes been called the process of rule making. From the point of commitment or covenant at international or epistemic level, the policy-making process cascades downwards to more specific legislation, regulation and program mandates at more local scale. This rule-making process increasingly hinges on intergovernmental administrative agreements or more formal instruments of delegation, or informal partnerships.

There are also dramatic institutional innovations occurring on the ground, in communities, at the point of actual implementation or program realization, where processes of community-based management are evolving. Questions of local level indicators of community health and ecosystem integrity, or reporting on progress toward sustainability as a result of actions taking place on the ground, are active areas of current research centred at this stage of the policy cycle.

There is a great deal of institutional structure and management linkage in between, and substantial puzzle around how all that is evolving. It seems to me that it is to this organizational linkage that much of the discussion of partnering or contracting for service delivery is directed, as in the other sessions of this workshop. But it is my claim that we have to judge the effectiveness of all this linkage, all these strategic alliances and public-private partnership structures, on the basis of their success in truly linking the ideals and covenants developed by epistemic communities at international level with the local knowledge and management decisions of communities of place at local ecosystem scale. It is fidelity or authenticity in the performance, on the ground, of texts elaborated in cyberspace that represents the ultimate test. If so, these are standards of performance that governments, administrative agencies and private organizations have not much faced before.

Epistemic Communities and International Covenants

So first, just a quick reminder of the vast array of new ideas introduced in recent years in international negotiations, especially those leading to multilateral environmental agreements (MEAs) and even trade deals.

Principles like those in the Rio Declaration, Agenda 21, the proposed Earth Charter, and so on, establish a growing concern for questions of sustainability and intergenerational equity. These lead on to articulation of principles of action such as the precautionary principle, increasingly expected to influence the fundamental balance in institutional decision-making in the face of risk, whether public or private. In addition, management principles are amended to reflect a need for integrated, ecosystem-based analysis and management. In an explicit way, these developments redefine the boundaries for social decisions and political action; but they do not eliminate them. They modify the definition of the spillovers and linkages that must be taken into account, they may accommodate more trans-border flow of information across borders, but those borders do not vanish.

These commitments and ideas mentioned above are now substantially reflected in national legislation, to be implemented by officials in a public service that has rarely been exposed to them, let alone become fully aware of the conflicting objectives and resulting tensions involved in carrying them forward.

But from this national legislation reflecting an underlying ethical orientation and international commitments, there is still a substantial apparatus of formal organization before one gets to see action on the ground.

Let me suggest just a few examples.

- Canada's new Oceans Act, which came into force in January 1997, explicitly establishes three over-riding principles or orientations to govern public policy and management in the field of oceans. It requires that policy and management follow an ecosystem approach, a precautionary approach and an integrated approach. It also mandates a more inclusive consultation-based process of policy development.

- Canada's new Environmental Protection Act includes reference to a precautionary approach, giving rise to considerable debate as to what this might mean operationally.

- Canada's Environmental Assessment Act requires synthesis and integration of traditional ecological and local knowledge with conventional science-based evidence in carrying out assessment of proposed developments.

- Health Canada now pursues a precautionary approach in its management of social risks to health, again raising heated questions about what this should mean in practice.

- All federal departments are now required to table every three years their sustainable development strategies and a Commissioner of Environment and Sustainable Development is required to review and report to Parliament on the adequacy of these and of the government's overall corporate approach to its sustainability responsibilities.

And so on. I know that much the same thing has been happening also in Australia for some time, and I look forward to learning more about these developments.

- At the provincial level, in British Columbia, similar developments are shaking up existing practices.

- A new Forests Act and Forest Practices Code[2] builds in (in its preamble, though not in its binding text) a legislated commitment to sustainable forestry.

- The Environmental Assessment Act demands exhaustive consultation and timely recommendations to Ministers on approval of development projects, taking into account impacts on the sustainability of communities and cultures.

- A Fish Protection Act proposes to regulate development activities at municipal level in order to protect fish habitat and assure sustainable fisheries. (Massive controversy surrounds the effort to write regulatory streamside directives to implement the intent of the legislation.)

Institutional Innovation on the Ground

Now let's look at what's happening out on the fringes. Take the example of Clayoquot Sound, on the West Coast of Vancouver Island. This region has now been designated a UNESCO Biosphere Reserve[3]. The history of the community processes and institutional development leading to this outcome is remarkable as an example of increasing community cohesion, emerging during an extended consensus-building effort following a deep and protracted period of conflict and civil dissent, leading to unanimous support among the seven distinct communities of the region – five aboriginal communities and two non-aboriginal communities – for the Biosphere Reserve nomination (such unprecedented unanimity being a condition before provincial and federal governments would submit the nomination formally).

Such an outcome would not have been predicted from the turbulent history over the last decade or two[4]. During that period, Nuu-chah-nulth First Nations, environmental groups and the logging industry have all been struggling to win influence in relation to government decision-making on land and resource use in the area.

As a result of a number of blockades by environmental groups and a growing public voice against old-growth logging, both locally and internationally, a number of dispute resolution roundtables or committees were formed in an attempt to reach consensus among all groups with an interest in sustainable development. These committees, which met off and on from 1989 through 1992, included representation from federal and provincial governments, local governments in the area, and stakeholders from the large number of sectors in the region.

These committees were unsuccessful in reaching consensus on any development strategy. (Part of this failure must be attributed to the absence of some major players: since the government refused to halt logging activity while talks were going on, most environmental organizations walked from the table in protest against the "talk and log" policy, a concern that continues to this day.) The final committee was disbanded in October 1992. However, the issue of sustainable development in Clayoquot Sound remained a priority for the British Columbia government and led to a cabinet land use decision for the region[5] and a public report by the Commission on Resources and the Environment (CORE)[6] in 1993. The CORE report recommended the establishment of a Scientific Panel to review current land use standards and to make recommendations for improvements for the area.[7] This panel was established in 1993, with the government committing itself to adhere to all its recommendations. When the panel finally reported in 1995, these recommendations included far-reaching principles for an ecosystem-based approach to planning, based on an integration of traditional knowledge with conventional science, using watersheds as the basic unit for planning and management, and for full recognition of the need to promote the cultural, social and economic well being of First Nations. The panel also recommended that land-use decisions must, to the extent possible, not prejudice or be subject to the outcome of comprehensive treaty negotiations,[8] which were just beginning to get underway. There is anecdotal evidence that government officials are determined to ensure that the precedent set by this process not be extended to other regions in the province. On the other hand, many voices that at the time complained that the panel was asked only how – not whether – to log in the Clayoquot Sound region now view the panel's report as establishing the baseline for responsible resource management everywhere.

The BC government and the Nuu-chah-nulth Central Region Tribes[9] commenced government-to-government negotiations on the co-management of the Sound in 1992. As part of these negotiations, an Interim Measures Agreement (IMA)[10] was signed in March 1994, creating the Clayoquot Sound Central Region Board (CRB).[11] The Agreement has since been extended twice, and ultimately, in March 2000, was replaced by the Clayoquot Sound Interim Measures Agreement: A Bridge to Treaty.[12]

The mission of the Central Region Board, created under this structure, is to manage land and resources in Clayoquot Sound, prior to the conclusion of a treaty, in a manner that:

- provides opportunities for First Nations consistent with aboriginal resource uses and heritage, and considers options for treaty settlement
- conserves resources in Clayoquot Sound and promotes resource use that supports sustainability, economic diversification, and ecological integrity

Major innovations in institutional structure have followed. The most dramatic thus far is the creation of Iisaak Forest Resources,[13] a joint venture of Weyerhaeuser with the Ma-Mook Development Corporation,[14] with the latter, a development arm of the Nuu-chah-nulth Nation, holding majority control. More recently, a community-based fisheries management structure, the West Coast Vancouver Island Regional Aquatic Management Board,[15] has been created as a pilot project by agreement of four orders of government.

In addition, as noted above, the community succeeded in coming together around a unanimous nomination of the region as a UNESCO Biosphere Reserve. This designation was formally confirmed by UNESCO in 1999, and a Canadian government financial contribution toward the funding for the creation of a Clayoquot Biosphere Trust as a non-profit society was announced by the Minister of Finance in the February 2000 federal budget.

UNESCO Biosphere Reserves serve to combine the three following functions:

1. conservation: contributing to the conservation of landscapes, ecosystems, species and genetic variation
2. development: fostering economic development which is ecologically and culturally sustainable
3. logistic support: research, monitoring, training and education related to local, regional, national and global conservation and sustainable development issues

Biosphere Reserves form a World Network. Within this network, exchanges of information, experience and personnel are promoted. Biosphere Reserves develop local solutions on conservation and sustainable development that can be shared with other Reserves.

The Clayoquot Sound UNESCO Biosphere Reserve has as a guiding principle the Nuu-chah-nulth First Nations philosophy *Hishuk ish ts'awalk*, or "everything is one." This stresses the importance of recognizing and learning about the interconnections within and between ecosystems in order to promote truly sustainable local communities and economies, while protecting the environment for future generations.

Through the web links set out in the endnotes to this paper one can find brief chronologies and details of these and other institutional developments in three selected sectors – fisheries, forestry, and integrated land use. In the fisheries domain, one can see in the pilot project a dramatic shift toward shared decision-making. With respect to forestry, developments have involved the joint venture just mentioned, and negotiation of codes of conduct or agreed standards of practice, in response to market measures at regional and global level (but also with substantial concern about capacity to monitor and report independently on actual practice, capacity to certify meaningfully, and capacity to engage in enforcement measures effectively). On the land use side, the search for effective land use planning at watershed scale, with reasonable integration of both terrestrial and marine components of coastal zone management, raises questions of local control potentially in conflict with province-wide policies as interpreted by provincial ministries.

These questions are explored a bit more fully in the following sections.

Governance Themes

These four (including the Biosphere Reserve designation itself) selected institutional innovations illustrate a wide range of organizational responses to the dramatic challenges of economic and social structural adjustment facing the region:

- The community initiative that led to the unanimous nomination of the region as a UNESCO Biosphere Reserve created an internationally recognized framework for land use generally consistent with the zoning framework established in the Land Use Plan established by cabinet decision (though there is, in any case, substantial doubt that the land use decision will ever be implemented).

- Strong pressure from the Nuu-Chah-Nulth people led to the negotiation with the provincial government of interim measures agreements and the creation of the Central Region Board as a voice for local control in integrated land use decisions.

- Pressure from Nuu-chah-nulth leaders, allying themselves with regional fishing interests, particularly through formation of the Regional Aquatic Management Society, succeeded in pushing negotiations for a Regional Aquatic Management Board to a successful conclusion, with formation of the Board accepted by the federal Department of Fisheries and Oceans as a pilot project.[16] Further pressure has led to a proposed decision-making process that would extend a participatory model of shared decision-making throughout B.C.

- And, following yet a different model, a major forest operator and the Nuu-chah-nulth development corporation formed a joint venture that successfully negotiated unprecedented Memoranda of Understanding with environmental organizations and with forest contractors or loggers to clear the way for continuing forest operations (neither federal nor provincial government was signatory to these documents, though the provincial government did approve the transfers of tenure involved[17]).

These four different models give rise to a number of observations and questions about governance mechanisms. A number of barriers can be noted briefly here and are explored in the next section.

First, these institutional innovations came only with difficulty, and continue to face serious practical problems because of the varying structures and cultures of the organizations involved. Existing administrative systems and accountability mechanisms are serious barriers to innovation. These administrative systems truly are caught in a sandwich between influences spilling over from distant stakeholders and strong pressures for local autonomy. The strains of the resulting cultural transitions are visible.

Second, as always, the tensions associated with power sharing are formidable.

It is important also to recognize that the cultural barriers to effective cross-boundary linkage apply not only to the organization and structures for operational management, as mentioned above, but also to a distinct, prior activity of building understanding, shared beliefs about facts and visions or norms, and indeed to an extended investment in building understanding and agreement around process and procedure. (Note that the CORE experience suggests something like 18 months is needed for this purpose simply of building trust and agreement around procedure – but if this investment is not made, the process will fall apart when it hits the first hard decisions that cannot be "win-win" on the first round for everybody. Indeed, this is the whole point – to build recognition that "win-win" solutions can only be possible in the context of a commitment to longer term processes promising a generalized reciprocity, not an assurance of favourable outcomes on a transaction-by-transaction basis.) For operational purposes, a pragmatic concern with timely decisions will view this development with some skepticism.

Can it be argued that this complex array of new institutions on the ground is itself coherent? Can there be a coordinated approach to the interacting, interdependent ecosystem dynamics at play? Is there really horizontal thinking here, or is it simply that integration is possible at a practical level when all these players are working at regional scale? It remains to be seen whether all these new institutions will simply gravitate toward a new elite, will in effect be co-opted in their turn by the existing large-scale formal institutional apparatus, as they become more abstract and distant in order to be effective in their linkage roles.

In all of this, however, the key point is that the importance of boundaries has not diminished – they may be in some ways more permeable, perhaps, and there may be many more mechanisms for bridging or linking across boundaries. But they remain significant.

If so, partnerships might be examined not so much as boundary-spanning mechanisms as boundary-enlarging – creating a new structure/alliance which brings inside new boundaries some groups or organizations that formerly were not part of so strengthened a membership. This leads to observation that boundaries are themselves socially constructed. Just as we recognize increasingly that our science is socially constructed, we see also that the boundaries to which we choose to respond – the communities of concern with which we choose to identify – are also open to social adjustment.

The dynamics of interaction between initial community pressures, government and corporate concessions; subsequent attempts to secure participation in the new processes; and fears of cooption are challenging concerns for all the organizations involved, but particularly so for the small civil society organizations. In the Clayoquot Sound setting, the interesting interaction between the reality of community pressures and the rhetoric of transformation in governance processes and government institutions is highlighted. Though the origins of these initiatives in community pressure is clear, ultimately the institutional innovations they drove find resonance in larger current campaigns for new modes of governance, subsidiarity and so on.

Issues for Discussion

To be sure, institutional innovations in community-based management in the Clayoquot Sound region have emerged out of a specific context, one determined in part by unique attributes and features that are products of particular circumstances. Yet conflicting interests, similar to those that drove innovations in the Clayoquot Sound region, are elsewhere being addressed in a similar way on a larger scale, for example now on the Central Coast of BC.[18] There, as in the Clayoquot example, discussions among formal stakeholders seemed to become more fruitful when First Nations and local communities were also brought into discussions with a focus on dialogue and a search for areas of shared common interests that could support innovative mechanisms such as green investment, community forests, cooperatives or trusts to institutionalize new relationships. Expectations of effective voice and shared decision-making appear to be growing throughout civil society, and the dynamics of the learning processes integral to the development of collaborative institutions in Clayoquot Sound are perhaps becoming more comprehensive and more inclusive, and spreading.

Still, the dust is far from settled on this story, and many questions remain. We should consider briefly at least the following.

- **Government's role.** Community visions of community control are, at best, rarely shared by governments. Many government agencies seem, perhaps understandably, still to be fearful of the existence, let alone expansion, of the model of local control and community-based management. Yet, new and larger accords (and global market influences) now seem to be driving the determination of corporate practices on public land without recourse to legislation or appeal to government authority.

  It is crucial to recognize how dramatic a change is being proposed in some of the discussion around these local institutional innovations. In the case of West Coast salmon fisheries, for example, some proposals for reform of decision-making processes envisage officials from both federal and provincial governments becoming advisory to a consensus-seeking process, rather than seeing the consensus-seeking process as advisory to them. Government officials (or Ministers) would be expected to exercise powers to make independent decisions only in cases where the consensus-seeking process fails to achieve consensus on necessary management action.

  "Perhaps we need a new institutional paradigm that sees management agencies not as providers of solutions, but as facilitators and partners with citizens (i.e. true 'civil servants') to help find joint solutions."[19]

  (One may also note here the growth of interest in mechanisms such as consensus conferences on the Danish model.[20] We return below to consider recent skeptical review of all this enthusiasm for consensus.[21])

- **Legitimacy, agency and accountability.** This development of participatory mechanisms of course leads to complex questions of legitimacy and agency amongst the formal civil society organizations and informal groups claiming places at the table and voice in decisions. Which groups speak for whom? Who speaks for the trees? How do we recognize the role of groups speaking for environmental concerns?[22] Which can claim to be representative, accountable and eligible to participate in the contested interpretations of uncertain evidence flowing from interventions as experiments? Who elected them? Are there limits to the tactics they might properly pursue in advancing their particular agenda in the face of general resistance?

- **Sensitivities.** From the uncertainties surrounding answers to these questions flow other concerns about sensitivities, rivalries and conflict within communities. Explicit protocols may be developed to bridge or reconcile some of the differing perspectives brought by various parties to processes of community-based management, but in other cases only long periods of institutional investment in building trust and confidence can establish the degree of shared commitment to joint undertakings that would be necessary to ensure that the process continues to be accepted as legitimate even though individuals may encounter adverse outcomes in particular cases. That is, it is crucial that participants become willing to stay on in the process even though they cannot win on every decision, or even avoid individual costs on some. What will motivate them to do so?

- **Fragmentation and horizontality.** The usual problem of diffuse and dispersed government responsibilities and mandates arises here in a crucial way, fragmenting attempts to deal in an ecosystem-based fashion with integrated resource management. For example, consider that the task of sustaining the fishery must be seen as sustaining fishing communities as well as sustaining fish stocks.[23] At what scale should the necessary integration and conflict resolution be attempted? The mandate of the Department of Fisheries and Oceans and the expressed priorities of recent ministers, for example, emphasize conservation. Should DFO itself attempt to balance these priorities against the concerns with sustainable coastal communities that should preoccupy social and economic departments? Have they the knowledge base and expertise to do so? How can departments or governments assure that their many representatives sitting at many different tables speak with one voice – or at least do not contradict each other in responding to or mandating needed community action?

- **Subsidiarity.** With the spillovers inherent in ecosystem-based resource management, can the authorities and autonomy necessary to effective adaptive management be exercised on the ground, within local decision-making bodies, without unacceptably fettering the discretion or pre-empting the responsibilities of ministers or governments? Are we already seeing bureaucratic efforts to contain this threat, for example, to reduce the impact of the precedents set by creation of the Scientific Panel or the Central Region Board?

- **Trusts.** A striking feature of some of the institutional developments sketched here is the manner in which they evolve toward an underlying structural theme, that of the trust as an alternative institutional mechanism. The formation of the Clayoquot Biosphere Trust was an institutional legacy of the UNESCO Biosphere Reserve designation. Forest trusts have been a solution emerging in the search for an end to the "war in the woods"; the British Columbia government has pursued trials of community forests as part of forest licensing and tenure reform discussions. Interest in the broader concept of a Community Ecosystem Trust is growing.[24] Aquatic Conservation Trusts to hold retired licenses at regional level have been proposed in the fisheries context as a means to preserve some community rights of access to the fishery in the face of the reductions in numbers of licenses and concentration in their ownership as a consequence of license buyback and fleet rationalization programs.[25] Discussion of a lands trust is being pursued as a way of resolving the most vexed and explosive of the land use issues in the Clayoquot Sound region, the question of Meares Island. (Note the provision in the Nuu-chah-nulth Agreement in Principle,[26] now in abeyance following its overwhelming rejection in early summer 2001 by Nuu-chah-nulth members eligible to vote.)

In reflecting on this concept of trusts identified as one general governance theme, it is important to note the significance of this development as a way of enabling devolution and decentralization, not to private corporations, but to other institutional forms more representative of a balanced community interest rather than only a possibly distant shareholder interest. This has the effect of recognizing not just financial capital or formal intellectual property, but the claims of other forms of capital – human, social, cultural and natural, as well as tacit and traditional knowledge. (And in this respect it has fascinating resonance with the emerging World Bank "many capitals" approach to measuring the wealth of nations and reporting on progress toward sustainability. One attempt to put the approach to work can be found in the ESDI project launched by the National Roundtable on Environment and Economy in response to Finance Minister Martin's call for environmental indicators to parallel the economic indicators on which budgets are based.[27])

- **Certification.**[28] The crucial role of certification processes and the flow of information have also to be emphasized here. Ultimately all these processes of market democracy, shareholder activism and similar approaches to reliance on decentralized decisions driven by the informed citizen rest crucially on adequate access to information enabling citizens to judge not just the products or outcomes of corporate or public decisions, but also the adequacy and acceptability of the means and the processes which generated them. But all these mechanisms also run up against the old reality of corporate control, and the separation of control from ownership, whether formal or virtual. Along with the movement to entrench investor rights, it might be argued, we are seeing also an attempt to counter the effectiveness of market democracy by extending the enclosures movement to the whole realm of knowledge as a global public good. What all this means for the role of the public servant in exercising discretion in resource management decisions is an important contemporary question. (One distinct but crucial illustration related to openness and the responsibilities of the public servant in possession of internal knowledge but participating in deliberative processes is explored in a separate paper.[29])

- **Realism: capacity.** Is there in fact adequate capacity to carry out the necessary shared decision-making as envisaged? Are there the resources to maintain the monitoring processes, data capture, information-sharing, synthesis and interpretation necessary to support ongoing informed deliberation, and can there continue to be, in an era of increasing government budget restraint? Is this an area where initiatives such as the Social Sciences and Humanities Research Council's innovative Community-University Research Alliance program (sadly now already a victim of questionable budget decisions) or the new Community-University Connections initiative[30] may make an important difference?

- **Realism: implementability.** Is it also possible to conclude that the consensus essential to community-based management may be achieved around decisions in principle, but will erode quickly as the hard choices of concrete implementation have to be faced? Is this more likely to be the case given the time scales involved with such resources as long-lived fish or old-growth forests and the limits on community capacity? How do we respond to the need for interim returns, early harvests, concrete evidence of progress and tangible benefits?

- **Realism: misguided objective.** The enthusiasm for community-based management and for extending its reach to inclusion of traditional knowledge and broadly participatory shared decision-making may have to be tempered by questioning their impacts on the quality of decisions themselves. Observers like Coglianese have argued that decision rules requiring consensus are neither necessary nor desirable.[21] Reasoning principally from work in regulatory rule making, Coglianese argues that such decision rules lead to lowest common denominator results that fail to address the difficult issues. (The point that is missed by these criticisms, of course, is that the concern is not with single decisions or particular outcomes; the focus is on consensus-seeking and learning processes. It is on relationships, not individual transactions; it is on building a track record, not recording individual victories; it is on a social context where mutual gains from continuing cooperation, not concentrated winnings from competitive victories, are the goal. Coglianese and others with similar criticisms fail to appreciate the difference between specific decisions demanding consensus and cohesion built by consensus-seeking processes.)

- **Realism: market tests**. Ultimately, market tests in some form must be faced. Despite the best hopes of smart growth advocates or ecological footprinters, regional self-sufficiency is not an option neither feasible nor desirable. The resources to enter into trade and commercial relations outside the region must somehow be earned. Will consumers really pay the premium involved in ecologically responsible resource harvesting? Can certification really force wholesalers to direct procurement to responsible producers? Can investors be persuaded to offer sufficient funding to purchase investment units embodying environmental values to the extent necessary to support viable commercial operators? Will sufficient philanthropic inflows be feasible on terms that do not conflict with local values and principles, and hence influence decisions towards activity unacceptable to community interests?

- **Realism: what community, what borders – colonialism by another name?** In the end, it seems, we still grapple with the core problem of institutions (multi-national enterprises, governments, civil society organizations) from far away doing deals about the exploitation and conservation of regional resources. Global transactions shape local life chances. Are communities of place any closer, as a result of all this institutional innovation, to real participation in the management of adjacent resources and the consequences for their own futures?

These questions and observations thus lead us back to the more extended context of social learning, and to the longer-term evolution of ideas and beliefs. In the case of Clayoquot Sound, we perhaps can see the effects of a dramatic evolution of ideas independently at two different scales. On one hand, we see an evolving view of universal rights and an expectation, within a globalizing civil society, that values can appropriately spill over from one community to influence – indeed, constrain – the conduct of activity (and hence public decisions) in another. Practices in Clayoquot Sound are thus forced to conform to the demands of distant markets reflecting the exhortation of distant advocacy groups. (For some prescient commentary on these developments one can see an old paper by David Cohen.[31]) On the other hand, at the same time, at a local scale, we note a heightening sense of entitlement to be not just involved in policy deliberation, but to be substantively engaged, with a significant degree of agency and autonomy, in policy formation and realization on matters that previously might have been thought to rest solely with ministers in Victoria or Ottawa.

This paper began with the problems of coastal communities facing the strains and challenges of transformation from an unsustainable model of resource exploitation and economic development to a vision of a journey to sustainability. Recognition of the problems of the old model and the essential shape of the new are both still contested, and approached from many perspectives. But a key element of the new vision is to see human relationships and institutions – the human subsystem – as embedded in the ecosystem as a whole, crucially dependent on relationships with the natural systems that form part of the surrounding biosphere.

In exploring this transformation, a key focus was the fascinating story of the development of new, more inclusive, participatory mechanisms for shared decision-making, involving a synthesis of traditional and local knowledge with information developed from conventional scientific methods.

One can argue the case for participation on three different grounds. The first is intrinsic, based on the inherent right of all individuals to have voice and influence in decisions that affect them profoundly. The second is substantive, based on the conviction that greater participation brings greater awareness, promotes synthesis of local and traditional knowledge with conventional science and hence leads to substantively better decisions. The third is instrumental, based on the belief that broad participation is essential to acceptance of the legitimacy of decisions and hence to compliance with them.

The transformation toward a sustainable path has not yet been accomplished. Indeed there must be reservations about whether any of the new institutions described here is really working well, really meeting the objectives set out for them. The old industrial model remains the driving paradigm, it seems, in almost all relevant decision-making quarters. Transformation of organizational cultures in the federal Department of Fisheries and Oceans or the provincial Ministry of Forests has not been achieved, despite pockets of evangelical promotion of sustainable management and participatory decision-making in each. Forest operators, fishing enterprises and land development companies, despite some participation in some of the new institutions explored here, remain largely constrained to a focus on industrial products rather than ecosystem values (though perhaps now more apprehensive about potential influences from market activism arising out of concern for the latter). Indeed, as First Nations and other community interests develop more immediate economic interests in the returns from production, pressures to deliver the fish and get the logs out now fragment pressures for sustainable management and create local antagonism to external exhortation about principles of sustainable development. The figure-ground reversal (or transformation of world view) that brings people to see economic activity as limited within the broader framework of continuing stewardship of a common heritage of humankind has not been achieved; the focus on cooperative action for mutual gain has not yet offset the drive to immediate short-term returns. The willingness to engage in true sharing of hierarchical power has not withstood the pressures of concentrated corporate interests and conventional bureaucratic mindsets.

On the other hand, to all these reservations and challenges it may be necessary to offer the same hopeful but incremental response. The hope here lies in social learning over decades or generations; the returns are not all in yet. There is a process of social movements attempting to establish a rules-based globalism that permits a social frame around the transactions of a global economy, a frame that ensures that economic and commercial relationships are pursued within underlying charter principles of social and ecological integrity. These influences on all formal institutions – governments and civil society organizations as well as corporations – are creating external realities to which institutional decisions must respond. Though there is a growing threat of institutional control of necessary information and access channels and consequent irreversible loss of citizen agency, this threat is not yet a reality.

Thus the challenge of drawing the right lessons from the fascinating recent history of the Clayoquot Sound region, and the institutional models and innovations presently in place (and the countervailing forces to which they may give rise), remains.

Conclusion

"Even in a live concert, the audience is separated from the individual voices. Only the performers are able to hear the person standing next to them singing a different harmony" (Janet Cardiff, from her notes on her work, Forty Part Motet (2001), included in the National Gallery of Canada exhibition, Elusive Paradise).

I would argue that the experience of Clayoquot Sound underlines the importance of processes of social learning in managing the impacts of human activities and dealing with the realities of collective action in a world of profound uncertainty. The over-riding feature of such management is to find order emergent, from the interplay of many voices, from participation and deliberation, not from expertise and calculation. The organizational challenge of accommodating the discretion essential to adaptive management is dramatically multiplied as both public expectations and legislative directives dictate vastly extended consultative processes, integrated approaches and synthesis of many forms of knowledge.

The dynamics of the processes in Clayoquot Sound are becoming more comprehensive, more inclusive, addressing more comprehensive tasks. The specific conflicts that drove developments and innovation in the region earlier are being addressed in a more abstract, institutionalized fashion at larger scale. The lessons, it seems, are being taken very seriously now on the Central Coast of BC. Newspaper stories recently have been reporting expectations of new and larger accords, driving the determination of corporate practices on public land without recourse to legislation or government authorities. Many government agencies may, understandably, still be fearful of this expansion of the model of local control and community-based management. But expectations of effective voice and shared decision appear to be growing, throughout civil society.

And perhaps this is an inevitable outcome as the performers become more aware of the power of the harmonies to be achieved by their many voices singing.

Notes

[1] This paper draws substantially from a larger monograph in preparation with Dr. Martin Bunton of the Department of History, University of Victoria. His contribution and helpful comments by Ross McMillan, formerly Co-Chair of the Clayoquot Sound Central Region Board, are gratefully acknowledged.

[2] Forest Practices Code (FPC): The Forest Practices Code refers to regulations made by Cabinet to regulate activities in the forest, particularly to reduce the size of clear cuts, strengthen requirements for reforestation, reduce the environmental impacts of logging roads, and protect water quality and fish habitat. Ostensibly, the code represents a "get tough"

approach to dealing with unacceptable logging practices. It was initially welcomed by environmentalists, but criticized by the forest industry on the grounds that the code is complex, unwieldy and imposes excessive costs of compliance. In its implementation it appears to be considerably less effective in protecting forest ecosystems than had been hoped.

[3] Clayoquot Sound UNESCO Biosphere Reserve: Biosphere Reserves are areas of terrestrial or marine ecosystems that are internationally recognised within UNESCO's Man and the Biosphere (MAB) Program for promoting and demonstrating a balanced relationship between people and nature. Individual countries propose sites within their territories that meet a given set of criteria for this designation. The Clayoquot Sound UNESCO Biosphere Reserve has as a guiding principle the Nuu-chah-nulth First Nations philosophy *Hishuk ish ts'awalk*, or "everything is one." This concept stresses the importance of recognising and learning about the interconnections within and between ecosystems in order to promote truly sustainable local communities and economies, while protecting the environment for future generations. http://www.clayoquotbiosphere.org/ and http://www.unesco.org/mab/wnbr.htm

[4] Clayoquot Sound Archive Project: The Clayoquot Sound Archive Project supports a web site index of documents relating to the recent history of Clayoquot Sound. http://sitka.dcf.uvic.ca/CLAYOQUOT/

[5] Clayoquot Sound Land Use Decision (CSLUD): After years of inconclusive discussion, the government of British Columbia made a decision in April 1993 on land use in Clayoquot Sound. As a result of the 1993 CSLUD, 34 percent of Clayoquot Sound is to be preserved for all time. The decision placed a further 21 percent of the Sound under special management, which allows some sensitive logging while emphasizing the protection of wildlife, recreation and scenic values. Before the land-use decision, the area assigned to general integrated resource management – the usual designation for logging and other resource extraction – included 81 percent of Clayoquot Sound. The government reduced this to 40 percent. First Nations were outraged at being excluded from the decision making process, and environmental groups were outraged that the plan permitted too much logging of old growth forest. While the provincial government's decision concerning logging in Clayoquot Sound has not been explicitly reversed, the government responded to the opposition by setting up the independent Scientific Panel.
http://www.for.gov.bc.ca/het/Clayquot/clay.htm#hpp
http://www.for.gov.bc.ca/vancouvr/district/SOUTHISL/Clayoquot/clayoquot_sound.htm

[6] Commission on Resources and the Environment (CORE): Established by the provincial government in 1992, CORE's mandate included the development of strategic land use plans in four of the province's most controversial regions (though Clayoquot Sound was excluded from its mandate). Although none of the regional land use planning processes initiated by CORE reached consensus at the table, the recommendations made by the commissioner were extremely influential in the final regional land allocations decided by cabinet. CORE was disbanded in 1996, with the expectation that the consultative processes would be carried on with the ongoing Land and Resource Management Planning (LRMP) process at the sub-regional scale.

[7] Scientific Panel on Sustainable Forest Practices in Clayoquot Sound: The Scientific Panel, which included First Nations resource management experts and leading scientists, was created by the BC government following the April 1993 decision on Clayoquot land use. The panel's mandate was to review current forest management standards in Clayoquot Sound and make recommendations for changes and improvements. The goal of the panel was to develop world-class standards for sustainable forest management in Clayoquot Sound by combining traditional and scientific knowledge. ftp://ftp.hre.for.gov.bc.ca/pub/clayoquot/clay1.pdf

[8] British Columbia Treaty Commission (BCTC): The BCTC is responsible for facilitating treaty negotiations in the province, not including the Nisga'a treaty negotiations. As the independent and impartial keeper of the process, the Commission is responsible for accepting First Nations into the treaty-making process. It assesses when the parties are ready to start negotiations, and allocates funding, primarily in the form of loans, to First Nations. The Commission monitors and reports on the progress of negotiations, identifies problems and offers advice, and assists the parties in resolving disputes.
http://www.bctreaty.net/files/bctreaty.html

[9] Nuu-chah-nulth Tribal Council: The Nuu-chah-nulth Tribal Council represents 14 first nations on the West Coast of Vancouver Island from Brooks Peninsula north of Kyuquot to Sheringham Point south of Port Renfrew. Five such groups make up the Central Region tribes in the Clayoquot Sound Region. http://www.nuuchahnulth.org/

[10] Interim Measures Agreement (IMA), Interim Measures Extension Agreement (IMEA): In 1994, a two-year Interim Measures Agreement (IMA) between the provincial government and the five First Nations of the Nuu-chah-nulth Central Region was signed. The IMA acknowledged that the Ha'wiih (Hereditary Chiefs) of the First Nations have the responsibility to conserve and protect their traditional territories and waters for generations that will follow. As a result of this agreement, the First Nations and the province became partners in a joint management process for land use planning and resource management in Clayoquot Sound to be carried out by a Central Region Board (CRB) composed of First Nations representatives and provincial government appointees. In 1996, because treaty negotiations were still in progress, an extension to the initial IMA was signed, known as the Interim Measures Extension Agreement (IMEA). In April 2000, this agreement was replaced by the Clayoquot Sound Interim Measures Extension Agreement: A Bridge to Treaty.
http://www.island.net/~crb/agmts.htm
http://www.gov.bc.ca/aaf/down/IMEA_Final4.pdf

[11] Central Region Board (CRB): The Clayoquot Sound Central Region Board was created by the 1994 Interim Measures Agreement and continued under the 2000 Interim Measures Extension Agreement: A Bridge to Treaty. Its mission is to manage land and resources in Clayoquot Sound, prior to the conclusion of a treaty, in a manner that provides opportunities for First Nations consistent with aboriginal resource uses and heritage, and considers options for treaty settlement; conserves resources in Clayoquot Sound and promotes resource use that supports sustainability, economic diversification, and ecological integrity; and encourages

dialogue within and between communities and reconciles diverse interests.
http://www.island.net/~crb/

[12] Clayoquot Sound Interim Measures Extension Agreement: A Bridge to Treaty
http://www.island.net/~crb/pdfimea/imea2000.pdf

[13] Iisaak Forest Resources: Iisaak was created to provide a new model of forest management in Clayoquot Sound, and is the direct result of commitments made by the Nuu-chah-nulth Central Region First Nations and MacMillan Bloedel Ltd. (now Weyerhauser) in the 1996 Interim Measures Extension Agreement. Through the joint venture agreement, the Central Region Nuu-chah-nulth First Nations own 51 percent through Ma-Mook Natural Resources Limited (Ma-Mook) and Weyerhaeuser (formerly MacMillan Bloedel Limited) owns the remaining 49 percent. In the Nuu-chah-nulth language, *iisaak* (pronounced E-sock) means "respect." "Iisaak Forest Resources is committed to *Hishuk-ish ts'awalk* (pronounced He-shook ish sha-walk), the Nuu-chah-nulth belief of respecting the limits of what is extracted and the interconnectedness of all things. This guiding principle of respect is the foundation for restructuring the economic, ecological and social elements of sustainable resource management in Clayoquot Sound." www.iisaak.com

[14] Ma-Mook Development Corporation: In 1997 Ma-Mook Development Corporation was established to represent the collective economic interests of the five Nuu-chah-nulth Central Region First Nations. In 1998, Ma-Mook Development Corporation and MacMillan Bloedel signed a shareholders agreement detailing their partnership in a joint venture company, Iisaak Forest Resources.

[15] Regional Aquatic Management Society (RAMS): Formed in May 1997, RAMS is a community-based organization with the purpose of establishing regional management of aquatic resources in Nuu-chah-nulth traditional territory on the West Coast of Vancouver Island. The society was a key participant in negotiations leading to the creation of the Regional Aquatic Mangement Board (RAMB).
http://www.RAMS-WCVI.org/RAMS/overview.htm

[16] Canada, Department of Fisheries and Oceans, "News Release: Pilot West Coast of Vancouver Island Aquatic Management Board to Proceed," February 26, NR-PR-01-021E (2001). West Coast of Vancouver Island Aquatic Management Board Terms of Reference http://www-comm.pac.dfo-mpo.gc.ca/english/release/bckgrnd/2001/bg009e.htm. As this text goes to press (September 2001) the nominations to the Board have yet to be completed.

[17] Forest Tenures: Forest tenures are the manner by which the cutting of timber and other user rights to provincial Crown land are assigned. Virtually all of the forested land in the province is covered either by volume-based licenses in Timber Supply Areas or area-based Tree Farm Licenses. Most of the timber harvested is transferred to processing facilities owned by large vertically-integrated companies, and processed into relatively low value commodities such as pulp and dimension lumber, mostly shipped to the United States, giving rise to the most divisive and protracted trade disputes between the two countries.

[18] An announcement setting out the marketing strategies motivating calls for cooperation on the Central Coast of British Columbia can be found at http://forests.org/archive/canada/bcecosgr.htm. More generally, the website http://forests.org provides documentation on forests sustainability issues globally. On the Coastal Forests Conservation Initiative launched by forest companies in BC, see http://www.coastforestconservationinitiative.com/, and specifically on the Joint Solutions Project undertaken by these companies with major environmental organizations, see http://www.coastforestconservationinitiative.com/pdf/Joint%20Solutions%20Project-%20march16.pdf.

[19] Barry L. Johnson, "Introduction to the Special Feature: Adaptive Management: Scientifically Sound, Socially Challenged?" *Conservation Ecology* 3, no. 1 (1999). http://www.consecol.org/Journal/vol3/iss1/art10

[20] Johs Grundahl, "The Danish Consensus Conference Model," in S. Joss and J. Durant, eds., *Public Participation in Science: the role of consensus conferences in Europe.* (London: Science Museum).

[21] Cary Coglianese, "Rethinking consensus: Is Agreement a Sound Basis for a Regulatory Decision?" Paper presented at a conference on "Environmental Contracts and Regulation: Comparative Approaches in Europe and the United States." University of Pennsylvania Law School, September 1999.

[22] Christopher Stone, *The Gnat is Older than Man*, (Princeton: Princeton University Press, 1993).

[23] R. Hilborn, J.J. Maguire, A.M. Parma and A.A. Rosenberg, "The Precautionary Approach and risk management: can they increase the probability of successes in fishery management?" *Canadian Journal of Fisheries and Aquatic Sciences*, 58 (2001), pp. 99-107.

[24] M. M'Gonigle, B. Egan, and L. Ambus, "When there's a Way, there's a Will." Report 1: Developing Sustainability through the Community Ecosystem Trust, 2001.

[25] L. Loucks and K. Scarfo, *Breaking the deadlock, building trust: framework for an Aquatic Conservation Trust.* A strategy for environmental, social, cultural, and economic balance. West Coast Vancouver Island Regional Aquatic Management Society and Community Futures, Ucluelet, B.C., 1998.

[26] Summary of the Nuu-chah-nulth Agreement-in-Principle is available at http://www.aaf.gov.bc.ca/news-releases/2001/ntcsummary.htm

[27] Robert Smith, C. Simard and A. Sharpe, "A Proposed Framework for the Development of Environment and Sustainable Development Indicators Based on Capital." Paper prepared for

The National Round Table on the Environment and the Economy's Environment and Sustainable Development Indicators Initiative, January 2001, updated July 2001.

[28] Certification: Sustainable forest management certification systems are still evolving. The standards currently most relevant in BC include:

The Forest Stewardship Council [FSC] certification standard was originally developed by environmental organizations (notably the World Wildlife Fund) in conjunction with a group of forest product consumers. Like the CSA standard, it provides for a local (regional or national) process to elaborate on a set of global principles.

http://www.weyerhaeuser.com/coastalwood/wycedar/cedar_cert.htm

http://www.interfor.com/managing_our_forests/bulletins/certification.html

ISO 14001: an internationally recognized standard for environmental management systems developed by the International Organization for Standardization. It defines the management system elements that an operation must adopt in order to attain environmental goals.

CSA Z809: a national standard in Canada for sustainable forest management. It was developed under the auspices of the Canadian Standards Association through a consultative stakeholder process, and is based on criteria approved by the Canadian Council of Forest Ministers, representing each Canadian province. Implementation of the CSA standard requires extensive local stakeholder consultation in setting management goals, measurable performance indicators and objectives.

Chain of Custody: a certification system that verifies a manager's ability to track the flow of raw materials from the forest to final product. It does not offer an assessment of forest management practices, but it is a necessary tool in allowing a manager to label a product as having originated in a certified forest.

[29] A. R. Dobell, "Social Risk, Political Rationality and Official Responsibility: Risk Management in Context." Paper commissioned by *The Walkerton Inquiry,* 2001. http://www.walkertoninquiry.com/part2info/commissuepapers/index.html

[30] Community-University Connections: A new initiative that explores the use of science in environmental and social policy, and facilitates collaborative research between community organisations and university-based researchers. The process draws on the successful European "science shops" model of community-based research. http://web.uvic.ca/~scishops

[31] David Cohen, "Domestic Land-Use Decisions Under International Scrutiny," in Rod Dobell, ed., *Environmental Cooperation in North America: National Policies, Trans-National Scrutiny and International Institutions.* Proceedings of a North American Institute Conference, Vancouver, Canada, 1996.

Building Community Based Resource Management into Contemporary Governance: the Australian Experience

Associate Professor Kath Wellman, Director, Centre for Developing Cities, University of Canberra

The Australian landscape is high in biodiversity and fragile. Farming based on ill-suited European models has exacerbated soil loss and degradation of both water and land systems. Major landscape transformation and degradation has occurred in the last century and has created critical conditions across much of regional Australia. Within this context this paper explores the development of relationships between government and communities in dealing with these regional landscape issues and the complexities that arise with shared responsibilities, but differences in agendas, accountabilities and requirements for transparency between partners. The first part of the paper looks at the history of community involvement in environmental conservation and some of the issues arising from the landscape scale of environmental issues. The second part explores issues that arise in partnerships between government and communities with particular reference to the Natural Heritage Trust grant scheme and incentive schemes for landholders.

Community involvement in natural resource conservation in Australia has a long history. In the later nineteenth century and the early twentieth century community groups lobbied colonial and state governments to protect forest lands and take these out of the control of lands departments. At the time government lands departments perceived forest lands and other natural ecosystems as largely uncleared farmland. Interest groups lobbied for national parks and wildflower reserves; they planted avenues of trees as war memorials along major routes and for amenity in urban areas. Small towns supported tree societies and naturalist clubs that had an interest in local conservation issues.

Federal government entered into environmental policy in the early 1970s through the National Parks System, through international agreements and through using its powers in export licensing to deal with environmental issues that had previously been seen as the responsibility of the states. It was a time of political activism inspired by the Whitlam government, which used the environment as a policy platform, and by activists such as Judith Wright.

Although there was a great deal of lobbying, communities were not actively involved in the management of public lands. Conservation of biodiversity was seen largely as a responsibility of government, through its reserves systems.

The 1980s saw the development of partnerships of non-government organisations and Australian farmers to deal with evident land degradation. An example of this is the Potter Farmland Plan, undertaken from 1984 to 1988 in Victoria. This was created through a partnership between the Ian Potter Foundation and farmers who had been locally identified as demonstrating best practice. The Ian Potter Foundation gave these farmers financial and technical support to develop and implement whole farm plans in return for these farmers encouraging and supporting their colleagues within the district to adopt better farming practice. Arising from this was Land Care, which was formed through a partnership between the Australian Conservation Foundation and the National Farmers Federation and was funded by a $340 million grant over ten years by Bob Hawke in 1989.

Land Care has had a marked effect on the perception of community conservation, and has done this both by absorbing the small community conservation associations that preceded it and broadening the base of membership. Strength lay in its national recognition and government support both at federal and state level (although the organisation at state level could differ from state to state). The community is seen not only as political lobbyists but also as active participants in conservation. Most activities have been on private or local government lands within the regions and state bodies have been reluctant in incorporating community management of lands, particularly in national parks. There are now 4500 Land Care groups in Australia, surpassing the original target of 2000 groups. Since Land Care began there have been a number of other community conservation movements such as Bushcare, Coastwatch, and Waterwatch that have had strong bipartisan support from government in Australia.

This sounds optimistic, but one of the problems of these organisations is that they have often been project focused, working on a local rather than a regional scale. Many of the major problems now facing the Australian environment are regional and national and require effective, integrated strategic approaches; this is further complicated by many of the problems originating or occurring on private lands. Toyne and Farley, who pioneered the Landcare movement, state:

> In retrospect, the goal of Landcare to achieve ESD on all properties in ten years was hopelessly optimistic . . . . While Landcare has been successful in providing information and stimulating attitudinal change, Landcare groups themselves have only had a marginal direct impact on environmental actions, which are on the whole initiated and paid for by individual farmers.
>
> A clear deficiency with the policy environment of Landcare has been the failure to properly articulate its place in the bigger picture. Structural adjustment, market systems, macroeconomic policy and economic incentives are all disconnected from Landcare policy. So too are issues such as State Government responsibilities, regional structures, service provision and incentives.[1]

In the past ten years both government and community have come to realize the issues are both complex and pressing. This is due to the sheer scale of land and water management problems in Australia and the growing realization of the governments' (both national and state) incapacity to deal with these problems without the assistance and support of the community. There is also a growing realization by the community, particularly the community on the land, that their life support systems are degrading and endangered.

In the 1996 census Australia's population was about 18.3 million. Australia has a land area of about 7.6 million square kilometres, an area of 0.42 square kilometres per person. In Canada with a population of about 31 million and an area of about 10 million square kilometres there is an area of 0.32 square kilometres per person. Australia is also one of 12 nations that is a major repository of ecological diversity and is the only developed country of that twelve. Estimates of biodiversity for Australia are 641, 488 species, which is a species for every 28.5 people, or if we want to look at it in relation to GDP, one species for every $1.095 million of GDP. These statistics show that the Australian population bears a large collective responsibility for biodiversity and landscape conservation and that this burden cannot be left to rural and remote Australia, which makes up only about 28% of the Australian population.[2]

Additionally there is a realization that traditional farming practice in Australia is unsustainable, both environmentally and economically. Australian farm businesses owed a total of $21.6 billion at 30 June 1998, an increase of 5% on 1996/1997.[3] The average gross indebtedness is $208,000 per farm. Farms subject to dryland farming have been losing soil for decades, and irrigation areas are now feeling the impact of rising saline watertables. Pastoral lands in areas such as South Australia are not economically, socially or environmentally sustainable.

Given the scale and severity of the issues it is important that resources that are utilised, whether from community, private foundations or government, are utilised as efficiently and effectively as possible. The national and regional nature of the issues means there needs to be strategic national and regional approaches rather than an approach aggregated of project fragments.

What is available to government, community and foundations to deal with this scale of responsibility? How can this responsibility be shared across all Australians? How can research institutions and universities assist?

Co-governance has been seen by many as the only way to deal with the reduced financial means of government and the scale of the problems that face Australians, particularly in relation to natural resource management. Here state and civil society share the function of decision making and service delivery. There exist major challenges in the relationship between government and the civil society, which can often vacillate between collaboration and confrontation, particularly where issues of power and finance are involved.

There are three levels of government in Australia – federal, state and local – and an increasing number of regional bodies with an involvement in governance issues in resource planning. Negotiating partnerships between these levels of government (particularly where they don't share agendas) and the community becomes particularly challenging. The challenge for government is to do this in a way that is accountable, transparent, democratic, predictable and equitous. It is important that this remains true for all partners. Breakdown will occur if, for example, in a federally initiated scheme the federal government was accountable and transparent and the state government was not. In this situation state government public servants have the possibility of acting as gatekeepers without the responsibility of ensuring the initiative works.

Governments utilise instruments to develop partnerships with the communities in relation to natural resource management. Two of these, grant schemes and incentive schemes for landholders, will be discussed here. These are chosen because they are currently the subject of discussion, particularly as a new grant scheme, the National Action Plan for salinity and water Quality in Australia, is currently being developed with funding of $1.4 billion over seven years. Other means to influence resource management on private lands, such as legislation protecting biodiversity or the development of markets (water, carbon sequestration, wetland restoration), will not be discussed.

Grants

Grants from government to the community have the potential to gain community support and action towards shared strategic objectives. Grants have the potential to target particular areas and government has the possibility to engage in negotiations related to outcomes. However, grants, particularly federal grants, can be seen by states and regional authorities as alternative funding for what are essentially existing state functions, and cost shifting can occur from state to federal government.

There have been a number of grant schemes to regional Australia over the past thirty years. Grants have been for Ecotourism, Regional Development, the Natural Heritage Trust Grants, Farm Business grants, etc. Generally there appears to be little communication across granting agencies in relation to the coordination or integration of grants, even though there is growing evidence of strong inter-relationships between, say, regional development, environment and farm business. Each grant system sets up its own operational system to contain accountability. These operational systems can ignore existing operational infrastructure, the recognition of which might make delivery more efficient and optimise resource use. The Natural Heritage Trust grants tried to overcome part of this problem by integrating the process over two government departments as well as state and regional bodies.

Grants can be used as a way for members of Parliament to communicate with their electorates and have been perceived to be linked to political advantage, particularly in marginal electorates. In other cases politicians like to support communities who are actively involved and dedicated to a pragmatic problem such as wetland restoration where the results are tangible. Members of Parliament's active involvement in grant schemes bring with it public scrutiny and a demand for transparency, equity and accountability. This has the potential to increase bureaucratic controls, increase approval times and limit particular partnerships that may not fit readily into these more process-oriented, rather than outcome-oriented, systems.

The largest grant system currently operating in relation to the Australian environment is the Natural Heritage Trust Grants, which initially injected $1.25 billion Federal money into 21 environmental programs for six years. This was later expanded to 1.5 billion over seven years. Funds came from Environment Australia and the Department of Agriculture, Fisheries and Forestry. The Natural Heritage Trust Grant scheme set up partnerships with state governments in each state with the idea of matching funds with state and regional agencies, thus leveraging Federal monies and ensuring a partnership between federal and state authorities. Its strategy was investment.

> The Commonwealth owes it to taxpayers to ensure that its investment leads to long term change towards sustainability. The Commonwealth investment of $1.25 billion will be directed largely through catalytic activities, which support and encourage stakeholders to overcome the barriers to sustainable management of land, water, native vegetation and biodiversity.

There are problems in setting up any grant system. It is extraordinarily difficult to set up a grant scheme that everybody is happy with or that will make a long-term impact. Inevitable tensions can result from conflicts such as the following:

- Development of new structure to support equity and accountability in grant distribution and existing operational structures, which they may compete with, duplicate or destroy.

- The need for a focus on strategic planning and integration of programs and the flexibility to respond to voices or issues in the community that initially might be thought to be outside the system.

- Issues of priority of need in relation to the severity of problems being addressed viewed against equity across all communities.

- The possible dominance of government organisations invested in established regional strategic plans over flexible response to communities input.

Additionally there is an expectation that community understanding of complex environmental and governance issues is the same as that of many experts and that communities have the ability to continue to expand this knowledge at the same rate as knowledge is being accumulated. This is a much greater request than asking communities to understand and be involved in small programs such as tree planting.

The Natural Heritage Trust grant system was ambitious in intent and extent. It was designed to achieve cultural change and it was highly fragmented. It was inevitable that it could not fulfil its original intent in the time allowed. One commentator on the grant scheme stated that it was like firing a shotgun one hundred metres from a shearing shed and trying to make sense of the result.

Later in response to the Mid Term Review the goals became a little more circumspect and a little less defined.

> The key element in assessing the performance of the Trust is its success in stimulating investment and activity – creating institutional frameworks and developing partnerships for the future. Achievement of the broader goals of conservation, sustainable use and repairs of Australia's natural environment will take many years and will also be in response to many factors in addition to the Trust's investments.[4]

What were the lessons learnt from the Natural Heritage Trust grant systems and how can these lessons be utilised to build community based resource management into contemporary governance?

The overall governance structure of the Natural Heritage Trust grant system is extremely complex, involving 12 layers between the investment decision of the Natural Heritage Ministerial Board and project delivery (see figure 1). It appears to be overwhelmingly dominated by government, particularly when you understand that assessment panels, one of the three layers that involved the community, were nominated by state government. It is based on the idea of partnerships between government agencies at a federal level and between the government at federal and state levels, but used primarily existing structures.

Figure 1: The Administrative Structure of the Natural Heritage Trust

Administrative Functions	Structural Units	Roles, responsibilities
Natural Heritage Trust Policy, Investment Criteria	Natural Heritage Ministerial Board	Sets directions, manages the Natural Heritage Trust of the Australian Reserve
Intergovernmental Policy and Administrative Framework	Ministerial Councils (ANZECC, ARMCANZ)	Communicates and collaborates on policy issues
Natural Heritage Trust Strategies, Direction, program Design	Environment Australia, Agriculture, Fisheries and Forestry Australia branch and Group and Division Heads	Develops and refines program strategies and guidelines
Natural Heritage Coordination and Collaboration	Commonwealth Team Leaders and Liaison Officers, Natural Heritage Trust Staff in State Agencies	Communicates program strategies and guidelines
Program Management- Lead Agencies	Program Managers in State Agencies (and Local Government)	Interprets and arranges program delivery
Project Assessment	State, Regional and Technical Assessment panels	Assesses and advises on projects
Regional planning	Regional, Catchment and Sub –Catchment Bodies	Prepares regional plans as basis for project proposals

Natural Heritage Trust Facilitators	Landcare Facilitators, State Bushcare Coordinators, Coastcare Facilitators etc	Stimulates community involvement, assists in strategy development
Project Advocates	Community organisations	Participates in planning, assists in project lodgement
Project Coordinators, Advisers	Program Coordinators	Provides technical advice and support
Project Delivery	Community Groups	People who have identified an investment need and want to act on it

Howard, in his mid term review of the grants system, states that this worked well at the policy and senior management level, because of goodwill and the commitment to ensure that the approach worked.[5] However he also states that the states had been developing integrated resource management strategies based on catchments in parallel with the Natural Heritage Trust initiatives. There was the potential for cost shifting from the state government to the federal government in relation to this and other areas of resource management. Many program managers interpreted the program as another grants program, not as an investment program, and this permeated down to community level.

One of the problems that Howard alludes to is the major role played by middle management, particularly at state level.[6] State government officials were involved in the coordination of the regional groups and the development of the assessment panels as well as the administration of the grants. This put a great deal of power into their hands without the requisite accountability and transparency of process.

The problem with the Natural Heritage Trust grant program was that it was too broad in scope, too fragmented across programs and was primarily project focused, rather than dealing with strategic regional plans. It tended to deliver a range of outcomes from extremely useful and highly thought out, through local action plans where communities took responsibilities for changing land and water management practice, such as the Angas Bremer Prescribed Wells Area Water Allocation Plan,[7] to projects which were badly documented, poorly managed and produced little to no result. Better results seemed to occur when communities had access to good scientific knowledge. Where local landholders had made a strong commitment in relation to local action plans such as the one for Angas Bremer Prescribed Wells, there was no mechanism for this to be further developed or implemented, with the potential for another government plan to be superimposed on this without recognition of what had gone before.

There was evident unevenness across regions and the states in relation to community capacity to take on a leadership role and active involvement in community conservation. However the trust did enable and support the development of regional community conservation groups such as the Blackwood Basin Group in Western Australia.[8]

John Fargher in the regional summary of the Mid Term Review of the Natural Heritage Trust[9] made the following recommendations, among others:

- Refocus the Natural Heritage Trust as an investment. Work with mature groups to develop and commit a share of investment to regional natural resource management investment prospectuses.

- Recognise community diversity. Commit to support a defined spectrum, certain activities that map out a path for regional communities to grow.

- Achieve institutional integration. Foster the development and implementation of integrated projects either by a process of funding components of integrated projects from different Natural Heritage Trust programs or by integrating Natural Heritage Trust programs themselves.

- Certify regional plans to formalise priorities. Develop and adopt a certification process for regional plans and negotiate compliance based on output-based investment agreements associated with a certified plan.

- Streamline responsibilities of groups through targeted investment. Invest in administrative and coordination support only at regional scale, through established regional organisations.

- Empower regional organisations and local groups through devolved grants. In consultation with regional organisations and state agencies, encourage consistent and widespread use of devolved grants for the implementation of small local projects that implement on the ground works consistent with a regional strategy.

- Work towards effective cost sharing frameworks. Include and enforce rigorous cost sharing requirements in partnership agreements.

To these recommendations, I would add:

- Ensure that technical assistance to the programs funded is consistent with the programs' objectives, such that there is a transfer of scientific knowledge to the community. There should be a strong tie between universities and research institutions involved in research related to natural resource management and the programs and the communities.

- Ensure a mechanism of accountability and review for each of the partners that is transparent. Information related to process and responsibilities and the possibility of appeal should be widely disseminated.

It should be noted that the Natural Heritage Trust has endeavoured to integrate across programs in the final years of the grants program by the development of the one-stop shop, which integrates grants over ten of the government programs, and has supported the targeting of programs to regional plans.[10] Some regional authorities, such as the River Murray Catchment Water Management Board, have also made this a prerequisite of their matching funds.

Incentives schemes for landholders

As noted in Toyne and Farley's paper, there has been a large burden placed at the feet of landholders in dealing with major environmental issues on their land.[11] Governments have been understandably reluctant to fund projects on private lands due to issues of equity and accountability. There is now, however, the development of structures that governments can use to assist and provide incentives for farmers to restore and conserve the health and biodiversity of their lands. Binning et al outlined these in detail in a number of publications.[12] They also note that the strengths of tax programs lie in their accessibility and capacity to recruit and reinforce the motivation of landholders to privately invest in public goods. Incentive schemes for landholders are seen as a complement rather than a substitute for the grants program. A diversity of approaches should be used to efficiently and effectively tap into community, industry and government resources.

The federal government under the Environment Protection and Biodiversity Conservation Act 1999 can enter into conservation agreements with landholders for the protection and conservation of biodiversity. Conservation agreements can only be entered into if there is a net benefit to biodiversity. Under such an agreement the Commonwealth Government could provide financial assistance for work entered into in pursuit of the conservation of biodiversity, for instance pay for fencing and conserving areas of remnant vegetation. A conservation agreement is binding on all later landowners.

There are also considerable tax incentives available for conservation on land where an agribusiness is being carried out because landholders in these circumstances can depreciate their machinery and equipment and deduct their operating expenses from their taxable income. A range of special incentives has been provided for the management of rural lands, such as the 34% rebate for Landcare works. These opportunities are not available to a landholder who is interested in conservation alone without a bona fide business.

Given the considerable land holdings that are private and the inability of government to own or manage land to conserve all Australia's biodiversity, it must rely on private involvement in landscape conservation. The government has recently amended tax laws to allow the following: an income tax deduction that can be apportioned over five years for non-testamentary donations of property (including land) with a value of more than $5000, regardless of when the property was purchased or acquired by the owner; a capital gains tax exemption for testamentary gifts of property donated to organisations, bodies or funds eligible to receive tax deductible donations and allowing for the establishment of private funds that are able to receive tax deductible donations.

These measures are a necessary precursor to the government recognising that the definition of property could extend to land, conservation covenants, bargain sales of lands (with a gap between sale price to a conservation trust and the market value), and donations of land with occupation right retained by the existing owner. If, for example, a conservation covenant was recognised and valued, it could be claimed as tax deductible if it was donated to an organisation such as the Trust for Nature (Victoria).[13]

Other incentives could be used to encourage revolving funds. This is a mechanism by which land is purchased, a conservation covenant is placed on the land and the land is subsequently sold. It has been used by conservation trusts such as The Nature Conservancy in the USA to protect biodiversity without tying up large amounts of finance and without the responsibility for land management. The person who buys the land with the conservation covenant is likely to value the conservation values that the covenant protects.

Another suggestion is the possibility of rate rebates for lands that have a high conservation value and that have been taken out of production to conserve these values. Rate rebates are not likely to win much support at local government level, as this is a source of their funding.

Conservation covenants in perpetuity lie at the foundations of many of these incentives. These covenants will need to be formed in such a way that they are binding on subsequent owners of the property. Who manages and monitors these covenants and how this management, monitoring and enforcement are financed will also need definition.

Conclusions

The burden of Australia's biodiversity falls primarily on landholders who do not have the means or the ability to reverse the land and water degradation that is occurring. Governments also do not have the resources to protect biodiversity within the reserves system. Co-governance, where responsibilities are shared between government and the community, is seen as the only possible path that will both conserve biodiversity and support regional communities. The regional and trans-state nature of degraded landscapes and water systems necessitates that governments find better ways of integrating programs across government in ways that ensure accountability and transparency at all levels of government and in the community. The challenge is to do this in a strategic and integrated fashion that has the flexibility to build on the strengths and successes of past work or local systems, deal with emerging and complex problems and allow communities tenure in decision making. This will mean looking critically at past systems or structures, trying to find new, inventive approaches that utilise, as effectively as possible, those resources, organisations or processes that are working well and ensuring that these processes have the transparency and accountability of good governance.

Notes

[1] Toyne, P & R. Farley, *The Decade of Landcare Looking Backward – Looking Forward*. The Australia Institute Discussion Paper Number 30, July 2000.

[2] *State of the Environment Australia 1996*. (Melbourne: CSIRO Publishing); *Australian Almanac 2000*, (Melbourne, Hardie Grant Books).

[3] *Australian Almanac 2000*.

[4] Australia, Natural Heritage Trust, Mid–Term Review of the Natural Heritage Trust. The Response, August, 2000.

[5] J. Howard, "Review of Administration," in *Mid term Review of the National Heritage Trust*, (1999).

[6] J.Howard, "Review of Administration".

[7] The Angas Bremer Prescribed Wells Area Water Allocation Plan was developed by the local irrigators and set environmental performance measures for irrigators within their area that were more stringent than could have been set through legislation. It is available on the River Murray Catchment Water Management Boards web page.

[8] R. Underwood, "Blackwood Region," in *Mid term Review of the National Heritage Trust,* (1999).

[9] J. Fargher, "Integrated Regional Summary Final Report," in *Mid term Review of the National Heritage Trust,* (1999).

[10] In *Natural Heritage Trust: Helping Communities Helping Australia, Guide to New Applicants 2001-200.*

[11] P. Toyne, and R. Farley, *The Decade of Landcare Looking Backward- Looking Forward.* The Australia Institute Discussion Paper Number 30, July 2000.

[12] C. Binning and M. Young, *Motivating people; using management Agreements to Conserve Remnant Vegetation.* National Research and Development Program on Rehabilitation, Management and Conservation of Remnant Vegetation paper 1/1997; C. Binning and M. Young, *Talking to the Taxman About Nature Conservation; proposals for the introduction of tax incentives for protection of high conservation value native vegetation.* National Research and Development Program on Rehabilitation, Management and Conservation of Remnant Vegetation paper 1/1997. C. Binning and P. Feilman. *Landscape Conservation and the Non Government Sector.* Report to the Land and water Resources R&D Corporation and Environment Australia National Program on Rehabilitation Research Report 7/2000.

[13] Trust for Nature (Victoria), Conservation covenants. http://www.tfn.org.au.

Commentary

Mr Roger Beale, Head of the Department of the Environment and Heritage, Government of Australia

---

There is an enormous amount in both these papers that I think is absolutely pertinent to the Australian circumstance. It is interesting, if you think of Kath's paper, that we entered the 1990s, spent much of the 1980s, talking about wilderness and forests and attempting to organise science and community discourse around those issues. There are very, very few extinctions in our great forest systems, and those that have occurred primarily have been because of invasive and feral species rather than logging per se. There have been many extinctions over that same time frame in the arid and semi-arid and coastal zones where there is been clearance for farming, for grazing, and urban growth. Right while we were spending our time focusing on woodchips and old growth, those losses were going on and gathering pace.

Clearly beginning in 1990 with the Decade of Land Care and increasingly through to the end of the 1990s We have shifted our focus to tackling these major issues – i.e. the management of landscape level systems, to combat soil and land degradation, loss of water quality, salinity, loss of environmental flows, loss of coastal wetland systems, turbidity, land-based pollution, etcetera, etcetera. Maybe this is part of the maturing of environment policy from "icons" to "sustainability."

When the Decade of Land Care started in 1990 it seemed like an awful lot of money and a big commitment. We ended the Decade of Land Care knowing much more about the problem and realising how little we had done to address it in real terms. In a sense, the Natural Heritage Trust story is not dissimilar. This is the biggest environmental investment, Commonwealth and state and community, that has ever been made in our 200 years. What have we achieved? I think we have achieved some very substantial things, not least is 300,000 Australians actually engaged on a voluntary basis on attempting to address these issues at their local level. But we know there is a huge task ahead of us.

What is the next stage? Well, I think it is very much – and you are seeing the beginnings of this in the prime minister's salinity action plan – engaging communities and creating governance at levels that are relevant to the ecosystem problems that you are attempting to manage. Now that is going to be both at a multi-state level and at a smaller, regional level. For example, we have to consider the Murray Darling Basin system as a system, as a basin and we have to consider the south-east region oceans as a system, even though they lap the shores of four states. But you then need to be able to focus as well down at the individual catchment level. You have to be able to get the communities owning the problems of unsustainable land and water use and accepting responsibility for becoming part of dealing with those problems.

So the National Action Plan on salinity is in the process of developing a new system of governance. The Commonwealth and the states are attempting to develop a framework that will enable us to empower regional bodies to contribute to catchment management and repair. These will sometimes, but more frequently not, be coincident with local government boundaries. We expect them to be joint signatories with the Commonwealth and with the states on integrated catchment management plans and to have a major role in sign-off on expenditure.

So far as the Commonwealth and the states are concerned, we are looking for transparency in financial commitments to these regions. How are the negotiations going? Well, all states and territories accept the plan in principle and we have got a number of states and territories signed up already, or about to sign up, to a more detailed Intergovernmental Agreement. In others, just those tensions that were spoken of by earlier speakers are still proving to be very difficult in getting the commitment by first Ministers at COAG translated into governance systems on the ground to try and address these issues.

It is important, though, that they are not seen just as local community bottom-up, if you like, initiatives, because if that happens we won't actually address the problems of basins. For example, you could have a high level of agreement in a local catchment group in Queensland in relation to the head waters of the Murray Darling System, that fails to deliver outcomes to sustain the Narran Lakes in New South Wales if the farmers say, "Well, that is New South Wales, isn't it. That is their problem. If we want to do flood harvesting to support new cotton development, that is our right. Look at all this water that is flowing past. Surely we are not making a difference." So success will lie in building layers of community and layers of governance. That is going to be tricky and take time.

If the prime minister's salinity action plan is a success, it should mean over the next four or five years we have got the agreements together, developed the communities' capacities, developed integrated catchment plans and deployed significant resources to support them. It is a thirty-year problem, so you are not going to solve it in the next four to five years. But if it is a success this architecture will hopefully provide the framework of the next generation of natural resource management programs between the commonwealth and the states more generally. Much more focus on region. Much more focus on consolidation of funding against accredited plans. Much less emphasis on the 21 individual programs that currently make up the NHT.

Just a final couple of comments before we start the discussion: Do we need a new sort of public servant, as suggested by Rod Dobell? In a sense yes, but in another sense no. I do not think we should ever forget – I wouldn't let any of my colleagues forget – that this is a representative democracy where it is the minister, under the constitution, who is actually responsible for much that we do. But if we turn around and say, "Well, how are we delivering these programs?" Well, a lot of them are not being delivered through public servants. Our land care facilitators and our community facilitators, by and large, are not employed by the department. They are engaged on contract – either directly or through community groups. They have clear objectives. But it is important that they are seen as community support. So it is devising new mechanisms that is important, rather than "reinventing" the core public service/servant.

I agree that it is important that we look at where things are working well, from a research point of view, but it is also very important that we look at the places where they are not working well, where there is a failure of governance as well as a success.

And, finally, in terms of communities as a focus for solving sustainability issues, it is important to be sceptical as well as positive. If we go back to where I started, you'll never address something like the logging or wilderness issue solely on the basis of local community engagement. You go to Pemberton (a logging town in WA) and engage with the local community and you'll get an answer that is very different from one that will keep the West Australian Liberals For Forests happy, who by and large reside in Perth not in Pemberton. So there is a need even at that level to understand that communities won't always exist simply at a geographic level. They can be communities of interest as well as geographic communities. This can make consensus, community based problem resolution, effectively impossible.

Discussion

Chair: Professor Mark Turner, Director, Centre for Research into Public Sector Management, University of Canberra and Deputy Director, National Institute for Governance

JENNY STEWART: A question for Rod Dobell. In listening to your presentation I was wondering to what extent you were talking about joint management of a UNESCO biosphere reserve at Clayoquot Sound, which is something that we are reasonably familiar with (i.e. bringing diverse bodies or groups together on a designated management task) and to what extent you are talking about partnerships and networks for integrated environmental management. I would see the latter as going a good deal beyond the former, in integrating decisions to do with fisheries, with decisions to do with forests, with broad decisions to do with land use. So is it the latter or a bit more of the former, or is it in a state of transition between the two?

ROD DOBELL: The purpose of these groups is to work towards the latter kind of understanding. With regard to integrated terrestrial marine land-use planning, the influence of the negotiators or communities' representatives in all of this is very strong. They have articulated the ideas around the integrated management of the resources, which means coastal resources, and also the habitat concerns arising from land-based operations and the offshore fishery implications. So the intention is to try to address these issues in an integrated management fashion. It is, to some extent, co-management in the sense of co-management of harvesting agreements. It is intended to be a community-based decision-making process with government representation, but not necessarily a structure in which the community process is merely an input into a government decision.

There are just lots of question marks around that structure, but the image that is held in the community is certainly one that would see those decisions made locally, and not in the senior reaches of the department, particularly if we are talking about fisheries, where the department is in Ottawa. There is a real concern that deals that are made around the table on the coast get undone in the corridors in Ottawa for reasons which no-one can quite work out. As long as that problem is there, the trust that is necessary to any of these operations will not be there.

So there are some interesting problems of working those co-management arrangements in a situation where there are still many voices on the ground but also many voices in the departments.

KATH WELLMAN: In Australia the federal government and the Bookmark Biosphere Reserve are doing a similar thing on a smaller scale, where there is a community group that has taken total responsibility for management of a very large station which is owned by the federal government. They have divided the station into paddocks and a community member has responsibility for a paddock. They have to meet particular benchmarks that they sit around a table and define, and they talk about management issues in relation to that.

That has been extraordinarily successful both from the community's point of view and also I think from the federal government. It has allowed a number of actions to go on within that reserve that would have not been resourced at a government level, things like feral animal control and restoration of habitat.

ROGER BEALE: I would like to add one very brief additional comment. I respect my colleagues in Ottawa and I'm sure that they'd have similar problems to those that we have in Canberra, namely that community groups can do deals on the ground that simply are not consistent with your international obligations. They have not sometimes faced up to the really hard issues.

You would have seen recently Robert Hill's push on prawn trawling in the Great Barrier Reef. He pushed a deal that was done at the community level, harder and further in the direction of what he considered to be consistent with Australia's world heritage obligations.

MICHAEL KEATING: I want to tease out this issue of whether you are governing for the whole of Australia, or the whole of Canada, versus a particular community. There are some issues where the whole of Australia and the community are pretty much in agreement. In principle, at least, everybody is opposed to increased salinity in the Murray Darling Basin. I'm prepared to accept that there are difficult issues in practice, but in principle there is not a huge difference between the respective parties. Maybe that was also true of Clayoquot Sound, Rod. I could understand if there is no fundamental difference. It is like the government of the whole of Canada, to use your terminology, telling its public servants to facilitate the community reaching its decision, not seeking to sway the decision.

Consider Sydney, where we want to have a second airport (if not today some time in the future there is going to be a second airport). I cannot think of any community that wants a second airport in their community. You can proliferate that type of example. So, how much power do you surrender to a community where there is a fundamental dichotomy of views between the interests of the majority and the interests of a particular group? A particular group is going to be more effective than any single member of the majority. After all, the majority is quite a big majority.

ROD DOBELL: That seems to me to be the interesting thing about trying to deal with these issues where we are looking at phenomena, which really can be contained locally, to concerns that are global. Certainly, when you are talking about the management of the fishery you are talking about what is supposed to be a resource managed for the benefit of the people of Canada. If you are talking about forests, provincial jurisdiction, it is the Crown and right of British Columbia whose interests in principle are being reflected in the management decisions. But the fact that all of those decisions are seen now in the context of global natural systems, they have implications and spillovers that go beyond the whole of Canada or the whole of Australia. We are left with the problem on each issue of being able to capture enough of the interests to have a reasonable discussion and be prepared to devolve authority for the decisions.

The problem is the same tension we have been talking about earlier. There is a sense of attempting to carry the integration as far as necessary. That leads you to a degree of centralisation, which precludes the kinds of timely action that you need for adaptive management purposes. So it is a question that probably cannot be answered on the basis of the existing constitutional structure.

We do have the communities of place. Increasingly they are driven by the communities of interest that were just mentioned, the virtual communities where the cross border information flows have to do with the values that other groups wish to impose on the operations locally. It is absolutely true that the community can arrive at decisions that won't be consistent with good practice or possibly even with international commitments.

At some stage there has to be the ability to exercise the authority. The state still has to have the authority to make those decisions in the end. But it seems to me the problem is that you cannot do that effectively now without the willing participation of stakeholders who previously could have been ignored. In some sense it is just a practical problem. To have effective public policy you must have established the legitimacy of trust and confidence. Otherwise the groups increasingly are saying, "We do not see those processes leading to decisions in formal agencies as reflecting the interests that we require to pursue."

You put your finger obviously on the tension that will be there throughout all of these decisions. It does not seem to me that there is an easy answer by looking to the formal constitutional authority. There is no easy answer looking to direct democracy either. So, it is some kind of participatory structure in between.

ROGER BEALE: Very simply, we are a nation of citizens as well as a community of communities. On some of these issues, speaking as a nation of citizens, we are going to tell communities what, as a nation, we believe ought to happen. The simplest example of that is probably the Tasmanian dams case. Very few people now, looking back, would say, "If only we had built the dams and cleared the wilderness." That is now one of our great world heritage sites. At the time if you had done a referendum in Tasmania you probably would have got an 80 percent majority for proceeding with the construction of those dams and the flooding of the wilderness. That was not a position supported by the majority of Australians. Now the rest of Australia ended up having to do a deal with Tasmania, but that was a deal that could not have been done without the national government exercising its constitutional obligations at some point to facilitate the outcome.

JOHN LANGFORD: My experiences with treaty negotiations in Canada show that, with regard to the issue of the natural interest, or the notion of a nation of citizens, the province is the level of government now prepared to accede more often to the local level. So that in fact it is leveraging its constitutional power in the constitutional mix. Almost every topic we look at now has some mix of state, federal or, in our case, provincial federal authority in operation. It is leveraging a local power by essentially acting as the spokesperson and providing an opportunity for local governments to have much more power than the constitution would suggest that they should have.

At the treaty table, I am faced with situations where the province is prepared to let a city government, or a small community association, dictate what the province will do. The Province could not in any realistic way be seen to be representing all of the citizens of British Columbia in these circumstances. It certainly makes it difficult for the federal government in a cooperative partnership treaty negotiation arrangement to represent all of the citizens of Canada. Does that ring true at all in Australia? It is certainly been a growing phenomenon in the Canadian context.

MARK TURNER: I would like to pick up on this idea of the new public servant. I was not clear whether the new public servant was the existing public servant who had been through a re-education course, whether the new public servant was completely different, whether they were citizens who were being deputised as public servants, or whether in fact it is all and any of these.

ROD DOBELL: The new public servant is was much more on the firing line, much more visibly having to take the responsibility for decisions that arise in public-private partnership kinds of structures. Here the responsibility for making a decision has been devolved sufficiently clearly that it does not make sense for the minister to assume responsibility. It is not possible for the responsibility to rest solely with the private partner. So, in effect, the neutral and anonymous and invisible public servant assumes a new and much more vivid set of clothes and is out in public.

I am referring to the role that is described for the public servant in the arrangements for these management processes. They simply envisage – and here I'm not talking quite so much of the existing structures as the proposed new structures for fisheries management – they envisage the departmental officials as playing an advisory and technical advisory role in a set of discussions that arrive at management plans. That will call for a slightly different attitude on the part of public servants. I'm not sure it calls for very different skills. As the public servant attempts to play a role in these participatory processes, there may be others arriving at consensus decisions while somehow preserving ministerial responsibility in the ultimate, and that, in itself, is a nice balancing act.

One interesting observation that struck me is the reference to the land trust in the Australian context. Each of the processes that I describe in trying to come to acceptable management structures in fisheries and forestry and in land use has given birth to proposals for trusts.

On the question of land use, Meares Island was the flash point for some of the dissent around land use in Clayoquot Sound. There is a proposal now for the creation of a land trust to manage this controversial piece of real estate, and the order of trustees will include equal representation of community and government. On the fisheries management side there is a proposal for the creation of a trust to carry the licences that are the rights of access to the fishery.

On the forest side, forest trusts are an initiative. They are being tested in a number of places in British Columbia. There are proposals around for very broad community ecosystem trusts. They seem to be a response to this sense that there are other forms of capital and other forms of ownership that have to be reflected in and represented in the decision processes.

So, you have all seen the World Bank's notions about the many forms of capital that represent the wealth of nations. The idea of social capital, the idea of natural capital, the cultural and traditional capital and so on are spreading quite widely. They give rise to the question of where the ownership of these sources of wealth rests. If you follow that line you find yourself thinking in terms of trust arrangements, where the owners of these other forms of capital sit at the table, along with the owners of physical capital, or the claims of financial capital. It seems to me an interesting straw in the wind and one to watch as we look at governance in the future.

PART 4

HORIZONTAL COORDINATION – HOW FAR HAVE WE GONE AND HOW FAR CAN WE GO?

Horizontal Coordination: The Australian Experience

Dr Jenny Stewart, School of Administrative Studies, University of Canberra

Approaching the problem

While coordination problems will be apparent in any organisation of sufficient size and complexity, they are particularly prominent in public sector contexts. This is because of the diversity of the activities governments undertake, the breadth of the values they serve, and the tendency of organisational forms and functions to proliferate and to persist long after the impetus that established them has faded from the public agenda. This means that when politicians or even public servants try to operate what they think of as the "levers" of government, they often get more (or sometimes less) than they bargained for, depending upon the organisational relationships which are already there.

Within political science, there has been a very long and inconclusive debate about coordination, which has revolved around the following questions:

- What "coordination" means (is it just a synonym for control?)

- How coordination is understood in the context of political management (generally as part of a synoptic decision-making process)

- How coordination actually occurs, if it happens at all (the empirical evidence suggests that it is as much "bottom-up" or possibly even "sideways" as it is "top down")

- How correct the assumption by most political managers is that coordination is always and intrinsically "a good thing" (coordination, especially if it comes from the top down, may be at the cost of responsiveness).

Institutionalist theory, with its emphasis on governance as opposed to government, is less likely than traditional public administration to pose "coordination" itself as a problem, or even as problematic. From an institutionalist perspective, such as we find in March and Olsen's *Rediscovering Institutions* (1989), coordination is not something we impose upon a structure, but an attribute which is generated from within it, and which is an outcome both of intrinsic design factors and the values generated by actors as they go about their business.

My approach is to examine, from a broadly institutionalist perspective, four kinds of coordination which I see at work in Australian governance, to give some examples of each, and to suggest some possibilities, some constraints and some patterns of change. I will, however, be careful not to confuse coordination with centralised control. Centralised coordination is important, but coordination can also occur – and has to occur – away from the centre and in a variety of informal ways.

Four kinds of coordination

The first is traditional coordination – well-established structures and practices that reflect the vertical chain of accountability in public sector and political management; the second is strategic coordination – the use of old, revamped (or sometimes new) structures to give effect to an overall strategy or plan; the third is coordination by ideas – a dominant paradigm is a powerful coordinating mechanism because it enables actors to "frame" problems in similar ways; and the fourth is network coordination – when actors form loose associations within agencies and also between agencies (both public and private), which are based on a congruence of interest and the mutually beneficial exchange of information.

None of these forms of coordination is particularly new. What may be new is an increasing role for network coordination, which is a far less top down form than the other three, and one that may be more suited than the others to addressing contemporary policy and management problems.

Why is coordination important?

Intellectually, it is difficult to imagine any area of policy that does not involve more than one agency. Institutional structures will always "slice up" policy problems because problems are systemic (that is, interconnected) while agency boundaries reflect a rough and ready division of labour based on administrative specialisation, the outcomes of previous turf wars and contemporary understandings of "what goes with what."

These problems should not be over-stated. Organisations in the public sector have formal boundaries so that each knows what it is responsible for, but as in the private sector, these boundaries may be quite fluid in practice, as functions are outsourced (or brought back in) and key tasks are performed by staff under contract.

In the policy sense, it is the functional division of responsibility that helps to keep problems manageable. We simply cannot comprehend the world as "one big system," nor is it readily possible to make trade-offs between the benefits to be obtained by, say, buying an extra aircraft as opposed to building a new hospital. Budget making makes these trade-offs manageable because they are implicit rather than explicit.

Nevertheless, there are many policy problems that transcend organisational boundaries – illicit drug use is an obvious one, because of the health and policing aspects. Environmental policy and management is another area that continues to strain integrative capacities. The recent discovery of "rural and regional Australia" by Australian politicians shows how easy it is for pressing social questions to fall through the cracks of conventional policymaking, particularly in a federal system as centralised as Australia's.

These kinds of problems may not be well-served by a system which tends to keep conflicting perspectives apart (because they are in different functional "boxes"), and which encourages the agency representing each perspective to defend its turf aggressively. To use some of the current British terminology, "departmentalism" or "the silo mentality" is at odds with the need for "joined-up" government.

In policy terms, then, it seems that the demand for coordination (or at least, for better-integrated decision-making) exceeds the supply. At the same time, the management of the public sector has been undergoing rapid change – in terms of the rhetoric at least, away from a centralised, bureaucratic model and towards one that is more flexible, customer oriented and devolved. The implications for coordination – at least for the centralised variety – are likely to be profound.

Coordination and change

Coordination means securing a consistent or coherent outcome in complex situations. Before looking at the four types of coordination in this context, it is worth reviewing the general effects of the two major changes to impact on the public sector in the past 20-30 years: new public management and new technology.

New public management produces a number of cross-cutting effects:

- Outsourcing to multiple agents makes coordination more difficult: a prime example would be the Jobs Network, where a multiplicity of contracts has replaced a single organisation – the Commonwealth Employment Service.

On the other hand, where a number of departments use a single agency (such as Centrelink) for service delivery, the potential exists for coordination at the delivery level.

- Agencies do not have to be "coordinated" when it comes to staff salaries and conditions.

On the other hand, there is evidence that new financial management techniques (particularly accrual budgeting, where a price is paid for a range of agreed outputs) may strengthen considerably the hand of central finance agencies.

- Meeting customer expectations suggests sensitivity to local conditions.

On the other hand, requirements remain for consistency of processing.

The effects of technology have been much less noticed by commentators. My sense of this issue is that new technology has powerful effects in relation to coordination. Bottom up or sideways coordination becomes more feasible because decentralised or sub-central IT applications allow for new and more diverse information flows.

- Single portals for a range of services (in theory) lessen the demand for coordination, because they allow a choice of programs to be tailored to individual circumstances.

- Communication between agencies is much easier than it used to be, because of the prevalence of email; this facility has obvious advantages for the formation and maintenance of networks.

On the other hand, IT has powerful centralising capacities and requirements. Potentially it offers the ultimate coordination – one number for every citizen's interactions with government. The challenge for policy and administration is to reap the potential efficiency and compliance advantages while at the same time safeguarding security and privacy.

Change is clearly pervasive. But it would be wrong, from a management point of view, to conclude that there is a trend – or even a demand – for devolved practice. Many issues can, and will, be handled quite comfortably using traditional techniques for coordination.

The capacity of traditional structures

Traditional, centralised structures for coordination are alive and well in Australian government. Cabinet, and in particular the prime minister, continues to be the main focus of control. At the departmental level, there may be fewer agencies than before (and centralised personnel controls are a thing of the past), but Finance continues to exercise control over money. The Department of Prime Minister and Cabinet can still involve itself as much or as little as it wishes in particular policy fields through its knowledge of cabinet business and its central role in the cabinet process.

Although their use is difficult to quantify, my impression is that inter-departmental committees, both formal and informal, continue to be the mechanism of choice for resolving policy issues where more than one agency is involved. It is on the management side that we find more diverse organisational forms being employed – for example, the partnership arrangements and Memoranda of Understanding devised for the implementation of the Natural Heritage Trust program.

While they are not, strictly speaking, coordination mechanisms, administrative restructures create new alignments and power balances that are reflected in changed budgetary trade-offs. Where previously separate agencies are brought together in a new entity, the hope at least will be that improved coordination between them will result. The creation of mega-departments in 1987 is a case in point. The coordination load on cabinet was significantly reduced because conflicting issues were resolved at portfolio or even agency level, reducing the requirement for separate cabinet submissions.

On occasion, separate coordinating bodies are created to oversee emerging policy fields, although their history is often not a happy one. The National Greenhouse Office, for example, seems to have disappeared from the federal radar screen altogether, as has the body charged with overseeing the outsourcing of IT.

Requiring departments to include specified impact statements in all cabinet submissions is one traditional mechanism for improving policy coherence. All current cabinet submissions, for example, must include a Regional Impact Statement.

Traditional coordination, with its apex at cabinet level, derives from, and is consistent with, the design principles of ministerial and cabinet responsibility. It does not deal with agency "silos" in the substantive sense so much as it provides arenas and mechanisms for sorting out disputes and for imposing budgetary discipline.

Traditional techniques provide a rough and ready form of control, but their defects are their lack of responsiveness, and their relative imperviousness to agencies' links with stakeholders and with customers.

Strategic coordination

Where there is sufficient political will, traditional bureaucracies show quite impressive capacities for strategic coordination, both in formulating strategies and (although less so) in implementing them across diverse groups of agencies.

The use of task forces has a fairly long history in this regard. The Ministerial task force on child support, in which Meredith Edwards was involved, is a case in point.[1] Task forces of the present era, though, are much more likely to include "outsiders" (industry leaders, or figures from the not-for-profit sector) than in the past.

In the UK, the Blair government in its first term commissioned numerous special task forces to address policy problems that had previously failed to progress because of entrenched departmentalism.[2] The Australian federal government has not been quite so enthusiastic, although I was able to find a number of task forces designed to come up with improved strategies for handling complex problems, and to improve coordination in implementation – the national illicit drugs taskforce and the task force on unauthorised arrivals are two examples.

The implementation of national competition policy through the Council of Australian Governments is another example of strategic coordination – the states in this case were forced to comply with the Commonwealth agenda through a mixture of threats and sanctions. Such is the coordinative strength of Australia's highly centralised federation.

Within agencies, strategic management, with links from general goals to corporate plans, has proved to be a successful mechanism for creating an environment conducive to change and, in some cases, for improving performance.

Strategic coordination is heavily reliant on the personality and priorities of the prime minister and of key ministers. In theory, strategy at cabinet level should mesh with agency strategies in a dynamic way, but so far at least, new public management has had less influence on the general workings of cabinet (as distinct from budgetary management) than might have been expected.

Strategic coordination can force participants – at least for a while – to forget their usual allegiances. But it requires a true sense of crisis (or an unusual convergence of interests) to succeed. Its defects relate to implementation: the impetus from the centre all too often dies, or turns into something else, by the time it reaches the periphery.

Coordination by ideas

Ideas are powerful coordinating mechanisms because they enable unwanted diversity to be censored out. The central agencies of Australian government, and a number of the line agencies as well, have long been coordinated by a dominant paradigm generally known as economic rationalism.

But there are other paradigms or ideas in good currency as well – mutual obligation, for example, is an extremely useful term because it gives an overall sense of how the government views social policy, particularly where the unemployed are concerned. Participation in what used to be called labour market programs is no longer a right to be taken up (or not) as desired, but a down-payment on support from government. There would be little point in any public servant working up an open-ended program aimed at the unemployed in this environment.

Coordinating ideas must strike a balance – not so general that they provide no guidance, but not so specific that policy-makers across a range of areas cannot identify with them. Where we lack a coordinating idea – for example in Defence, or in Regional Policy – a great deal of policy churning results.

Complex conditions may, of course, not be amenable to a single co-ordinating idea –

"sustainable development" contained too many contradictions to be useful. But it is difficult to mobilise the power and resources of central government without a catchy way of indicating the overall intention.

Network-based coordination

In one sense, policy networks have been a long-standing part of the informal coordination that took place in and around the traditional structures. In another, they represent promising new ways of bringing about a new kind of coordination – not coordination in the sense of "one size fits all," but a way of forming and implementing policy through loosely articulated structures "on the ground." It would be fair to say, though, that these arrangements are still very much in their formative stages and, at least so far, have been used as adjuncts to more traditional approaches to coordination rather than as replacements for them.

I want to discuss two aspects of these developments: delivery networks (such as the Jobs Network) and moving beyond programmatic thinking.

Delivery networks

It is easy for departments to call outsourced service delivery arrangements "networks." However, many of these networks exist more in the eye of the department sponsoring them than as a reality for participants or for clients. If you set up networks that have the department as a hub but no connections on the perimeter, you do not have a true network at all because the constituents do not talk to each other. Indeed, because they are competing with each other, the description "managed market" would be more apposite.

The network concept (as a formal management tool) may have more relevance for information gathering, and for projecting the presence of a federal agency (headquartered in Canberra) into the state capitals and regions. An example of an information-gathering and "road-testing" network (or potential network) would be the Area Consultative Councils set up by DEWRSB (Employment, Workplace Relations and Small Business). Family and Community Services' (FaCS) use of its state offices for "Network Management" as reported in its 1999-2000 Annual Report suggests that at least some policy agencies are seeing the potential of these somewhat neglected parts of their operations.[3]

Moving beyond programmatic thinking

Much policy is program-based – money is allocated in specified ways to bring about desirable results. From the point of view of the applicants and recipients, on the other hand, there may be a plethora of programs available, but none to address the problems they actually have. Moreover it is not uncommon to find programs that overlap or which sometimes even conflict.

A "one-stop shop" is a popular way to attempt to resolve the first part of the difficulty – single portals might be the electronic equivalent. But using programs to address systemic problems is not the way to achieve "joined-up" government. A good example of the difficulties involved is the Natural Heritage Trust.

The Natural Heritage Trust (NHT) supported the spending of over a billion dollars (obtained from the part sale of Telstra) on the rehabilitation of the Australian natural environment. The NHT probably represents the apotheosis of the programmatic approach – an enormous variety of projects were funded, covering five main areas of activity. The administrative arrangements were complex, involving partnerships between Environment Australia and AFFA at the federal level; between federal and state agencies; and between government, community and other groups involved in regional assessment panels.

However, viewed from a regional perspective, the whole proved to be somewhat less than the sum of the parts. A review concluded that the program's primary purpose as a vehicle to invest in the restoration of the natural environment had been adversely affected by a lack of integration between projects, and by selection criteria that did not sufficiently acknowledge regional differences in circumstances and capacity.[4]

In this, as in other areas, it would clearly be preferable if ways could be found (while maintaining accountability) to customise what is on offer to particular communities. One way of doing this might be to use public servants in information or brokerage roles, which they exercise on behalf of a number of agencies. FaCS's thinking about Community Capacity Building seems to have elements of this approach, as do the Regional summits sponsored by Transport and Regional Services.

Nevertheless, this kind of systemic coordination, with both top-down and bottom-up elements is difficult to reconcile with the traditional role of the Australian states (very important in regional and community matters) and, if money is involved, with principles of upwards accountability. If a community wanted money to be spent, say, on ten different projects in very different fields, ten different organisations would have to be accountable for the funds expended.

A cynic (or is it a sceptic?) might also point out that it is somewhat ironic that some federal agencies are trying to undo the damage caused, at least in part, by the policies of the central agencies of government. Creative regional coordination is of little point if the strategic priorities of government lie with policies such as deregulation and national competition policy, which tend to pull investment and activity out of "uncompetitive" areas.

Policy networks have been the subject of much excited academic truffle hunting. But the reality is one of cautious, incremental change with an overall system that remains inevitably minister-centric.

Conclusion

When they wish to use them, governments have considerable capacities to coordinate decision-making between agencies. These capacities have probably increased rather than declined over the past twenty years. For the most part, however, they are reliant on the exercise of control (or power) in various forms, and operate in a highly centralised way.

The construction of markets and the use of price-based signals to achieve results (as, for example, in the reform of Water policy) suggest one way in which this might be done. But the complementary challenge is to find ways of assisting the growth of adaptive capacity without throwing money at separate segments of the problem.

The argument I am advancing here suggests that very complex problems require a new approach to coordination that starts from the bottom up rather than the top down. In particular, what I call programmatic thinking may have had its day. There are some signs that the use of networks and partnerships by many agencies offers a first glimpse of what a devolved form of joined-up governance might look like. At the same time, there is a requirement for an overall framework that maintains some level of strategic consistency and accountability.

Notes

[1] Meredith Edwards, *Social policy, public policy: from problem to practice,* (Sydney: Allen & Unwin, 2001).

[2] D. Marsh, M. Smith, and D. Richards, "Joined-up government under Labour," Paper delivered to Australasian Political Studies Association Conference, Australian National University, October 2000.

[3] Australia, Department of Family and Community Services, Annual Report 1999-2000 (Canberra: 2000).

[4] Dames and Moore, Mid-term review of the national [sic] heritage trust – integrated regional summary, Natural Heritage Trust website www.nht.gov.au/review (2000).

Culture, Control or Capacity: Meeting Contemporary Horizontal Challenges in Public Sector Management

Professor Evert Lindquist, School of Public Administration, University of Victoria, Canada

Introduction[1]

The challenge of working across the traditional boundaries of government to deliver public services has seized the attention of political and administrative leaders across Canada. This encompasses designing and delivering a wide variety of programs across agencies, levels of government, and with partners in other sectors. Many different phrases are invoked to describe the challenge and purported solutions: horizontal government, collaborative government, "joined-up" government, and public-private partnerships. The term "horizontal" arguably now challenges "strategic," "performance," "cost effective" and "results" as the top adjective for describing the directions for public sector reform, and is often invoked as a noun – "horizontality" – in effect, a condition, desired state, or mind-set for those working in the public sector.

In drafting this paper I have sought to suppress the natural reflex of practitioners and academics to critique the next overarching concept to sweep discourse in the field of public administration. Nevertheless, it is important to carefully understand what is meant by "horizontal challenges" for three reasons. First, horizontal challenges are very diverse and evolutionary in nature, and thus difficult to categorize. Second, horizontal issues have always been with us, and therefore we should come to grips with why there is such widespread interest in the concept at this point in time and discern whether there are factors and opportunities that are materially different. Third, developing a better understanding of horizontal challenges – both as individual experiences and as a collection of phenomena – should allow for determining more effective and sensible ways for governments to tackle the challenges they present.

This paper reviews how the Canadian government has recently attempted to address the modern challenges of horizontal management. It begins by reviewing examples of horizontal initiatives, identifying some concepts to motivate analysis, and sets out several premises regarding the nature of horizontal management challenges. I review recent reports produced by the public service and by the auditor general of Canada on horizontal initiatives, and argue that public service leaders have primarily focused on inducing cultural change, while the auditor general, who is critical of how the government has managed horizontal issues, does so from a control paradigm. I suggest that a middle ground exists between the cultural and control perspectives, which involves creating sufficient capacity to manage horizontal initiatives. Accordingly, this chapter sets out elements of a strategy for how the "centre" might better support at the system level.

I conclude by encouraging readers to consider what might be in store for horizontal management by engaging in some preliminary scenario-thinking. The four scenarios that emerge suggest that, along with the idiosyncratic and evolutionary nature of horizontal initiatives, further variability may derive from the different "system" environments in which they proceed.

Contemporary Horizontal Challenges: Definitions and Premises

Any public servant or informed observer of government can recite without much prodding the arguments for horizontal or collaborative public sector management: increasingly demanding citizens, new information and communications technologies, continuing pressure on public sector budgets, experimentation with new ways to deliver services, and greater recognition of the complexity of social problems and the range of expertise from different institutions and sectors required to tackle them. All of this creates increasing demands for governments to work across the traditional boundaries of the public sector – departments, agencies, portfolios, and other levels of government – as well as the non-profit sector, private sector, and larger public sector, and often other countries. The availability of new ICTs has forced re-examination of all linkages, since vertical channels within government are no longer the only way to advance on issues.

While these themes are well known, it is often difficult to get a precise grip on the nature and diversity of the challenges of horizontal management. In this section, I provide some examples of horizontal initiatives and then consider to what extent they actually represent a new development in public sector governance. I conclude by proposing some premises to guide analysis of how to improve how governments can support horizontal management.

Some Examples of Horizontal Challenges

Defining what constitutes a horizontal initiative, let alone trying to develop workable taxonomies, constitutes a "horizontal management challenge" on its own terms. The best way to proceed is to review examples of horizontal management identified by the CCMD Roundtable to motivate its own deliberations,[2] although I hasten to add that they do not exhaust all the examples examined by the Roundtable, nor do they fully reflect what are undoubtedly hundreds of such initiatives under way at any given time in the Canadian government. Here are brief sketches of eleven of the examples that were considered:

- *The Trends Project.* An initiative of the Policy Research Secretariat (PCO) and the Social Sciences and Humanities Research Council which funded the development of several multi-disciplinary networks of policy researchers to identify and probe key trends affecting policy-making in Canada. This process also engaged federal officials across the public service as well as representatives from the nonprofit, private, and think tank sectors. This was closely linked to the Policy Research initiative.

- *Team Canada.* An initiative of the prime minister to coordinate federal and provincial governments, along with business leaders from across the country, in a series of visits to foreign countries in order to expand markets for Canadian business. The Government of Canada takes the lead in coordinating the delegations. These high profile events include meetings with foreign governments and business associations, and usually involve the signing of a multitude of contracts and MOUs.

- *Urban Aboriginal Strategy (Saskatchewan).* Announced in 1998, the goal of the UAS is to deal with needs of urban Aboriginal people at risk. This involves working with many different federal departments, Aboriginal communities, and provincial governments, to coordinate and tailor programs and services for specific communities. The federal Saskatchewan Regional Council developed a subcommittee first to coordinate federal action but later expanded to embrace the other actors. Later a Working Group, led by the Western Diversification Office, assumed the lead for implementation and coordination.

- *Science and Technology MOU for Sustainable Development.* First signed in 1995, and renewed in 1998, this MOU involved five departments to support better science to deal with issues associated with sustainable development. This agreement emerged from the S&T Review and the Program Review processes in 1994, as well as prodding from the auditor general of Canada, pointing to insufficient collaboration and management of the S&T capabilities of the federal government.

- *Implementing the Oceans Act (1997).* This has led to the development of the Oceans Management Strategy, with the Department of Fisheries and Oceans as lead department, but requires collaboration with 23 federal departments and agencies (10 are key players), provincial governments, and non-governmental groups. The challenge is to coordinate existing statutory authorities, share information, and promote accountability (which rests fully with DFO). The goals are improving ocean ecosystems, educating children and youth, conservation, economic development, and sustainable costal communities.

- *Search and Rescue – Swissair 111 Disaster.* The Rescue Coordination Centre of the Department of National Defence has responsibility for coordinating the activities of federal and other government agencies to handle disasters. In this case, RCC dealt with seven departments, agencies and other organizations, involving well over 1000 people.

- *Rural Team New Brunswick.* Emerged in 1999 from the Canadian Rural Partnership dialogue process (1997-98). The goal is to increase access for rural communities and business to government programs, and to expand the capacity and leadership in those communities. RTNB involves thirteen federal and seven provincial departments, which have developed a strategic action plan. Federal activities were coordinated through the NB Federal Regional Council.

- *Voluntary Sector Task Force.* An initiative of the Canadian government and various representatives of the voluntary sector. Co-led by representatives from the government (eventually 23 departments were involved) and the voluntary sector, the process involved creating several tables for sponsoring and reviewing research, discussion, and developing recommendations. The process led to a report, *Working Together*, which outlined a comprehensive set of recommendations.

- *Regional councils.* Informal councils of representatives of federal agencies were created in the early 1980s as part of economic development initiatives to encourage information sharing within provinces. In recent years the breadth of regional council activities have expanded, and they been used more regularly by the Treasury Board Secretariat and other central agencies in support of implementing system-wide reform initiatives, and to assist with specific horizontal initiatives in the regions. To some extent they are tapped into as sounding boards and for advice on management and, sometimes, policy initiatives.

- *The Leadership Network.* Established in June 1998 with a two-year mandate, TLN is to further renewal of the federal public service (initiated as La Releve Task Force in 1996) to foster leadership and to support the ADM community. Its work proceeds alongside the authorities of PCO, TBS, PSC, and CCMD, and works in a collaborative and catalytic mode. TLN sponsors or co-sponsors many events and has developed an impressive portal web site with great resources relating to learning and professional development.

- *St. Lawrence Action Plan.* A five-year collaborative exercise among eight federal and five Quebec departments and agencies to improve the water quality of the St. Lawrence River. This project has proceeded through several phases since 1988 and has involved harmonizing and coordinating policies across organizations and governments, as well as non-governmental organizations, resulting in a five-year plan and a results framework.

These examples show that horizontal challenges are incredibly diverse. A similar set of cases, with some overlap, was reviewed for CCMD, The Leadership Network, and the Government of Canada's Quebec Regional Council on collaborative basis by researchers at Ecole nationale d'administration publique.[3] The cases included: (1) federal-provincial strategy to improve income security for the First Nations of Quebec and Labrador; (2) improving federal government visibility in Abitibi-Temiscamingue; (3) federal action strategy for Greater Montreal; (4) the Youth Café in Montreal; (5) St. Lawrence Action Plan; (6) Team Canada Inc.; (7) creating Quebec Maritime to promote tourism; (8) establishing the Health Canada Development Centre to promote employee self-learning; (9) Museumobiles, a traveling museum for senior citizens; (10) the Lower St. Lawrence Model Forest, a national program that in this case has forty partners; (11) the Saguenay-St. Lawrence Marine Park agreement between Canada and Quebec, involving many public partners; (12) locally-shared support services delivered in Shawinigan by ten federal departments; and (13) a similar arrangement for Estrie.

The CCMD Roundtable suggested that its cases could be grouped into the categories of service, research, policy, internal support, emergencies, and multi-faceted projects. An early background report prepared for the Roundtable provided several typologies for categorizing initiatives based on (1) *function* (information, resources, work, authority), (2) *goals* (support services, knowledge, policy development, program and service delivery), and (3) *mechanisms* (a menu of formal structures and processes, and informal coordinating devices).[4] However, these typologies are insufficiently robust – each initiative outlined above is complex, and their goals and structures, whether formal or not, evolve over time. In plain terms, a typical initiative will involve several of these goals or activities:

- Developing policy
- Collecting data, research
- Exchanging information
- Marketing
- Consulting with citizens
- Sharing financial resources
- Delivering services
- Managing human resources
- Monitoring results

Moreover, dealing with any one or more of these specific challenges takes on very different dimensions depending on the partner institutions involved. Horizontal initiatives can proceed across departments and agencies, across governments, and with organizations in the non-profit and for-profit sectors. It is for these reasons that attempts to produce typologies to neatly categorize horizontal initiatives are usually unsatisfying; they are almost as complicated as the challenges themselves, and fail to usefully simplify the phenomena under consideration.

Are Horizontal Challenges New? Beyond Coordination and Mutual Adjustment

Horizontal initiatives and working across the boundaries are certainly not a new challenge for modern governments. Indeed, standard textbooks on public sector management delineate the many formal mechanisms that can facilitate collaboration. They include the following:

- Ministerial portfolios and committees
- Structure of departments, agencies
- Central agencies and specific bureaus
- Task forces, committees, working groups
- Cross-governmental committees, groups
- Sectoral councils (comprised of non-governmental and governmental actors)

Moreover, cabinet and central agency decision-making systems can develop formal processes for ensuring that proposals receive vetting from pertinent departments and agencies, and that required consultations with other governments and non-governmental actors take place. Prime ministers and central agency heads often use these structures and processes to designate lead agencies or to ensure that collaboration occurs. More generally, it is well understood that formal structures and processes do not work well without the informal sharing of information and relationship building.

One commentator has cast horizontal management as "coordination," a matter of politics; another has conceptualized it as "mutual adjustment" across departments, about getting specific tasks, often government-wide priorities, accomplished across boundaries.[5] But these depictions fail to capture the full essence of the challenge: managing horizontally is more than coordination and mutual adjustment across government departments, it is also about mobilizing and aligning capacities across organizational and institutional boundaries, and it is about getting specific tasks, often government-wide priorities, accomplished across boundaries. This surely involves the matching of expertise and authorities across departments to the complexity of the task at hand.

Horizontal management has taken on new meaning for different reasons. First, there has emerged a view that more of the work proceeding in the middle of public service institutions, as opposed to at the apex (previously involving ministers and deputy ministers) now has horizontal components. There is greater awareness of the complexity of policy and service delivery issues, which require tapping into the expertise of many departments and other actors. Moreover, there is a perception in Ottawa that structural solutions (new departments, agencies, ministries) are not necessarily a productive way dealing with modern horizontal challenges, and thus require different approaches. Accordingly, there has been considerable interest in finding ways to create and foster a culture more disposed to horizontal and collaborative management. This also comes in response to the growing interest in identifying and measuring results across program areas, governments, and sectors. Finally, the very complexity of horizontal initiatives has led to increasing worry about accountability and oversight on the part of Parliamentarians and the auditor general of Canada.[6]

Some Propositions on Horizontal Challenges to Consider

In the sections that follow, I review different approaches that have been taken or proposed for improving horizontal management in the Canadian government. However, I believe that there are several premises – often unstated in discussions of horizontal management – that influence the what system-wide strategies get proposed. I state them below in the form of ten propositions:

1. *Public servants, and the larger institutions of which they are a part, have considerable experience working across boundaries.* Whether celebrated or not, public servants have led or been involved with many horizontal initiatives, and considerable wisdom exists already within the public service. This suggests that such knowledge needs to be identified, shared, compared, and then distributed to colleagues across the system.

2. *Demands for horizontal governance and collaboration will continue to multiply.* Although governments have long had to manage horizontally, the premise is that many of the factors noted above will increase the amount of horizontal work that needs to be accomplished by public servants and their departments. Another way to put this is that, while executives have long been involved in horizontal management, "horizontality" now affects the work of middle and front-line public servants.

3. *Horizontal initiatives outweigh the capacity of departments and the centre to manage.* The cases reviewed above do not fully represent the diversity nor the sheer number of horizontal challenges, which will tend to be smaller and more distant from executive ranks. Casting a broader net will surely tax central monitoring and oversight capacities. For this reason, a more promising strategy is to cultivate new values, identify relevant pockets of knowledge, and link mentors to managers with new horizontal challenges.

4. *Vertical structures, incentives, and accountabilities will persist.* The expanding number of horizontal projects, or greater demand for horizontal competencies of officials at all levels,

does not mean the end of "vertical government." Accountability and resource allocation is exercised in a top-down manner because of our system of Parliamentary government and because we need hierarchy to coordinate and organize vast amounts of expertise across a large country. Thus, improving horizontal management will not, and should not, supplant vertical systems, and therefore strategies must work within and supplement vertical systems to better address contemporary policy and service delivery challenges.

5. *Too many "heavy" coordinating mechanisms may complicate or crush promising horizontal initiatives.* The challenge of coordination is not new, and the demands on executive teams and central institutions are enormous. Moreover, subjecting all horizontal initiatives to "one-size-fits-all" rules or oversight by central institutions is bound to be counterproductive, even though accountability and oversight remain important objectives. Thus, executive support must be strategic, and itself is likely to be horizontal.

6. *Every horizontal initiative will have different leadership and management challenges than its predecessors; there must be multiple ways to secure advice and support.* It remains difficult to discern how knowledge and advice get applied to solving problems and learning because use is highly situational. What we do know is that useful connections are serendipitous, and obtain in very different ways. Any strategy should support multiple channels of influence.

7. *Good horizontal management may simply be good management, but leaders must understand unique horizontal challenges.* To adapt Aaron Wildavsky's famous phrase: "if horizontality is everything, then maybe it's nothing." If we believe good horizontal management differs from management, then efforts should be made to ensure that any new training and resource capacities add value with respect to the particular challenges of managing horizontal issues.

8. *Timely executive support of horizontal initiatives is crucial for success.* Most horizontal initiatives seem to be precarious, requiring considerable nurturing and support. The lower the profile of an initiative, and the more remote from the centre, the less likely it is to receive support crucial for success at any phase. Additional "system" capacities should assist smaller and less proximate initiatives, and make executives and managers across government better aware of the resources and knowledge at their disposal.

9. *System supports for horizontal initiatives are investments.* Central support should take the form of investments to assist with specific projects at crucial moments and to ensure that managers are better trained and that executives are more supportive. Resources for delivering mature "horizontal" programs should be handled through operating budgets.

10. *Political posturing and policy conflict across governments will continue.* Too often calls for improving horizontal management are accompanied by the expectation that political leaders, as well as bureaucratic leaders, will repress tendencies to protect turf and vigorously advance the causes of their departments. A more realistic premise is that such behaviour constitutes a condition, and the challenge of horizontal management is to develop strategies and supports that increase the chances for success in the face of such behaviour.

These premises, in addition to the specific substantive and political challenges associated with each horizontal initiative, present significant barriers for public servants to overcome. This rest of this paper describes recent thinking at the upper echelons of Canada's federal public service about how to inculcate more horizontal ways of working among public servants in the face of complex demands, and contrast that with the model of horizontal management espoused by the auditor general of Canada, which emphasizes the need for more control and transparency.

Promoting Horizontal Management as Culture and Competency

The management of horizontal issues has moved increasingly highly on the agenda of leaders of the federal public service in Ottawa. This interest has been revealed most concretely with the Deputy Minister Task Force on Managing Horizontal Policy Issues,[7] the release of a study on *Managing Horizontal Government* by the Canadian Centre for Management Development,[8] and more recently with CCMD's Roundtable on the Management of Horizontal Issues, which was initiated in early 2000 and completed its work just over a year later.[9] Other studies have been sponsored by the Treasury Board Secretariat and the Federal Regional Councils,[10] and jointly by CCMD, the Leadership Network, and the Quebec Regional Council.[11]

These developments are doubly interesting because the 1996 Task Force report was initiated by Jocelyne Bourgon, then clerk of the Privy Council and secretary to cabinet, but was led by Mel Cappe, then deputy minister of the Department of Human Resources Development of Canada. Bourgon is now the president of the Canadian Centre for Management Development, and Cappe has since become clerk. So these issues have been top of mind at the apex of the public service.

The Task Force on Managing Horizontal Policy Issues (1995-96)

The Task Force was launched during an era of great change within the federal government. The Program Review process had been initiated in 1994 under the Liberal government, which entailed a concerted government-wide effort to reduce the federal deficit (citation). Each department had to meet strict expenditure reduction targets ranging from 20% to as much as 50% over a three-year period. To meet these targets, ministers and departments submitted plans for overhauling or even eliminating programs (the phrase "alternative service delivery" vaulted to the top of the lexicon), first to a committee of senior deputy ministers, and then to a committee of ministers. The results of these decisions were announced in the February 1995 Budget.

The Program Review process is generally hailed as a success, despite the many difficult decisions made in a relatively short period of time. The process, as well as the Expenditure Management System that accompanied it, are credited with turning around the fiscal fortunes of the Liberal government. However, public service leaders worried about the process for several reasons. First, they wondered what implications these decisions had for the shape the "new" public service would take beyond the immediate planning horizon. Second, they believed that most Program Review decisions were informed by analysis of their impact on other programs (i.e., two departments cutting back or retaining similar programs for the same clients). Finally, they worried that even if there had been demand for such analysis, the public service could not have supplied it -- the capacity to undertake high quality policy analysis and medium-term planning had steadily declined as a result of managerialist reforms during the previous decade.

It was in this context that the Clerk launched several task forces in late 1995, led by deputy ministers, on a variety of topics linked to the future of the federal public service. One of them focused on horizontal policy issues, and its final report entitled *Managing Horizontal Policy Issues* was completed in December 1996. The forward noted that there had been no shortage of other initiatives designed to work across the boundaries of departments, such as the Council on Administrative Renewal, Personnel Renewal Council, and the work of federal Regional Councils. But this only underscored the focus of the exercise: the matter of managing horizontal issues at this point in time was attached to the question of how to better manage horizontal policy issues, not "horizontality" more generally. It is worth reviewing the contents of this report in some detail in order to set the stage for further analysis.

The task force reviewed best practices in recent horizontal initiatives as a basis for making its recommendations. It recognized that the extent of "horizontality" for each policy issue would vary greatly, depending on the scope of the problem, the authorities assigned to departments and ministers, their respective capacities, the nature of stakeholders, and whether the issue at hand was a central priority of the government. The review of recent practice pointed to the importance of properly defining issues, identifying lead institutions and providing proper mandates to lead officials who would deal with the issues, and securing the right level of support from central agencies (which could be assigned the lead, if necessary). The task force also recognized the need for ministers and deputy ministers to not expect the impossible: there had to be realistic time frames and expectations, and sufficient resources to support initiatives. Finally, the task force called for proper accountabilities to be delineated in advance, to be followed by reviews once horizontal policy exercises were completed.

The task force resisted the reflex to achieve better management of horizontal issues by re-organizing the structure of government, a reaction to the massive restructuring of the federal public service in June 1993, still causing indigestion across the public service in 1996. Rather, the goal was to strengthen the "interdepartmental policy-making system" by streamlining the cabinet and expenditure management systems, better utilizing the Coordinating Committee of Deputy Ministers (CCDM) and the ADM Forum to manage such issues, and striking standing committees or temporary task forces when required. Together, these recommendations implied that the Privy Council Office needed to develop a more collaborative approach in its capacity as strategic coordinator, better engaging ministers on horizontal issues and systematically using COSO committees and temporary task forces to support such work. Indeed, the task force recommended that a deputy minister committee on long-term planning proceed under auspices of COSO Policy Committee.

Perhaps the most interesting aspect of the report was its conclusion, based on workshops held in collaboration with another Task Force on Alternative Service Delivery, that departments were overly focused on turf protection and positioning, that there was too little genuine collaboration across departments, and that there were insufficient incentives to encourage collaboration. The remedy was multi-faceted. Public servants were to take courses, adopt horizontal perspectives as part of their value system, take up new appointments across departments, and get appraised for their ability to work collaboratively. The emerging policy community was to foster networking, hold more events to discuss issues, and support more professional development. Executives were to serve as models of good collaborative colleagues, recognize horizontal achievements, and ensure that sufficient resources were deployed to support horizontal initiatives. Pilot projects to be identified (under the auspices of

CCDM Policy) and more training opportunities relating to horizontal policy issues were to be developed under the aegis of a Treasury Board Secretariat Advisory Committee. All of this had implications for central agencies: PCO was to anticipate and trouble-shoot on horizontal issues, TBS was to facilitate mobility of executive recruits and incorporate horizontal issues into the learning policy framework under development, the Public Service Commission was to include competencies relating to teamwork and horizontal issues management for promotion in executive ranks, and CCMD was to fold this into its courses and seminar series.

The task force recognized that success depended on deputy ministers: they had to "walk the talk" when dealing within their departments and working with other departments. The task force challenged deputy ministers to inculcate a new culture within their departments by encouraging executive teams to identify horizontal issues (perhaps by designating an ADM to play a lead role in monitoring and challenging the department on such issues), initiate reviews of department programs and initiatives in order to determine the extent of horizontal qualities of programs, and take a government-wide view when proceeding with departmental business. Other suggestions included obtaining input from stakeholders and experts from inside and outside government, encouraging ADMs to join interdepartmental committees, including horizontal activities in departmental appraisals to inform appraisals and promotion decisions and developing training programs and rotational assignments to facilitate horizontality. Finally, deputy ministers were asked to assess whether departments have the capacity to undertake short-term policy analysis and longer-term policy research, and to engage in longer-term anticipatory thinking

In short, while the Task Force report was partly informed by case study information, it focused less on how to better manage specific projects, and more on building a "culture" across the public service that would be conducive to handling horizontal issues and policy initiatives. As the Task Force completed its work, the clerk created the Policy Research Committee, comprised of ADMs and other officials, to undertake the "Canada 2005" scanning exercise, a precursor to the Policy Research Initiative (PRI) and later the Policy Research Secretariat, which reached out across departments and to think tanks and universities, with the Trends Project and other activities.[12] The themes of horizontal policy development were soon echoed in the Annual Reports on the Public Service from the clerk to the prime minister,[13] and the idea of a "borderless institution" became part of the mantra describing federal public service.

The CCMD Roundtable on the Management of Horizontal Issues (2000-01)

The 1996 Task Force report called for a progress report to be prepared two years later in the name of "continual improvement."[14] However, to my knowledge, so such review was undertaken. However, the new president of CCMD initiated a year long Roundtable on the Management of Horizontal Issues in November 1999 to "distill and assess the state of practical experience with managing horizontally in the government of Canada."[15] The Roundtable was led by an associate deputy minister and consisted of ADMs, directors and two academics, supported by a small secretariat CCMD. The group was provided with a review of relevant literature, received written summaries and presentations on case studies of different horizontal projects, organized several consultations with officials in summer and fall 2000, and produced a practical guide for public servants.[16] There was considerable interest among federal public servants on issues of horizontal management, thereby bolstering the work of the roundtable.

The Roundtable arrived at several conclusions. First, not only is each horizontal initiative unique, but their character and associated managerial challenges varies over time. Second, successful horizontal initiatives require leadership, teamwork, and considerable energy by staff to deal with the challenges of working across boundaries, not the least of which is meshing with the vertical system of incentives and accountability of public service systems. Finally, success depends on building trust among partners, securing sufficient financial and human resources, and having champions at the executive level.

The Roundtable made several general practical recommendations for improving the horizontal management of projects, in the following categories:

1. *Mobilizing teams and networks.* Perhaps the most crucial aspect of working horizontally, building teams requires not only strong leadership, but shared leadership that reflects the capabilities of each representative. Despite coming from different organizations, members need to cohere as a team, by developing trust and loyalty though continuous dialogue that focuses on mutual interest, and through rewards and recognition of team accomplishment. All of this must be accomplished while reporting to and serving well their home institutions. It was found that champions at senior levels in home institutions could be crucial to success at critical moments.

2. *Developing a shared framework.* Horizontal initiatives are greatly facilitated when the team develops a common understanding of issues and its own vocabulary, even while relying on "creative ambiguity" if issues are unresolved. Shared frameworks also help to clarify roles and responsibilities, and deal with accountabilities including measuring results. Reconciling collective responsibility of the team with respective accountabilities of governments and departments is difficult to resolve, yet crucial. Difficulties often derive from vertical reporting requirements, and so effort must be made to tailor reporting for a given initiative. Horizontal teams need sufficient resources to support accountability and management requisites, and to undertake business planning and reporting.

3. *Matching support structures to evolving needs.* There is a large menu of structures (formal and informal) available for coordinating horizontal initiatives, and choosing one depends on the tasks at hand and the nature of partner institutions. Too much formal structure and process, particularly early in a process, can suffocate initiatives. It is more important to ensure regular contact and ongoing sharing of information, which helps develop focus and a sense of purpose. Agreements must emerge about how to share resources, create necessary capacities, and make decisions consistent with home institutions. Structures should be allowed to evolve as project demands change, including the possibility of building in a sunset date for the initiative.

4. *Maintaining momentum.* Participants in horizontal initiatives must be prepared for setbacks, turnover in members, evolving needs, and unanticipated challenges. Leaders are thus crucial in motivating the team, facilitating flow of information, chairing productive meetings, meeting deadlines, and supporting members with their home institutions. Due to the lag in achieving goals, a sense of momentum can be generated on the team by celebrating small victories and marketing these accomplishments to home institutions and other stakeholders. Opportunities should be provided for reflection and adjustment.

In contrast to 1996 Task Force, the Roundtable report offers a "bottom-up" view of the progress to date on furthering horizontal initiatives. Pressures for horizontal management have not declined, but "horizontality" is no longer a novel concept. Rather, the focus of the Roundtable was less on how to instil a new culture disposed to horizontal ways of working, and more on how to make horizontal projects work better and to ensure that public servants are better prepared to shoulder such responsibilities in the face of complicated challenges and vertical structures and incentives.

Missing from the analysis, however, was an assessment of how the "system" might increase the ratio of successes to failures, how to reduce exposure to unnecessary risks without dampening innovation, and how to encourage and reward innovation. Perhaps the most telling observation was that "horizontal management still depends too much on heroic individual effort. More support is needed from departments and the system in general." In other words, the challenge is not just to ensure that horizontal teams work better, though this remains critical; it is also about fostering an environment to support the leaders of horizontal initiatives.

Conclusion: Federal Public Service Initiatives in Perspective

Public service leaders in the Canadian government have invested considerable energy in thinking about how to manage horizontally. Indeed, the 1996 Task Force and the 2000 CCMD Roundtable each reflect horizontal, collaborative approaches to dealing with public-service wide issues, relying on deputy ministerial leadership and ADM-level engagement. Although both initiatives were broad in scope, the Canadian government first broached horizontal management with respect to moving forward on government priorities for policy issues. Only later did the horizontal management of a broader set of issues, broadly and deeply understood, get broached. However, despite the promulgation of government-wide key results commitments, relatively little attention has been directed to the question of accountability for performance at this level.

Generally, Ottawa's approach has focused more on altering the culture of public service leaders, as opposed to adopting a new generation of structural solutions, in order to create an environment conducive to facilitating horizontal management. Under this model, cultural change is effected by new leadership exemplars, better training, a broader range of assignments, and appraisal and promotion that recognizes horizontal experience. Whether this choice has proven effective is an entirely different question, and, in the next section, we review the assessments of an influential observer of the government's performance.

Horizontal Management and Accountability: Control and Results

A close observer of developments and progress in public sector reform in Ottawa has been the auditor general of Canada. Under the "value-for-money" precepts it has the mandate to audit how well the Canadian government is progressing with management reforms and reporting. Following the Program Review progress, the government entered into alternative service delivery arrangements across departments, with other governments and partners. This led to a smaller core public service, poorer access to information, and often murkier accountabilities.

The auditor general has asked increasingly tough questions about how well the government manages these arrangements. These questions have also been tied to an abiding interest in results reporting. The auditor general has advocated and collaborated with central agencies to put in place a new Estimates reporting regime as a follow-up to the adoption of the new Expenditure Management System in 1995.[17] The auditor general has emerged as a strong critic of how Ottawa has handled horizontal management, fearing that the government has insufficient control and reporting on these initiatives. In what follows, I review two key reports recently published by the auditor general, but it should be noted that these reports draw on a larger set of audits.

Perspectives on Collaborative Government

In his 1999 report the auditor general noted the trend towards "collaborative government" by the Liberal government and observed that they could be "an innovative, cost-effective and efficient way of delivering programs and services."[18] However, the existence of more alternative service delivery arrangements, and the promise of more to come, led the auditor general to worry about more risk to taxpayers and the public. Since the government is typically only one of several partners in such arrangements, the auditor general saw increased potential for the diffusing of accountability to Parliament. The rationale of the report was to provide a guide on how to better participate and manage the risks in collaborative arrangements and to provide a checklist of questions to inform scrutiny of these arrangements by Parliamentarians.[19]

Interestingly, the auditor general chose not to review collaborative arrangements with other governments, conventional contractual arrangements, grants and contributions, or arm's length organizations – the test was that decisions and oversight had to be jointly managed with another federal departments. The programs used as examples included the Infrastructure Canada Works, the Model Forests program, the National Action Program on Climate Change, the Labour Force Development Agreements, the Canadian Industry Program for Energy Conservation, and the North American Waterfowl Protection Plan. Although not stated explicitly, in carrying out the study, the auditor general set a low threshold: one would expect that collaborative arrangements would more likely be better managed *among* federal departments and agencies.

The auditor general reviewed the challenges inherent in managing collaborative arrangements, noting that they are more challenging to manage then conventional programs because:

1. a vision and effective leadership among several partners had to be developed;

2. there is more complexity since each partner has their own goals, interests, authorities, administrative styles, and accountabilities;

3. coordination costs are relatively higher and there is greater potential for conflict, and these in turn require more capacity to manage; and

4. building trust and confidence are essential ingredients for collaboration, and take time.

The auditor general seems to have developed a reasonable view of the challenge confronting those who manage such arrangements, but for the same reasons he anticipates much greater risks.

In developing a framework for assessing collaborative arrangements, the auditor general relied on lessons learned from previous audits and built in around the themes of serving the public interest, developing effective accountability arrangements and greater transparency. While the report goes into greater details concerning examples and best practices, for our purposes it is best to review the summary questions prepared by the auditor general:

Serving the Public Interest

- Are objectives being met?
- Is the collaborative arrangement the best way to do it?
- Is serving the public interest being given appropriate emphasis?
- Are public service values being maintained?

Effective Accountability Arrangements

- Are the objectives, the expected level of performance and results and the operating conditions agreed to clear?
- Are the authorities, roles and responsibilities of each partner clear?
- Are the expectations for each partner balanced with its capacities?
- Can performance be measured ad credibly reported to Parliament and the public?
- Has adequate provision been made for review, program evaluation and audit?

Greater Transparency

- Have the information needs of those affected been recognized?
- Is appropriate and sufficient information being disclosed to Parliament and the public?

All of these questions seem very reasonable, and the implication is that, if several cannot be answered, the government either should not have entered in the collaborative arrangement in the first place, or should invest considerable energy in improving its administrative regime. The problem, though, is that the auditor general believes that these questions should be answered at the *outset* of collaborative arrangements, and yet everything we know about horizontal initiatives suggests that they take time and much dialogue to establish. Providing complete answers to all of these questions would be a tall order for programs solely based in departments, even if political sensitivities were not an issue. Moreover, these initiatives tend to evolve significantly over time, and different partners may have varying confidentiality needs where information is concerned. It is presumed that Parliamentarians, the public, and the media clamour for this information, and yet the evidence to date suggests this is not the case.[20]

Given the inherent challenges of developing and implementing horizontal initiatives, the criteria actually raises the bar higher than for traditional programs because the transaction costs to secure agreements and information are necessarily greater – not only does the auditor general argue that departments have the same reporting obligations to Parliament, but they should also ensure that partners can live up to these reporting standards as well. Although he does not invoke this phrase, what the auditor general places paramount emphasis on is "control" as opposed to the flexibility required for innovation and management.

Horizontal Initiatives and Results Reporting

The latest contribution from the auditor general was released in early 2001, not long after the return of Parliament following a federal election.[21] Among the 18 chapters released at this time was a report that, interestingly, focused jointly on the progress that the government had made on department results reporting and, more specifically, on the challenges with respect to reporting results on horizontal issues.

There is no need to review, in detail, the history of the auditor general's involvement with the introduction of results reporting in Ottawa. Suffice to say that the Office was closely involved in the pilot projects and the eventual rollout of new Estimates documents, including department plans and performance reports since 1997 under the Improved Reporting to Parliament project. The December 2000 report is best understood as an audit of the progress made to date. While the auditor observed that departments had embraced results reporting, he raised concern about the extent to which it is actually utilized for the purposes of accountability, monitoring, and planning by departments and central agencies. The auditor believes that the government and departments fail to clearly set out expected results, that program evaluation is insufficiently used, and calls for the government to move beyond a "persistent state of planning" for results reporting.[22] The Treasury Board ministers and its secretariat are singled out for insufficient leadership in moving results reporting to the next level by sharing information and practices across departments.

The more interesting part of the chapter focuses on the auditor general's interest in how results are managed when the government is involved in horizontal issues. The report notes that many recent commitments of the Canadian government require horizontal policy coordination and implementation, notes recent initiatives of the Alberta government to raise as higher priorities selected horizontal issues, and refers directly to the recommendations of the 1996 Task Force report *Managing Horizontal Policy Issues*. With respect to the latter, the auditor reminds the government of its call for an accountability framework, consultation with stakeholders, setting realistic expectations for complex projects, providing sufficient resources, offering incentives and rewards for such activities, and the importance of evaluation and other information-sharing.

The purpose of the audit was to explore how results are used as a management tool in horizontal initiatives and the impediments to their use. This was done by reviewing three case studies – the Family Violence Initiative, the Disability Agenda, and the Canadian Rural Partnership – as well as drawing on other work done by the Office. Once again, the auditor focused on initiatives that tended to involve only federal departments and not other levels of government, and assessed them with respect to (1) coordination and management structures, (2) leadership from senior officials, (3) accountability frameworks, and (4) reporting frameworks.

While the auditor recognizes that informal coordination may be less burdensome and more productive, it is clear that he prefers structured coordination revolving around shared frameworks, roles, responsibilities, and decision-making protocols, and that all of this is connected to a defined government strategy. This requires identifying a lead department and providing dedicated staff support to the initiative. The auditor observes that coordination takes considerable time and energy to achieve, often longer than expected, which poses a challenge for results reporting. Like the 1996 Task Force, the auditor calls for strong executive champions of these initiatives, which helps with securing resources and supporting managers.

The auditor noted that formalizing accountability frameworks is useful for more complex undertakings, particularly with regard to securing financial or other support for initiatives that are not funded centrally. While incentives and tools are necessary to achieve success, the auditor argues that horizontal managers usually do not have access to these tools and therefore central agencies need to play a greater role.

The most critical remarks, however, come with respect to results reporting. On the basis of the cases examined, the auditor concludes that little reporting of results has occurred with the three horizontal initiatives, in part because each partner institution has different reporting regimes, and in part because in takes time to develop a credible collective results regime for such initiatives. He also noted that partners in such initiatives resist developing detailed frameworks, results and other information. The auditor, of course, called for more systematic reporting for horizontal initiatives because there is insufficient knowledge of the actual costs of delivering these programs from the home departments. Due to turnover, the auditor worried that there was insufficient institutional memory that could provide lessons for the next incarnation of these initiatives and from the experience of other horizontal initiatives. Finally, despite acknowledging that TBS had taken leadership in identifying and supporting horizontal initiatives, the auditor worries that not all initiatives receive appropriate scrutiny because many do not secure funds or approvals through the submission process, and that TBS approaches horizontal initiatives in a "piecemeal" manner. The auditor calls for TBS to adopt a strong central leadership and a more strategic approach, to ensure that the resources are made available to ensure that proper coordination and reporting of results takes place, and to facilitate the sharing of lessons and best practices

Like the report *Collaborative Government*, Chapter 20 on results and horizontal issues sets out clear markers for the government, public sector leaders, and managers. The auditor general indicates what questions it will ask and what standards it will invoke when reviewing horizontal initiatives. While possessing a shared view of the difficulties of managing horizontal files, the tenor and emphasis of the auditor general is clear: there must be much more of an emphasis on transparency and results reporting, and strong central leadership and support for these initiatives.

Beyond Culture and Control: The Capacity Argument

While the focus of deputy ministers has been on changing the culture of the public service and removing barriers in support of horizontal initiatives, the emphasis of the auditor general has been on ensuring accountability, reporting of results, and strong central leadership. We should not be surprised, of course, that the auditor general and the government are odds over a complex challenge like horizontal governance given their respective institutional histories and interests, even though there seems to be a common understanding of what challenges managers have to overcome when working across boundaries.

Here I want to consider whether or not there is some common ground between these respective lenses on horizontal management. Let me simply assert that the government, deputy ministers, the auditor general, *and* working managers have a common interest in ensuring the appropriate capacities and resources are dedicated to horizontal initiatives. A common complaint from the managers of these projects – even if they have not yet been subjected to more onerous reporting requirements – is that they find themselves managing horizontal projects "off the corner of their desks" and find it difficult to secure attention from department executive teams and the centre, unless they qualify as a high-profile initiative.

The question is where and how should such capacities be installed? The auditor general clearly believes that the Treasury Board Secretariat should take a more active role in this regard, and provide greater oversight and support. However, one premise I outlined earlier in this chapter suggests that the sheer number of horizontal initiatives could easily overwhelm central agencies, if only because of their diversity. Moreover, as the 1996 Deputy Minister report suggests, some departments or other central agencies may be better positioned to take the lead responsibility depending on the project. Although the CCMD Roundtable did not have as part of its mandate responsibility for proposing how central agencies could create a more supportive environment for horizontal initiatives, some follow-up work did proceed.

What follows are my own suggestions about how to strengthen "system support" of horizontal initiatives. The suggestions are as follows:

1. *Support a training program on horizontal management.* CCMD, the Learning Network, and Training and Development Canada should collaborate to create courses (some distanced-based) for leaders and staff involved in managing horizontal issues. They would build on the literature, case studies, and the reports produced and collected by the Roundtable. If possible, participants should be encouraged and supported to write up detailed accounts of the projects they managed, and add to the corpus of practitioner knowledge on horizontal management. This is a recommendation of the 1996 Task Force that has not been actively pursued.

2. *Support a network or mentoring program on horizontal management.* The Roundtable succeeded in identifying several cases and a network of people with considerable expertise on horizontal management. This network could be galvanized for two purposes. First, the training program proposed above should be closely aligned with a network of individuals who have relevant experience in managing horizontal projects. Some of them could be called on to teach courses, serve as guest lecturers, or be advisors to students in courses, who are developing strategies or new skills. Second, the network would stand ready for individuals seeking advice on horizontal projects, but who are not taking training courses.

3. *Develop a central reserve/capacity to support and recognize horizontal initiatives.* The reserve could be accessed by managers of horizontal projects (or their champions) in order to provide limited-term assistance for staff support for stretched managers and performance pay for managers and their teams. Applications for "investment" support could be vetted through either a CCDM committee or TBS Advisory Committee. The program would be handled within TBS by a small Horizontal Management Secretariat (HMS), perhaps adjacent to the office serving the Federal Regional Councils. HMS would also provide advisory support and/or connect managers to members of the proposed network. Receipt of funding would trigger reporting requirements consistent with TBS/OAG guidelines (which would have to be streamlined) and keep policy-makers informed about horizontal challenges.

4. *Matching machinery to specific horizontal management challenges.* The list of candidates to take the lead on horizontal initiatives is long: regional councils, headquarters or regional operations in departments, central agencies, Coordinating Committee of Senior Officials, the Treasury Board in its capacity as management board, intergovernmental affairs units, etc. My sense is that some leaders of federal regional councils worry about taking on more responsibility in this regard, even though they have key facilitating roles, largely

because they want to maintain their brokerage and advisory bodies.[23] Each horizontal initiative emerges for unique reasons, and the candidates for oversight should vary accordingly. The goal should be to connect the managers of new horizontal initiatives with the right mentors, and to inform them of training, knowledge, and financial resources that could be at their disposal.

5. *Communications and educating executives and their managers.* Enhancing system supports will not achieve its full potential if managers with horizontal challenges are unaware of their existence and of the expectations promulgated by TBS/OAG. Accordingly, the HMS would have responsibility for ongoing communication of these expectations and resources. Much of this can be accomplished through other institutions, programs, and courses, but the secretariat should constantly remind executives and managers alike of these expectations and resources. Recognition awards are also a means for accomplishing this objective.

6. *Encouraging better reporting and accountability.* The recent interest of the auditor general and the Treasury Board in better managing horizontal and collaborative projects has led to a long checklist of good practices and reporting requirements. However, to busy front-line managers, such checklists are often daunting and inevitably compete with other demands on their time. This does not lessen the importance of those practices and requirements, but suggests that HMS find ways to assist managers in meeting those expectations in realistic ways. This might include developing templates and other tools that can be readily applied and adapted by busy managers and their partner organizations.

7. *Enhancing existing recognition programs.* Great strides have been made by the government and the leaders of the federal public service to recognize exemplary work and innovative management practices, and many horizontal projects undoubtedly have been celebrated. However, perhaps a new category should be created to recognize horizontal initiatives, if one does not already exist; this is simply a question of aligning rhetoric with the reality of horizontal challenges. Moreover, the proposed Horizontal Management Secretariat would be ideally positioned to administer recognition awards for best practices in this area.

These initiatives have been presented in an integrated manner, with linkages built in across them, as elements of an overarching strategy. However, each could be de-coupled from the others and proceed as an independent initiative. The proposals noted above are mutually reinforcing, but they are not predicated on any one model of engagement. Each horizontal initiative will emerge in very different ways, requiring different kinds of support, and leaders and champions could seek out or be advised to tap into "system" supports in myriad ways.

Central to the "integrated" strategy outlined above is establishing a Horizontal Management Secretariat (HMS) in the Treasury Board Secretariat. This is properly conceived as a focal point and liasing capacity on these matters. It would work with central agencies and advisory entities to develop training programs, to review candidates and identify priorities for "investment" support and mentoring contacts. It would have the primary responsibility for communications, web site development, general advice, reporting assistance, and recognition programs associated with horizontal initiatives.

A Speculative Conclusion: Possible Futures for Horizontal Management

Rather than review the main arguments of this paper, I would like to conclude on a more speculative note and encourage discussion. What does the future hold in store for horizontal management? This paper began by reviewing several trends in public sector governance that have been leading the Canadian government to think more carefully about how to improve horizontal management. By now, these trends are familiar to the reader:

- Increasing complexity, interdependence
- Increasing demands for better service
- Pace of technological change continues
- Increasing demands for accountability and results reporting
- Political and policy conflict will continue

All of this points to increasing demands for collaborative governance, and hence continuing and even accelerating interest in ensuring that the skills and supports for fostering better horizontal management of issues are in place.

However, relying on trends is not a useful way to think about the key contingencies that might affect horizontal management. One creative and stimulating way to think about the future is to develop plausible scenarios; scenario-builders do so by making a distinction between trends and critical uncertainties.[24] Here I would like to suggest that, generally, the most critical uncertainties confronting public sector managers with respect to grappling with horizontal issues have to do with the political environment in which such activity proceeds.

One critical uncertainty involves the nature of discourse on policy issues that straddle boundaries within and across governments – it easy to imagine that governments might descend into more turf-oriented debates, or they could respond by developing more collaborative approaches. The other uncertainty has to do with whether citizens take a greater or lesser interest in the policy regimes that guide policy development and service delivery. One can surmise that citizens, if buffered from the real work of our governments by technology and intermediaries, will have decreasing knowledge of how public services are delivered. Conversely, they might develop a better understanding due to better access to information on the performance of governments and become an important source of pressure for greater coordination across institutions.

Figure 1   Four Different Future Environments for Horizontal Management

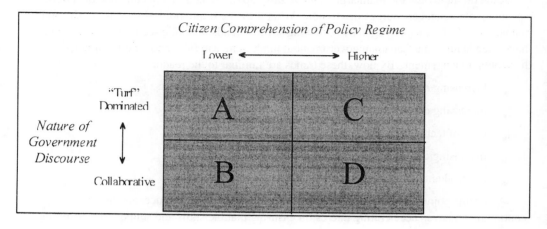

When these possibilities are combined, one can conceive of horizontal management proceeding in four very different environments, illustrated in Figure 1. Public service managers would contend with all the trends identified above in each scenario, but what would change is the amount of "system support" for middle managers as project leaders of horizontal initiatives:

- Scenario A suggests a future where governments openly and continually squabble and citizens become more detached about how governments deliver services. Deputy ministers would focus more on securing strategic and tactical advantage in a federal system, and less on supporting collaborative initiatives. This would not put an end to horizontal management, but rather it portends uphill struggles for those who are tasked with leading those initiatives or who advocate bottom-up horizontal solutions to policy and service challenges.

- Scenario B indicates a future where citizens either ignore or take for granted the policy and service regimes of governments, but ministers and public sector executives attach considerable importance to well-managed programs and utilizing resources across their agencies and levels of governments as effectively as possible. In such a climate, there may not be strong, explicit public demand for horizontal initiatives, but a new spirit of professionalism emerges that not only encompasses horizontal precepts, but also supplies sufficient moral and other forms of support to such initiatives.

- Scenario C promises a future where more discerning citizens develop increasingly better knowledge and higher expectations about policy and programs, but become frustrated with insufficiently collaborative governments. Public servants become more frustrated because they cannot fully respond to citizen demands and implement new ideas, partly because they do not receive requisite support but also because there are few incentives for ministers and public service executives to lend support for such initiatives.

- Scenario D augers for considerable public sector demand and government support for effective horizontal initiatives. To be sure, this would invite greater scrutiny of the performance of public sector managers, but it would also lead to more supports, such as training and investment capital, and attention in the form of oversight and mentorship, all directed to ensuring that horizontal initiatives succeed.

This exploration of scenarios is only exploratory and suggestive, and could be greatly enriched with more extensive and layered analysis. For example, the health of relationships between governments and other sectors may not be the only force that either promotes or militates against collaborative and horizontal government. Indeed, the prospects for the extent to which public sector managers can proceed with horizontal initiatives and secure necessary guidance and support may have a lot to do with how prime ministers organize and manage their cabinets. If supportive and collegial cultures do not emerge at this level, the leaders of central agencies and operating departments alike will struggle mightily to collaborate, even if they believe it to be a prudent course of action. More generally, how cabinets function and are led can have significant implications for intergovernmental relations,[25] and the prospects for collaborative and horizontal government.

In short, although the trends and challenges confronting governments in all jurisdictions point to increasing need for better horizontal management, scenario-based speculation suggests that the ability of governments to develop cultures, exercise control, and provide sufficient support for better managing horizontal initiatives may vary dramatically. This, of course, does not mean that public sector leaders and central agencies should not find ways, regardless of which future might unfold, to better support horizontal management. But it does suggest that, along with anticipating the highly idiosyncratic and evolutionary nature of horizontal initiatives, public sector leaders should recognize that the trends may manifest themselves differently at the system level and thus provide very different opportunity sets for managers grappling with these issues.

Notes

[1] Many of the examples of horizontal initiatives and some of the insights presented in this paper derived from my participation in the Roundtable on the Management of Horizontal Issues, which proceeded under the auspices of the Canadian Centre for Management Development during the year 2000. The roundtable deliberations culminated in Mark Hopkins, Chantal Couture, and Elizabeth Moore, *Moving From the Heroic to the Everyday: Lessons Learned from Leading Horizontal Projects* (Ottawa: Canadian Centre for Management Development Roundtable on the Management of Horizontal Initiatives, 2001). The report can also be found at http://www.ccmd-ccg.gc.ca/pdfs/horinz_rt_e.pdf. However, the views presented in this paper are mine alone and do not represent the views of Roundtable members or the Government of Canada.

[2] For similar summaries and other examples, see *Moving From the Heroic*, pp.43-48, 55-61.

[3] See Jacques Bourgault and Rene Lapierre, *Horizontality and Public Management* (Ottawa: Canadian Centre for Management Development, December 2000).

[4] Canadian Centre for Management Development, "Horizontal Management: Issues, Insights, and Illustrations – A Background Paper" (Draft for Discussion – no date, c.2000).

[5] See Guy Peters, *Managing Horizontal Government: The Politics of Coordination*, Research Paper No. 21 (Ottawa: Canadian Centre for Management Development, January 1998); and Mark Sproule-Jones, "Horizontal management: implementing programs across interdependent organizations," *Canadian Public Administration*, 43, no.1 (Spring 2000), pp.93-109.

[6] John English and Evert Lindquist, *Performance Management: Linking Results to Public Debate*, New Directions Series, No.2 (Toronto: Institute of Public Administration of Canada, 1998).

[7] Canada, *Report of the Task Force on the Management of Horizontal Policy Issues* (Ottawa: Privy Council Office and Canadian Centre for Management Development, 1996).

[8] Peters, *Managing Horizontal Government*.

[9] See *Moving From the Heroic*.

[10] See Luc Juillet, "The Federal Regional Councils and Horizontal Governance," a report prepared for the Federal Regional Councils and the Treasury Board Secretariat (Ottawa: Canadian Centre for Management Development, Sept. 15, 2000) at http://www.ccmd-ccg.gc.ca/pdfs/Horiz-RegionalCouncils-REV.PDF.

[11] See Bourgault and Lapierre.

[12] Herman Bakvis, "Rebuilding Policy Capacity in the Era of the Fiscal Dividend," *Governance*, 13, no.1 (January 2000), pp.71-103.

[13] For example, see Jocelyne Bourgon, *Fifth Annual Report to the Prime Minister on The Public Service of Canada* (Ottawa: Privy Council Office, 1998).

[14] Canada, *Report of the Task Force on the Management of Horizontal Policy Issues*, p.31.

[15] The roundtable was part of a larger initiative; three others were established that year on The Learning Organization, Risk Management, and the Social Union Framework.

[16] The work of the Roundtable was inductive, rooted in the experience of colleagues with recent horizontal experience. This stands in contrast to the deductive approach employed by Sproule-Jones, "Horizontal management," which is a very promising avenue for future research.

[17] Evert A. Lindquist, "Getting Results Right: Reforming Ottawa's Estimates," in Leslie A. Pal, ed., *How Ottawa Spends 1998-99: Balancing Act: The Post-Deficit Mandate* (Toronto: Oxford University Press, 1998), pp.153-190.

[18] Auditor General of Canada, "Collaborative Arrangements: Issues for the Federal Government," Chapter 5 in *Report of the Auditor General of Canada to the House of Commons,* Volume 1, April 1999 (Ottawa: Minister of Public Works and Government Services Canada, 1999).

[19] Ibid., pp.7-9.

[20] Lindquist, "Getting Results Right."

[21] See Auditor General of Canada, "Managing Departments for Results and Managing Horizontal Issues for Results," Chapter 20 in *Report of the Auditor General of Canada to the House of Commons,* Volume 3, December 2000 (Ottawa: Minister of Public Works and Government Services Canada, 2000).

[22] Ibid., p.25.

[23] See Juillet, "The Federal Regional Councils and Horizontal Governance."

[24] See Kees van der Heijden, "Scenario Thinking About the Future," in Steven A. Rosell, *Changing Maps: Governing in a World of Change* (Ottawa: Carleton University Press, 1995), pp.147-162; and Kees van der Heijden, *Scenarios: The Art of Strategic Conversation* (New York: Wiley, 1996).

[25] See the seminal article, J. Stefan Dupre, "The Workability of Executive Federalism in Canada," in Herman Bakvis and William Chandler, eds., *Federalism and the Role of the State* (Toronto: University of Toronto Press, 1987), pp.236-58.

Commentary

Dr Michael Keating, Research School of Social Sciences, Australian National University

Now that I'm no longer the head of a coordinating department the rebel in me is tempted to try and make out the case for less coordination. I mean that quite seriously. As Evert just said, coordination is expensive. It occupies people. But, more than that, it is expensive in the sense that it can operate to stultify initiative, responsiveness and flexibility. So I think we do need to consider seriously the case for coordination.

My worry is that too often coordination is being used as an instrument for central agencies, particularly to get involved in other people's business without very much thought as to the reason why. That is why I very much identify, Evert, with your comment about horizontal management; that it is a matter of trying to mobilise capacity and capabilities to achieve specific goals. I think that is important, whether we are talking about horizontal management or coordination, we do need to think about what it is exactly we are trying to achieve.

To my mind it means that the way you approach coordination should depend upon the nature of the problem or the issue at hand. Fundamentally I think what you are after with coordination is a degree of consistency, and I think, Jenny, you said that. I also think you put the emphasis on consistency of outcomes. I agree with that, and think we ought to be a bit more flexible by allowing a variety of means or methods. But it is important to think about what it is you are trying to get consistency about, at what level, and your approach to coordination ought to take that into account from the outset.

For what it is worth, while I have not heard the auditor general for Canada speak for himself, I think if the questions were posed in that dimension then he might need to shift his position somewhat. But we could pursue that further, if you wish.

Let me say a few words about coordination of policy formulation, one end of the spectrum, and a few words about coordination at the policy implementation service delivery level at the other end of the spectrum. I think it is fair to say, Jenny, you mainly focussed on policy formulation in your comments. I recognise the four types that you had there. For what it is worth, I just say I do not see a big difference between what I think you call "traditional" and "strategic." I think they shade into each other. But the other two, which is the significance of ideas as a coordinating mechanism and networking as a coordinating mechanism, I think they are very worthwhile contributions.

I would like to take a minute just to talk about cabinet. If you read Evert's paper, the conclusion of the paper does bring out the importance of cabinet as a coordinating mechanism. Cabinet is a very long and tried mechanism for coordination dating back, at least in Britain, for over 150 years now. And I think the point that Evert was making in his paper at the end is that cabinet has an enormous influence on the approach taken by actors below the cabinet level. If you think of cabinet as the pinnacle of policy formulation, it influences very heavily the approach taken by the various departments who report to the ministers, who are members of cabinet. I would take the view that the development of cabinet as a system of government in the last 20 years now allows it to perform that coordination task better than it did, say, 40 years ago, which is as far back as my firsthand memory goes of the Public Service.

The cabinet processes have improved. They have been more formalised. And, by the way, Jenny, this was a key part of the management performance reforms – something we again can take up, if you wish. The fundamental endeavour is to ensure that there are no surprises, that when a minister goes into cabinet he's not going to get ambushed in some way, or she's not going to get ambushed in some way or another. I wouldn't want to say for a moment that that never happens, but I think it is less likely to happen than it used to be.

I won't go through all the details of those particular reforms, but let me just conclude on this point, that I agree with Evert that you can have all the rules you like, but how well they are observed depends fundamentally on the prime minister of the day. His department can assist him in enforcing the rules but, in the end, he has to back them up.

The other element of cabinet I want to refer to is some of the developments in budget making. Now, I accept that coordination isn't only about budget making but it is an important part of where priorities are brought together, and I think there have been quite significant improvements there. The one I want to refer to in particular is the notion of what we might call "financial envelopes." Canada had some experience of this back in the 1970s. We were terribly interested in Canada's experience then, but I think in the end we thought it was not working.

I say that our more modest attempt at financial envelopes has worked on the whole. Essentially what happens is the government identifies that here is a cross-cutting problem – if that is the right piece of jargon – which they want to elevate to a priority. They are going to do something about it. And they recognise that there are, say, several ministries that need to be involved. We'll call it an "innovation statement," because the prime minister had one recently. And while I have no knowledge of how they did it, my hunch is that the way this statement was put together has not changed much from when I was around. In practice there is a degree of iteration between the proponents of the policy package and the rest of cabinet as to broadly how much ought to be spent on it. But the relevant ministers who are directly involved then meet to work out a coordinated response. At the end of the day they are delegated a fair amount of authority to determine the priorities within the agreed budget for the package.

Now, that system is used more or less exclusively for high priority problems spanning more than one ministry. Working Nation was done that way. The former Labor government also had an innovation statement that was developed that way, and one could proliferate the examples. That seems to me a very good way of, if you like, getting trade-offs and priorities coordinated by getting ministers and their senior officials working together. And I do not recall that more than 20 years ago. In fact, I do not recall it even less than 20 years ago.

Another device I just mention is where the taskforces are put together. I think there are a number of reasons why taskforces are meant to be more productive than IDCs, and I think Meredith has elaborated this in her recent book. But one of the things I would mention is much more attention to the terms of reference, because when terms of reference are extremely general, like "fix the drug problem IDC," there can be enormous scope for debate about what you ought to be doing. Whereas, if the government is prepared to lay down the terms of reference rather more specifically the public servants will get on and do the job.

An example I just quoted is the setting up of ANTA, which was a commonwealth/state initiative. ANTA, for those who do not know, is the Australian National Training Authority. Essentially the commonwealth wanted to get involved more directly in training. It initially made a bid to take over training from the states. Surprise, surprise, the states wanted the money but they did not want to give up the power and there could have been a turf war forever. But in the end the COAG ministerial council basically wrote pretty specific terms of reference that instructed the heads of the commonwealth and state departments to go away and fix it. The public servants could not have a theological debate about what ANTA should do or it shouldn't do. Instead we were instructed to work together to produce a unified training system for Australia.

Finally, just a few words on coordination at what I'll call the policy formulation level. In Australia when I joined the Public Service, which is now over 40 years ago, I was told by my then departmental head about how my career should progress until I retired at 65, which I still have not reached. But essentially the assumption was that I, like everybody else, would remain in that department for the rest of my working life, which would continue to age 65. It was unheard of for people to transfer from departments, and if you ever did leave your department you were blackballed by it.

Now today the culture is quite different because there is an attempt to rotate people, move them around. At the senior levels it is quite deliberate. I mean, people are identified their personal development would be improved by being moved around. At the level of departmental head it is quite unusual for someone to be appointed head of the department that they are currently working in. And that does change the culture of tribal loyalty to your department, come what may. In my view the ethos of the services has changed enormously, precisely for that reason.

Let me now turn to service delivery. The point has been made already, and I hesitate to say it again, that we have shifted from that bureaucratic approach of same treatment for all and that the focus is now much more on outcomes. I believe that should ease the accountability problem. In the end I think it is quite appropriate that governments set standards of what they expect to be achieved in terms of outcome and monitor performance in terms of those standards. But you can have quite a lot of flexibility in terms of means, so long as they can be defended in terms of due process.

I'll skip over a couple of points about IT and how centralising it is, Jenny. I personally consider that IT, on balance, has enabled an enormous amount of devolution because it allows people at the top, who are ultimately responsible and who are going to be saddled with accountability, to devolve a lot of decision-making whilst still keeping track of what is going on. They can then meet their responsibilities accordingly.

Centrelink as a one-stop-shop is a device for coordination, as has already been mentioned by Jenny. It is interesting in the case of Centrelink that I asked them, "How do you choose when two departments are asking you to deal with their program or problem first? You have got to please one. You cannot please the other." Centrelink tell me they have worked out what they call a hierarchy of programs, which is agreed by the various departments, and it tells them which department's program they should use in relation to each specific case. They have different hierarchies for different situations. But they have confronted this issue and they have a set of rules that are conveyed to the staff.

I want finally just to say something about purchaser/provider models and, perhaps more importantly, case management. My fundamental contention would be that coordination for service delivery is best done at the lowest level possible. I do not believe with the best will in the world you can coordinate service delivery from here in Canberra or Ottawa. I could agree with my counterpart – another head of department – that our two departments will work closely together, but often nothing happens on the ground in my experience. Jim's probably got the same view when he was minister.

The advantage of case management is that you put someone to work with the client to coordinate the set of services that each client wants and best meets their particular needs. And I would contend that approach is working for Job Network, notwithstanding some comments earlier today that it is not.

But let me give you another example: health services for those people who have serious ongoing health problems that require multiple services. They represent about 10 percent of the population and a significantly higher proportion of health expenditure. There have been trials going on, which I would regard as quite promising, that involve case management for these people. However, for that case management to work the dollars have to be appropriated in the end to the case manager or the client and not to the service provider. The service provider then finds it very much in their interest to cooperate, because if they do not cooperate their services won't be bought. That sort of coordination I think is probably the way to go with service delivery. Thanks.

Discussion

Chair: Professor Patrick Weller, Director, Centre for Australian Public Sector Management, Griffith University, Australia

DAVID GOOD: No one is talking about coordination without a coordinator. We are talking about coordination with a coordinator. It is a bit like the potluck supper. In coordination without a coordinator you may end up with a lot of desserts and no appetizers and the appetizers, if they arrive, come too late.

The strategic question in the system becomes: whom do you ask to be the coordinator? What is the capacity within governments to have multiple coordinators, depending upon what they want to achieve? Do you pick the guardians? Do you pick the spenders? Do you pick certain individuals, certain ministers and certain situations? It seems to me that the capacity to say in certain situations, "Yes, we want the prime minister's office to coordinate this" or, "we want the department of finance to do it" or, "we have a strong social policy capacity and let's let that agency coordinate it" or, "in delivery we have very strong local capacity, let's let that do it" is very important. There must be the capacity within the corporate structure of a government to do the horizontal coordination that is required.

RICHARD CURTAIN: Evert, has there been any attention given to the question of how you measure coordination and horizontal policy making? If, in fact, people are going to be rewarded for doing it, how is it actually measured?

JIM CARLTON: Professor Lindquist at the beginning of his remarks raised the question as to whether the term "horizontal management" was useful. By the end of his presentation and the description of a lot of taskforces and round tables, I came to the conclusion tentatively, without re-reading the full paper and the comments of the auditor general, that it would be better to spend more time working out how to manage the various policy problems that come up – the design of policy, the implementation of policy, of which horizontal coordination is an inevitable part in everything you do and always has been.

I have managed in private, public, NGO sectors. As I understand it horizontal management is the kind of coordination you need, regardless of whether you are doing it within one department that has sub-departments, whether you are doing it across departments, whether you are doing it across states, or federally, it is always there. To single it out as an object of study or being something particularly new strikes me as a very rank waste of time.

I have started reading Meredith Edwards' case study book on development and implementation of policy within the Commonwealth Public Service. While reading about how they got through cabinet certain quite important structural changes, I do not recall the word "horizontal management" being used in the text. Maybe it was, but as an automatic process of coordinating both the policy development, the consultation, the getting it through cabinet, the implementation, and the evaluation. Each one of those involved coordination of one sort or another. The requirements of coordination in each were different and particular to the problem.

In response to your original query as to how valuable the concept was, I came out thinking that maybe I will forget it and go back to worrying about how you actually solve problems, how you recommend policy, how you get policy accepted by cabinet and how you implement it, coordinate it and evaluate it.

PAT BARRETT: Why is this an issue at the commonwealth level? It is an issue of devolution of authority and the tensions associated with principles-based legislation, which makes it clear that individual agency heads are responsible for what happens in their agencies. While we have always recognised there has been coordination, the fact is that there are now tensions when you have shared responsibilities. Who is actually accountable? That is where the tension arises.

In a purchaser/provider situation there is even more tension, and the notion of contracts or agreements between agencies in themselves are points of tension that are not being satisfactorily resolved. That is why you have this issue of horizontal management. I do not care what you call it, but the fact is we have a tension and that needs to be resolved. The private sector model focuses very much on the institution. You might ask, "What does corporate governance mean if you have shared responsibilities?" It comes back to who is the coordinator and who is responsible and where is the shared responsibility.

There are performance contracts for individuals. Tony Blair in the UK is talking about how he will manage this for a joined up government. There will be a clause in the performance contract that says "How much did you contribute to joined up government?" I'll leave it at that.

JOHN HALLIGAN: My question follows on from Pat's because this process of reviewing horizontal management seems very typically Canadian, in so far as they were among the first to identify this as a problem. They spent a lot of time investigating it, but the follow through does not seem to have registered a great deal of change. This led me to make a comparison with the UK, where they have developed a range of mechanisms for following through on joined up government. It has been driven more politically. They have certainly been focusing rather more on the implementation end. Interestingly, the big debate when I was there later last year was what had happened to cabinet, because there seemed to be less reliance on cabinet as a central mechanism for coordination and direction. How significant is the lack of the results focus in the Canadian context? This reflects Pat's point about there being a lack of edge – a lack of an incentive to require people to deliver on these things.

Finally, I was interested in your range of capacity building devices, because they seem to be a mixture of culture, control and structure, and a very judicious one.

JENNY STEWART: I'll address the question about who is to be the coordinator. I agree, that is an important question to answer, but only if you see coordination as being a form of control. I would argue that that is just one variety of the genus. If you are going to seek coordination as a form of control then it has to be clear in advance whose values are to dominate in the given policy or even delivery situation.

Secondly, the nominated coordinator has to have sufficient clout to make the control stick. If neither of those two conditions is met there can be some rather egregious problems. Consider the National Greenhouse Office, over which the Australian federal government was to have some sort of coordinative role in relation to the devising of the federal government's response to greenhouse issues. But those two conditions I mentioned were conspicuously not met and that organisation has faded from the scene.

There is some merit in the sort of institutionalist focus here, which sees coordination as more an emergent quality of a structure and a system rather than something that is imposed upon it. I'm particularly attracted to the idea of appropriate incentives in that context.

Your performance agreement might specify: "What have you done during the term of this agreement to bring about joined up government?" In some ways, having to report on that might even kill the impetus towards it. That is a very significant issue. At the moment, at whatever level you talk about, particularly possibly at the lower and middle levels of organisations, the incentives seem to me to be very much aimed towards pleasing superiors and towards meeting performance criteria which are always seen as emanating from the top. So, local heroes notwithstanding, what incentives are there for you to try and relate your activities to those of other agencies which you know very well are operating in your field?

It seems to me that government has quite a bit of capacity when it comes to that control sort of coordination. We still need to find appropriate cultures, to develop appropriate cultures, and to bring about more consistency of outcome. Maybe we are just talking about an operational kind of compromise that will do for the time, given that values are so diverse in many of these areas.

EVERT LINDQUIST: First, on the issue of who coordinates, I do not think there can be one answer. Ultimately, it is the judgment of prime minister's office and the secretary to cabinet and, in the case of Canada, the Committee of Senior Officials (COSO), as to who should take the lead on a high-priority horizontal initiative. Moreover, the responsibility for leading a horizontal initiative could change over time.

Second, the question of how we can measure coordination and horizontal policy-making is very interesting, and very complicated. Let me suggest that how one attempts to measure for the purposes of reward will depend on whether or not the focus is on the progress of the project as opposed to personal performance or the evolution of the larger organisation. In other words, middle managers may discuss in advance with their superiors or executives "How am I going to use my next year or two here?" and "Will I sit on interdepartmental committees, get involved in internal horizontal reviews, and have some time off to train in one of the disciplines of horizontality?" Evaluating performance (for promotion or perhaps performance pay) will thus have as much to do with how individuals utilized the experience as well as judgments on the success of in the initiative.

Third, my sense of the source of the clash between auditors general and executives in government has to do with deciding when to apply the rigour of results management and controllership paradigms. Auditors general want to insinuate such rigour to begin with, whereas most managers know (and auditors general know this, too) that many horizontal management regimes take time to coalesce. Leaders begin with seeds of ideas and strategies and then they grow in certain directions, and it may take a couple of years to get the MOU that provides sufficient clarity for a results framework to emerge. So we need to develop a better understanding of mutual expectations. It still will not remove the tension, of course.

Finally, I want to take issue with the idea that "horizontal management" is an empty or superfluous concept for two reasons. First, one could say the same thing about the "learning organisation" which can apply just as universally to all of our organizations. Invoking these precepts may not change underlying organizational realities, and may not lead to results that are measurable by some standard, but we may well think differently about our workplaces. I think that it is admirable when executives in a public service say, "We need to stop and think about this for a while and see how well we are doing it," and initiating such reflection and dialogue should not be construed simply as wheel-spinning.

Second, executives may think such precepts add little value because they have always done horizontal management. This may be true, but what has changed is that horizontal management has become a requisite for middle managers, where the rubber hits the road – this is where people are getting burned out. Managers at that level are wondering, like the auditor general, "Where is the capacity to handle this and to do a really good job?" In my own school, which is not large, we have faculty and professional staff with all kinds of good ideas for initiating projects that span our respective domains. At some point, though, just as with larger bureaucracies, we all look at one another across the table and say, "So, who is going to do it? And can we do it well?" This is where this interest in horizontal management is coming from, from the middle.

MARK CONSIDINE: The consistency of outcomes issue seems to me to be a very important dimension. If we look at it from the point of view of the purchaser/provider devolved system versus centralised system, old bureaucratic versus new governance, hierarchical versus horizontal, there are a series of conditions that need to be established before we can decide which of those various innovations are going to be appropriate. It does not often get talked about in these terms, but clearly in a program where the costs or the risks of failure for some individuals are very high you would prefer a system that delivers average type consistent results, not one that produces some very high results and some very disastrous ones. Part of the problem with setting an appropriate performance and incentives structure is that when governments take on these new ways of doing things they often then try and diffuse them across a whole different set of environments and terrains.

This was brought home to roost in a discussion I had with some people in the corrections area a year or so ago. They pointed out that it did not much matter in their area whether their rate of rehabilitation went off the graph if one of the costs of the more case-managed, devolved system was that the number of escapes also went off the graph. So we must consider the degree of vulnerability of the clients, and the degree of the risk for poor performance. Are we really prepared to sacrifice one or two smaller species in order to get some very spectacular results on other fronts? I suspect the answer would be no.

Finally, to be an unwilling advocate for the older bureaucratic centralised system, there is comparative information certainly in the Australian case that average type consistent results are often easier to get in that type of system than in the much more complex, horizontal, multi-actor, different cast of characters every year type of environment. That does not mean it will always be thus but that is certainly how the data look so far.

ROD DOBELL: I'm brooding about Paul Barratt's observation that the head of an agency is responsible for what happens in the agency. I'm thinking about the fisheries management situation where it seems as though ocean regimes have shifted and ocean mortality for fish have changed, and the managers on the ground and the harvesters on the sea are looking at outcomes. Something has happened for which, it seems to me, it is very hard to attribute responsibility.

If I look at the folks that have lost their jobs in the forest industry, in part it is because somehow Green Peace Germany succeeded in persuading a lot of people that the clear cutting on those particular mountainsides was immoral. How exactly the responsibilities for the outcomes that flow from that change in regime are to be assigned is a very interesting puzzle. I wonder whether we aren't chasing a lot of questions to which there are unlikely to be any really very good answers.

How would you know how much you contributed to joined-up government? How do you answer that question? And if you cannot answer it then what do these structures we are talking about really mean?

MICHAEL KEATING: I agree you cannot measure coordination and effort. My own view is that you can measure the outcome of a policy. Then you can say, "Well, why did it not work?" That might lead you to a view about whether the coordination was adequate or not. You can measure outcomes.

My problem with coordinating agencies is they often do not focus on what they ought to be trying to coordinate. When departments wanted to shift money from postage stamps to telephones they had to go to the Department of Finance to get permission. Now, that particular piece of coordination contributed exactly nothing, except a waste of public money. Since then the Department of Finance got better control of the budget bottom line. I take the view that governments ought to control their budget bottom line. But Finance did get better control of budget bottom line when it stopped trying to control shifts of money from postage to telephones, because such detailed controls effectively gave managers an excuse for not even being able to manage. So managers weren't responsible for controlling their bottom line and in the end the government lost control of its bottom line.

The point about average type results is a very good point. Obviously governments are going to be concerned about particular types of risks. What I find difficult to establish as a theoretical proposition is that one type of coordination is necessarily better than another type of coordination in that context. I think you have to look at it case by case.

I cannot say axiomatically the old style Public Service is bound to be better at risk management or even risk avoidance than some of the devices we have deployed for devolution.

I would like to comment on the point about how long it takes to work up policy solutions and how you are learning by doing. I empathise with this. With the most interesting problems you do learn by doing. You do not have an end solution when you start dealing with the problem and some, I suspect, will never have an end solution. With some problems, relatively early in the policy process you can at least reach an agreement on what it is you are trying to achieve, even though you want to experiment in a variety of ways with how you get there. It is important to get the focus on what you are trying to achieve and measure performance in terms of outcomes relative to what you are trying to achieve.

JENNY STEWART: I just want to make a concluding comment about this really interesting question of risk. I would agree with Mike that we do not have much of a feel for the answer to the question as to whether a traditional bureaucracy necessarily operates in a more risk adverse way than a more devolved, contractually based delivery system. The key question here is how do we think about risk regardless of the type of system we might wish to create to manage it. In other words, the choices we make about the level of risk we want to have are really not choices at all. They are implicit in the things we set up. We do not have good ways of bringing those questions out into the open. Here the question of educating the political executive is absolutely critical. Political executives cannot continue to have it both ways: devolving power and even responsibility and then crying foul when something goes wrong, when the prisoner escapes.

Risk assessment relates to values. I keep coming back to that word. So it is a very difficult debate to have. If we can move it a bit from the technical arena in which it tends to be lodged and see it in more political terms, that would be refreshing, at least.

EVERT LINDQUIST: Well, two points. I want to go back to Mark's question. One of the decisions I had to make when drafting my paper was whether to stick with what the round table was examining, which was more of a bottom-up perspective based on experience and practitioner "rules of thumb" and provide some historical perspective on how Canadian officials have broached this subject, or whether I would take a formal modelling approach, drawing on a tremendous literature on network and organisation theory from the past twenty or thirty years on these issues. I chose the former approach because I believed that it would provide a better basis for exchanging ideas on Australian and Canadian experience to date.

More formal modelling, if done well, can lead us to think better and more systematically about horizontal management and different dimensions of the challenge. You could think about the number of stakeholders and some of the resource and power asymmetries there. You could think about some of the risks, and then you could also think about the available coordinating capacities in the system. It would be a combination of a formal modelling and a rational choice approach. The result would not, of course, be definitive answers on how to coordinate horizontally, but there would be more clarity. Like any matter of machinery-of-government, it is ultimately an art.

Finally, I want to come back to the question that John Langford posed earlier about how we address horizontal management in MPA programs. Some time ago I gave a talk at a meeting of a federal-provincial citizen-centred service delivery network. They had been doing remarkable things in terms of measuring service to citizens – an issue equally as important as horizontal management. I wondered where in our MPA program, do we really expose students to service delivery precepts? Should we have a separate course, and if so, should we put it in the core curriculum or should it be an elective? Should we simply tell students that the challenge is out there, or should we salt as many parts of our curriculum with examples of this kind of problem? We could devise a course that looks at the suite of skills required to better train the next generation of public servants with respect to horizontal management or managing public/private partnerships, but should that course supplant more traditional core courses on quantitative analysis or microeconomic policy analysis, or law and public policy? I think few of us would be willing to make that dramatic a step. What we can do is make each of those courses more interesting and relevant to the issues we have been discussing in this symposium by using examples and cases, and inviting speakers to show how tools are used to address these new governance challenges.